Rethinking equality

Manchester University Press

Simon Tormey and Jon Simons · series editors

The times we live in are troubling, and as always theory struggles to keep pace with events in its efforts to analyse and assess society, culture and politics. Many of the 'contemporary' political theories emerged and developed in the twentieth century or earlier, but how well do they work at the start of the twenty-first century?

Reappraising the Political realigns political theory with its contemporary context. The series is interdisciplinary in approach, seeking new inspiration from both traditional sister disciplines, and from more recent neighbours such as literary theory and cultural studies. It encompasses an international range, recognising both the diffusion and adaptation of Western political thought in the rest of the world, and the impact of global processes and non-Western ideas on Western politics.

already published

Radical democracy: politics between abundance and lack
Lars Tønder and Lasse Thomassen (eds)

Chris Armstrong

RETHINKING EQUALITY

The challenge of equal citizenship

Manchester University Press

Manchester and New York

distributed exclusively in the USA by Palgrave

Published by Manchester University Press
Oxford Road, Manchester M13 9NR, UK
and Room 400, 175 Fifth Avenue, New York, NY 10010, USA
www.manchesteruniversitypress.co.uk

Distributed exclusively in the USA by
Palgrave, 175 Fifth Avenue, New York, NY 10010, USA

Distributed exclusively in Canada by
UBC Press, University of British Columbia, 2029 West Mall, Vancouver, BC, Canada V6T 1Z2

British Library Cataloguing-in-Publication Data
A catalogue record for this book is available from the British Library

Library of Congress Cataloging-in-Publication Data applied for

ISBN 0 7190 6924 6 *hardback*
EAN 978 0 7190 6924 6

ISBN 0 7190 6925 4 *paperback*
EAN 978 0 7190 6925 3

First published 2006

15 14 13 12 11 10 09 08 07 06   10 9 8 7 6 5 4 3 2 1

Typeset in Minion by Action Publishing Technology Ltd, Gloucester
Printed in Great Britain
by CPI, Bath

Contents

Acknowledgements

Many people have assisted the birth of this book, whether knowingly or not. I have benefited greatly from presenting the various chapters of this book at a number of seminars and conferences, and I would like to extend my thanks to audiences at Queen's University Belfast, the University of Wales College, Newport, the University of Granada, the University of Leeds and the University of Newcastle, as well as to the members of the Equality Studies Centre at University College Dublin. I would also like to thank the following people for reading one or more chapters and for offering invaluable feedback: Sophie Armstrong, John Baker, Keith Breen, Terrell Carver, Clare Chambers, Vince Geoghegan, Andrew Mason, Cillian McBride, Susan McManus, Shane O'Neill, Anne Phillips, Simon Thompson, Simon Tormey and Iris Young. Many of these people may disagree with many of the things written here, but I have found their responses stimulating and helpful nonetheless. Finally, I became a parent at the same time as beginning this project, and spending time with my family has helped put the work of writing the book into perspective, as well as being a wonderful time in itself. I would like to dedicate the book, then, to Sophie and Felix, for all the love, support and encouragement you have given me.

A version of Chapter 2 previously appeared as 'Equality, Risk and Responsibility: Dworkin on the Insurance Market', *Economy and Society* 34(3): 450–472, 2005. Chapter 3 draws extensively on 'Opportunity, Responsibility and the Market: Interrogating Liberal Equality', *Economy and Society* 32(3): 410–427, 2003. Both are reprinted with kind permission of Taylor and Francis, www.tandf.co.uk. A version of Chapter 5 is forthcoming in *Political Studies* under the title 'Opportunities, outcomes and democracy: Young and Phillips on equality'.

Introduction

EQUALITY stands in an uncertain position at the beginning of the twenty-first century. Since Rawls's *Theory of Justice* (1971) there has been a prolific philosophical debate on the meaning and demands of equality; and some even claim this debate has played a key role in reviving the normative ambitions of political theory. At the same time, though, discourses of equality have come under sustained assault from at least two directions. On the one hand the ideal of equality has been challenged from the political 'right', particularly as a result of a resurgent neoliberalism which from the 1970s mounted a serious attack on the limited equalities achieved within many contemporary welfare states. Several decades on, the aspiration towards equality threatens to disappear entirely from the rhetoric of contemporary centre-right or centre-left political parties, and as a result the most prominent egalitarian theorist working today has proclaimed equality 'the endangered species of political ideals' (Dworkin 2000: 1). On the other hand, the ideal seems to have been steadily supplanted within what we might call the 'radical imaginary' by rival ideals such as inclusion, justice, the politics of difference or the politics of diversity, radical democracy, recognition or redistribution (see Cooper 2000: 250). Rather than simply reflecting academic fashion, this dislocation of equality is informed by a series of challenges to mainstream egalitarian theory emanating from the political 'left', from feminism, critical race theory and post-structuralism. The language of equality is criticised within the 'equality/difference' debate for being an inherently assimilationist ideal, implying that equality for women can only mean an impossible aspiration towards a male norm (see e.g. Flax 1992). Within the more recent 'recognition/redistribution' debate too, the language of equality seems to be, if not rejected, then at least relegated down the pecking-order of critical concepts (see e.g. Fraser 1995). And in a related argument mainstream egalitarian theorists have been condemned for pursuing a narrow and intro-spected politics of 'distribution' at the expense of crucial issues of sexual, racial or cultural justice (see e.g. Young 1990).

Although these radical critiques often hit the target when aimed at mainstream theories of equality they do not, in my view, necessitate a rejection of the language of equality itself (indeed they sometimes betray a concealed commitment to equality themselves: at the same time as given theories of equality are rejected as restrictive, normalising or foreclosing of political possibilities, the promise is held out of more radical, inclusive or transgressive conceptions). Beyond the confines of the academic world, equality remains hugely salient as an organising concept for the struggle against capitalism, racism, sexism, cultural oppression, political marginalisation and against the continuing rise of neoliberalism and the widening global inequalities that accompany it. The question, then, is not whether equality is dead or dying – whatever that might mean – but whether theorists can supply a vision of equality that takes on board these critiques, and harnesses some of the critical force of movements for radical change. In order to address this question I want to differentiate, first, between two broad approaches to equality. The usual provisos apply: I will not claim that these exhaust the theoretical possibilities, or that all egalitarian theorists can neatly be slotted into one or other of these categories. But the distinction is, nevertheless, worthwhile. The first approach can be called the 'equality of what?' approach.

Equality of what?

Taking its lead from Rawls, the liberal debate on equality, largely employing the tools of Anglo-Saxon analytic philosophy, has endeavoured to discern the underlying meaning or logic of equality by asking what it means to treat individuals as equals (see Kymlicka 2002). When conceived as an issue of distributive justice the central question has been what, if we are interested in equality, individuals need equal shares *of* – or, to reflect the terms of the debate more precisely, what it is that individuals need equal *opportunities* to obtain. This produces the hugely influential 'equality of what?' debate (Sen 2000), and putative answers have ranged from welfare (Arneson 1989), to resources (Dworkin 2000; Rakowski 1991), through intermediate, and somewhat 'amorphous' conceptions such as 'advantage' (Cohen 1989), or 'capabilities' (Sen 1992). The 'equality of what' debate has been hugely prolific, but in recent years the dominant position has been occupied by a school of thought known as 'luck equality'. Luck equality as a philosophical doctrine claims to capture not just an important part, but the very essence of what it means to be an egalitarian. On this view, the aim of equality is to extinguish the influence of brute luck on distribution, to make the distribution of goods, or happiness, or abilities responsive to individual effort or ambition alone, and not the arbitrary circumstances in which we find ourselves. Crucial to this doctrine is the 'discovery' of the importance of individual responsibility and choice for egalitarian theory – a discovery which, for Dworkin (2000), means that equality is no longer vulnerable to conventional criticisms from the 'right'.

Despite its prominence, some persuasive critiques of this model have emerged in recent years. For one thing, although most of the protagonists agree on the centrality of responsibility and choice, a definitive answer to the 'equality of what' question has not been forthcoming, and it is increasingly unclear that the search for one pristine good or principle of distribution could ever succeed in capturing the egalitarian impulse (as Walzer 1983 suggested early on). It has been successfully argued that the monomania of the luck egalitarian project does violence to other egalitarian commitments, such as a concern for individuals' self-respect, or a hostility towards desperate poverty even when this might be construed as 'voluntary' in origin. John Baker (1990) asserts, to the contrary, that the egalitarian tradition is 'pluralistic, non-foundational and mutable'; there is no one 'stuff' about which equality is concerned, and the various commitments of the egalitarian tradition cannot be translated into a single super-principle. The proponents of this debate may be gradually realising this themselves, with one prominent figure suggesting that we must be concerned about a plurality of 'stuffs' though not, necessarily, a plurality of principles (see Cohen 2004).

A second set of problems concerns the exclusions or marginalisations that attend this way of formulating the pursuit of equality. As has been widely noted, the 'equality of what' debate stands largely disconnected from parallel debates about democracy and participation (see e.g. Gutmann 1980; Levine 1998). To be sure egalitarians often argue that a commitment to equality *entails* a defence of formal democracy – but it is not at all clear that the *achievement* of equality is seen as an inherently democratic project. A more troubling question is whether since Rawls liberal egalitarians have significantly circumscribed the proper bounds of political action and contestation, at the same time as narrowing the remit of theoretical inquiry. On a related theme, Iris Young's (1990) critique of the distributive paradigm of justice certainly suggested that egalitarian theorists have neglected hugely important issues which do not fit into a 'distributive paradigm', and inadequately theorised those they have discussed – thereby producing political conclusions that fail to challenge the basic institutional structure of contemporary societies. It has been suggested that mainstream accounts of equality ignore or are ill-placed to deal with issues of 'culture' (see Young 1990; Fraser 1995), as well as 'sex' or 'race'. Given the subsequent emergence of what Kymlicka (1998) has called the 'liberal (multi)culturalist consensus', this critique may now appear a little sweeping. But whilst liberal egalitarian theory has increasingly, albeit slowly connected with issues outside of a conventionally 'distributivist' frame, it is far from clear that it possesses the theoretical resources to deal with them appropriately. It is worth noting that although answers to the 'equality of what?' question vary considerably, the framing of the question seems destined to ensure that the approach taken is a 'possessive individualist', rather than a relational or institutional one: equality concerns the things we have, want or succeed in consuming individually, and not the question of whether we stand together in relations of freedom or subjugation. On this theme, it will be argued that the recent focus on issues of choice and responsibility represents an adoption of, not a challenge to, a broadly neoliberal sensibility.

The third objection concerns the intellectualism of the literature. Rawls himself has long been a target of criticism on this point, with Ted Honderich's

(1999) caustic rejection of his work as 'doctrinally burdened' representing but one example. But such views seem just as applicable to the luck egalitarian literature, and even as sophisticated (and at times difficult) a philosopher as Susan Hurley (2006) has argued that whilst the 'equality of what' debate has generated a good deal of philosophical sound and fury, it is not at all clear quite how or whether the rival positions would differ in practice, still less whether they could ever be implemented. More worryingly yet, Hurley argues that the literature has become divorced from the realities of human suffering, and from the brute facts of poverty and inequality which it does little to analyse or to explain. Have liberal philosophers, in their insistence on a watertight resolution of the egalitarian 'puzzle', in fact bypassed the rather simple facts of human suffering? Relatedly, does the methodological individualism of luck egalitarians allow them to adequately capture the nature of the complex inequalities that characterise contemporary societies? This question has recently been answered, persuasively, in the negative (see e.g. Phillips 2004; Young 2001).

Equality, democracy and citizenship

I would endorse these critiques and attempt to extend many of them in the chapters that follow. But the second approach to equality may be more successful in avoiding such problems. This approach seeks to employ citizenship as an organising principle for egalitarian politics. Baker (1997) argues that equality is a 'clustered' concept, with the various elements of egalitarian politics sharing a 'family resemblance' rather than being united by some putative super-principle or super-good. The impulse towards equality concerns not just possessions but also social relations, the nature of institutions, complex social structures and indeed the very ideas and concepts of social life. But if this is the case, what is equality 'clustered' around? A variety of answers might be given, and I aim to investigate but one possibility – could *citizenship* work as an organising principle for egalitarian theory? Could a commitment to a democratic, egalitarian form of citizenship give focus and force to a critical egalitarian politics? If so, might this allow us to remedy some of the problems of the liberal literature, and move forwards in the light of contemporary challenges? Many contemporary critics of the 'equality of what' debate suggest that the answer is yes. Here we could mention Elizabeth Anderson (1999a), Andrew Levine (1998), and Samuel Scheffler (2003), all of whom have argued that equality makes most sense when allied to a conception of citizenship or membership in a democratic community, and who have used that intuition to extend a critique of the luck egalitarian position. As Scheffler has argued, 'equality so understood is opposed not to luck but to oppression, to heritable hierarchies of social status, to ideas of caste, to class privilege and the rigid stratification of classes, and to the undemocratic distribution of power' (2003: 22). For Levine (1998: 128), rather than seeking to elucidate some pristine distributive principle, 'In the end, what egalitarians want is a democratic community of self-realizing, morally autonomous agents' that underpins a substantive form of equal citizenship.

Though it has recently re-emerged in response to the 'equality of what' literature, this idea has a long heritage. A rhetorical link between equality and citizenship can be found in the work of Marx and Rousseau, in the socialisms of Tawney or Titmuss, and in the New Liberalism of a century ago the link between equality and citizenship was explicit (see Simhony and Weinstein 2001). John O'Neill asserts that whilst 'traditional egalitarianism' sought to minimise the impact of structural social factors on individuals' lives, it did not seek to extinguish the influence of 'brute luck' in any metaphysical sense. Instead the idea of equality implied 'the creation of a particular form of community in which certain forms of power, exploitation and humiliation were eliminated, relations of solidarity, fellowship and mutual aid were fostered, and basic needs universally satisfied' (O'Neill 2000: 307). More recently, the concept of citizenship has continued to provide a site for the elaboration of a diverse set of radical theoretical concerns. Many feminists, anti-racists, multiculturalists and egalitarians are engaged in attempts to rethink and reconstitute what it means to be a citizen; all the while informed, as Werbner observes, by an understanding that 'Struggles over citizenship are ... struggles over the very meaning of politics and membership in a community' (Werbner 1999: 227, 221; see also Mouffe 1993).

It might be said that the distinction between the two models has been overstated, and that both approach much the same issues, albeit from different directions. It may indeed be the case that the concrete suggestions of one or other of the theorists mentioned above depart from those of liberal egalitarians by degree rather than by kind. Nevertheless, I would assert that the way the problem of *inequality* is framed is fundamentally significant (see Bacchi 1996, 1999), and that the second approach opens up avenues of thought that remain foreclosed on the first. On the first model the 'problem' of inequality is defined in terms of the unequal possession of something (especially *opportunities* for resources, welfare or functionings). Here any inequalities that do not arise from choice, however small, are illegitimate – but by the same token any inequalities that do arise from free choice, however large, *are* legitimate. On closer inspection, the 'problem' of egalitarian politics frequently ends up being located in the properties of individuals – in their tendency to make bad choices, to fail to show ambition or to act with the requisite rationality. The result is that serious attention to structural inequalities gradually ebbs away. On the second model, equality is a relational, as opposed to a merely comparative concept: on this view inequality occurs when we can identify oppression, when individuals or groups exist in relations of hierarchy, or are prevented from standing together as peers. Devising ever-more precise metrics for eradicating any differences that do not result from free choice is not the burning issue here; rather, the focus is on struggling against the forms of oppression, hierarchy and privilege that blight people's lives across the world (and the working assumption is that the latter goal cannot be captured in the language of the first). This suggests that a focus on citizenship might represent a promising terrain for organising resistance to racism, sexism and a whole host of other inequalities, as well as an arena for challenging the discourses of neoliberalism. However, much remains to be said about what a progressive conception of citizenship might look like; some of the arguments presented in this book attempt to put a little flesh on the bones of that ideal.

Citizenship: between equality and hierarchy

The subject of this book, at its broadest level, is the relationship between the concepts of equality and citizenship in contemporary egalitarian theory. Over recent years there have been extensive theoretical debates on the concepts of both equality and citizenship; the two debates, though, have often remained separate. The literature on citizenship has chiefly been informed by sociological theory, and particularly by the legacy of T.H. Marshall's work on citizenship rights, though recently theorists have tried to broaden Marshall's influential framework to incorporate considerations of gendered citizenship, industrial, cultural, ecological and technological citizenships, consuming, affective and embodied citizenships. The dominant liberal debate on equality, on the other hand, has tended to revolve around a slightly different, and more philosophical set of questions, as shown above. Whilst the philosophical literature on equality has also gradually oriented itself towards issues of gender, culture and global justice, for instance, it has tended to move along its own discrete trajectory.

In many ways this disparity is surprising, since in the modern era at least the relationship between the two concepts – equality and citizenship – is intimate, as Bryan Turner (1986) has argued. This is because, firstly, modern conceptions of citizenship gesture towards, and imply – in theory at least – various forms of equality. And, secondly, the notion of equality seems to conjure up a notion of interaction as peers – usually within a democratic polity – that has clear affinities with the idea of a common citizenship. Certainly the two ideas have grown up together as concepts and are still co-implicated. Or at least in theory, anyway: for the egalitarian specification of citizenship has been partial at best, and historically citizenship has also functioned as a category of exclusion, hierarchy and privilege. For Etienne Balibar (2002: 114), the fact that each incarnation of citizenship has its own inclusions and exclusions means that citizenship always embodies both equality and hierarchy. Citizenship is continually contested, and serves as a counter in various political and discursive projects. On the one hand, it has often been a tool of social control (Mann 1987), for the exercise of social and economic discipline, which has in the past elicited extraordinary sacrifices and stifled social unease. On the other hand, it has functioned as a tool for advancement and emancipation, as individuals and groups seek inclusion in the realm of citizens, or the eradication of divisions between 'first-' and 'second-class' citizens.

As I employ it, the concept of citizenship has two uses. The first is expressed by Turner as 'that set of practices (juridical, political, economic and cultural) which define a person as a competent member of society, and which as a consequence shape the flow of resources to persons and social groups' (Turner 1994: 2). Citizenship refers to the way in which a variety of institutions – most typically the state, historically at least – apprehend and incorporate individuals as equal members of a polity, rather than outsiders. In its second sense, citizenship refers to a 'status' – or more precisely to a complex and shifting set of statuses (see Lister 2003: 102) that determines a set of rights and responsibilities, and the relation of individuals to the state, and to each other. Here it is important to recognise that citizenship has always been defined *against* something: citizenship represents a political identity which some agents succeed in constituting as 'virtuous, good, righteous, and superior', and differentiate from the identities of 'strangers, outsiders, and aliens who they constitute as their alterity'. As such, 'citizenship and its alterity always emerged simultaneously in a dialogical manner and constituted each other' (Isin 2002: 36, 4). The nature of citizenship is not simply defined in isolation, with the side-effect that some categories of people are excluded. To the contrary, the exclusions of some play a vital part in defining the citizenship of others, and the construction of citizens plays a vital part in defining the excluded.

These exclusions are of two types: 'external' exclusions – those abroad or exiled, the genuine outsiders who live beyond the geographical borders of the political community. But there are also 'internal' exclusions. Some people are present, and presumed at the founding of citizenship regimes; but simultaneously absent, and excluded from citizenship as a practice (Isin 2002; see also Yeatman 1994). In classical citizenship, one obvious example would be slaves, who were not just excluded from the status of citizenship but made that status possible precisely by their very exclusion; the classical ideal of political virtue was underpinned by freedom from economic necessity, bought at the expense of others' servitude. Through to the middle ages and later still, 'Women and slaves, servants and propertyless white males, non-Christians and non-white races were historically excluded from membership in the sovereign body and from the project of citizenship' (Benhabib 2002: 451–452). All of these categories of people were, to use Kant's notorious phrase, 'mere auxiliaries to the commonwealth', and hence to citizenship. The effects of slavery and the accompanying exclusions continue to be felt in the USA of course, where the majority of black Americans were still disenfranchised and systematically disadvantaged a century after slavery officially ended. Here, the fight against racism and segregation was explicitly framed – and continues to be framed – by the language of citizenship, and it seems that the promise of genuine citizenship for black Americans would require fundamental social and political change to achieve fruition.

Each citizenship regime has its accompanying inclusions and exclusions, but this book is principally concerned with *liberal* discourses on citizenship, since these play a key role in constituting citizens, non-citizens and less-than-full citizens in the contemporary world. The most notable characteristic of liberal discourse on citizenship is that it has been profoundly dualistic (Faulks 1998). Many inclusions and exclusions have accompanied the project of liberal citizenship, but I want to note just a few now by way of example.

Class

Socialist theory has frequently condemned the hollowness of modern citizenship in the face of vast economic inequalities. The classic statement of the simultaneous inclusion and exclusion of the poor within modern citizenship remains Karl Marx's *On the Jewish Question* (Marx ([1843] 1994: 28–50). For Marx, pre-modern citizenship is simultaneously political and economic – to put it sweepingly, one is either wealthy, and a citizen, or poor, and not. But in modern times this connection is broken as voting rights are gradually detached from property qualifications. Political citizenship is extended to the poor, despite their lack of property. This is a positive step, but it also means that liberal citizenship holds out a radical promise which it never fulfils: for Marx, the merely political citizenship of modern times was simply bourgeois and false if it remained married to economic servility. Nevertheless this critical gap immediately opens up grounds for immanent critique. It inspires the demand that the dualism be closed, rendering citizens genuine political equals by effecting substantial economic equality.

There is some evidence that this was a strategy that appealed to Marx, and that despite its failure to 'materialise', Marx had at least a grudging respect for the ideal of equal citizenship. But we can certainly associate such an approach with Rousseau ([1762] 1978), who understood equality primarily in relation to citizenship. As such, equality 'must not be understood to mean that degrees of wealth and power should be exactly the same, but rather that with regard to power, it should be incapable of all violence and never exerted except by virtue of status and the laws; and with regard to wealth, no citizen should be so opulent that he can buy another, and none so poor that he is constrained to sell himself' (Rousseau 1978: 75). Thus Rousseau derives two specific egalitarian commitments from the overarching ideal of egalitarian citizenship. Firstly, equal citizenship implies a commitment that state power might only be wielded as the result of democratic participation. Secondly, the political equality of citizens entails a cap on material inequalities, without which it would inevitably be compromised. This implies that equal citizenship is endangered not only by the poverty of the poor, but also by the wealth of the rich. Taken together, both are intended to enact the vision of genuinely equal citizenship (see Green 1998: 5–7). We can also identify such a strategy in the writings of contemporary theorists such as Anne Phillips, whose work I examine in this book. There is, as Phillips (1999: 126) argues, 'a great deal of unfinished business in working out what it means to treat citizens as equals', and this 'working out' in practice provides shape and force to egalitarian concerns.

Culture and ethnicity

Other exclusions relate to the cultural or ethnic bases of citizenship. To be sure, this is not always evident in the realms of liberal theory, given that there has been a 'nearly complete neglect of problems of membership and exclusion in predominant theories of justice' until very recently (Bader 1995: 213). Insofar as this is the case the conflation of citizenship and nationality is presumably simply taken for granted, allowing liberal theorists to preach a doctrine of separation of ('private') culture and ('public') state even though the two have been fundamentally interconnected. It scarcely risks overstatement to assert that modern states would not exist without their active endorsement, even creation, of cultural identities. Indeed even liberal defenders of the nation now admit that states have largely built nations, rather than vice versa (see e.g. Miller 2000). In the nineteenth century in particular, citizenship was constituted around racial divisions, excluding outsiders on the basis of ascribed ethnic identity (Turner 2001: 192), and allegiance to the traditions of the state is still actively pursued. The effects of this can still be keenly felt; the most explicit examples being provided by citizenship education and oaths of allegiance. But this is just the tip of the iceberg. Nationality policies based on blood or birth, and often linked in turn to policies on marriage and the family, have been absolutely key to building the contemporary world of nation-states (see Stevens 1999 for an excellent account).

The continued link between culture and citizenship is endorsed within popular discourse on citizenship. According to Conover, Searing and Crewe (2004: 1061), the empirical evidence shows that for many actual citizens, citizenship is strongly linked to cultural identity. Popular attitudes to citizenship bear witness to politically salient distinctions between 'legal' and 'proper' citizenship, and the substance of that distinction refers to compliance with or deviation from standards of culture, customs or birthplace (see also Shafir and Peled 1998). As Narayan (1997) argues, whilst citizenship has been used as a critical tool by groups seeking to achieve inclusion and participation within a given community, it has at the same time functioned as a mechanism for excluding minority groups (the exclusion of black Americans was briefly discussed above; see Smith 1989 and Gordon 1989 for two accounts of the ways in which citizenship has functioned as a counter in 'race politics' in Britain).

Nevertheless, several recent trends, sometimes grouped under the potentially misleading category of 'multiculturalism', place strain on these identifications. It may be that multiculturalism symbolises the end of the grand vision of a culturally homogenous nation state. The collapse of this grand vision would be welcomed if it allowed us to unearth the previously hidden cultural assumptions of the state, and begin a more inclusive negotiation of common political identities. But if this is the promise, its course has not run smoothly. For at the very same time as many have proclaimed the emergence of post-national or post-ethnic forms of citizenship, 'in a reactive move, one finds the traditional superposition and amalgamation of ethnic, "racial", cultural, and national identity and citizenship becoming even stronger' (Bader 1995: 212). And as Lister (2003: 44) rightly asserts, 'in an era of extensive migration across an economically polarised world, the boundary-staking functions of citizenship as a legal status have become more prominent'. Although a post-national or post-ethnic citizenship remains in many ways an attractive prospect, its inception remains a relatively distant one.

Gender and sexuality

It is by now widely accepted that citizenship is a pervasively gendered institution, and more recently the connections between discourses of citizenship and sexuality have also been unearthed. From the 1970s onwards feminist historians of political thought successfully exposed the pernicious ambiguity of major Western theorists on the question of sex. The pre-liberal canon presents a fairly (though not completely) uniform impression of contempt for, and marginalisation of, women. Within the liberal literature, however, a slightly different problem often presents itself, for a characteristic theme of liberalism as an ideology is the rejection of traditional hierarchical forms of government and their replacement by a rational order of at least formal equality for all citizens. Such citizens are conceived of as possessing the potential for rational self-government; as such, each should be treated by the political and economic order fairly and on his own merits. The problem lies with the 'his'. There is a constant – and some would say constitutive – slippage on the question of whether women are included or excluded from pronouncements about citizenship, and the rationality (and therefore equality) of individual subjects. This ambiguity is ever-present, and continues to pervade the work of liberal theorists well into the twentieth century; Kate Nash (2002), following Derrida, calls this the 'liberal undecidability of women'. Even after citizenship ceased to formally exclude women, their association with the private realm has played a crucial role in the project of citizenship in the modern West. For Pateman (1988), the association of women with the private sphere has been absolutely central to constituting modern citizenship. As with slavery in classical citizenship, modern citizenship is often therefore said to presume, but exclude, women (and as Collins 1999 shows, the gendering of citizenship is also overlaid with assumptions about race and culture).

An awareness of the ways in which dominant discourses of citizenship have been predicated on the inequality of women leads, in feminism, to 'Wollstonecraft's Dilemma' (Pateman 1992), and to the 'equality/difference debate'. Both of these wrestle with the consequences of seeking inclusion into a regime of citizenship that threatens to grant only formal, as opposed to substantive, equality for women. Instead, genuinely equal citizenship is said to require radical transformation of the nature and assumptions of citizenship. As Phillips puts it, 'Why should equality mean women shaping themselves to a world made for men? Why shouldn't the world be made to change its tune?' (Phillips 1992: 219). For some at least, the answer has therefore been a broader, more gender-sensitive notion of citizenship (e.g. Pateman 1988). It is now commonly argued that citizenship might provide the only remedy to the intractability of the equality/difference debate (see Voet 1998; Siim; 2000). In the words of Longo (2001: 270), 'feminists need to intervene at the conceptual level to highlight the way in which a restricted notion of equality allows "difference" to be set against it and sets limits on the possibility of genuine reform'. The most valuable political tool here, Longo asserts, is that of citizenship: 'a genuinely democratic kind of citizenship in which both sexes are full citizens and their citizenship is of equal worth to them as women and men' (2001: 272). As Yuval-Davis puts it, 'in spite of the deeply exclusionary nature of citizenship, the actual couching of the discourse on citizenship in universal terminology would prove a lever that was later used by a variety of the social movements of the excluded, including women' (1999: 121). Much more recently, similar conclusions have been reached on sexuality. As with gender, modern liberal citizenship is said to be organised around the ideal of 'normal' heterosexual marriage (Turner 2001), or heterosexuality more generally (see Evans 1993; Waites 1996; Richardson 2000). But at the same time, citizenship is increasingly turned to as a language for critique and reformulation (see e.g. Monro and Warren 2004).

These dualisms are pervasive, and each has deeply inegalitarian effects. But what are the prospects for transcending them? What would be the implications for future citizenship(s)? The first step is obviously to work to bring these dualisms to the surface, and to understand the ways in which contemporary citizenship regimes have depended upon them. Dominant groups have in many different contexts peddled visions of universal citizenship which in fact universalise their own particular identities, experiences or desires (Young 1997b); if we do not reveal this fact, we can hardly challenge it. As Frazer and Lacey (1993: 76) put it, 'Liberal theory begins with the conviction that all persons are equal in essential respects, and ends with the normative conviction that they should be treated equally, irrespective of their race, sex, moral creed, and so on ... this normative gender (and race) neutrality effectively means that liberal theories do not see and cannot take account of the realities of power exercised along these dimensions'. Merely 'absorbing' non-citizens threatens to disguise – and hence preserve – unequal relations and as a result radical critics argue that such inclusions must simultaneously be transformative. The first critical move is therefore always one of excavation, followed by genuinely democratic reconstruction. As Patrizia Longo eloquently puts it, 'difference can only stop mattering when we have effectively addressed the deep and subtle ways in which it does matter' (Longo 2001: 272).

What the above theorists agree on is that, despite its previously exclusionary incarnations, citizenship does provide tools for further immanent critique. A modern – and specifically democratic – conception of citizenship seems to contain within it the promise of a single, non-hierarchical citizenship status. The modern conception of citizenship sets itself – in theory, if never wholly in practice – against the hierarchies of status, class or caste that have characterised all societies (Walzer 1983: 277). But the idea of citizenship is also indirectly egalitarian in a whole variety of ways, since the protection of the equal status of citizens is argued to involve a series of prerequisites. In this way commitments to various equalities are 'read off' from the notion of citizenship within a democratic polity. As Marshall (1950: 29) put it, citizenship represents an ideal 'against which achievements can be measured and towards which aspirations can be directed'. Different visions of citizenship incorporate within them, as Werbner and Yuval-Davis (1999) note, specific horizons of possibility, immanent ideals, blueprints, even utopias.

John Hoffman (2004: 138) suggests that citizenship, like equality, is a 'momentum concept'. Such concepts, he argues, may be figured in various ways but are always potentially progressive: 'They "unfold" so that we must continuously rework them in a way that realizes more and more of their egalitarian and anti-hierarchical potential.' This seems to suggest not only a progressive deepening, but also an expanding frontier of citizenship. This raises the question of whether we can moderate or abolish the *external* exclusions of contemporary citizenship practices, and brings us to the final dualism: the *geographical*, as opposed to social, differentiation of insiders from outsiders. In fact the inclusivist and emancipatory social citizenship of Western states often creates and requires 'exclusionary tendencies' towards non-citizens (Werbner and Yuval-Davis 1999: 23). As such we can say that the privileges of Western citizens have historically been bought at the expense of non-citizens, and still are. But is a purely national version of citizenship tenable in what is euphemistically termed an 'interconnected' age? Or does the national focus of discourses of citizenship mean that it will remain a category of hierarchy rather than equality? As Judith Squires observes, it is often thought that 'citizenship [is] increasingly unable to deal with important issues ... beyond territorial boundaries' (Squires 1999: 192). But such questions refuse to go away. In a world of transnational flows of capital, information and (to a lesser extent) people, even a national border is an international institution, and one that needs defending by force and by moral argument. Over recent years a growing literature on 'global citizenship' has emerged, which is addressed at the end of this book in order to examine the resources its offers for contemporary egalitarians.

Structure of the argument

This book will pursue two broad, but inter-related sets of issues. My first major concern is to explore whether explicit engagement with the practice and potential of the ideal of equal citizenship might be productive for egalitarian theory. Are the broad problematics of egalitarian theory transformed once we shift the frame to the theorisation of equal citizenship? More positively, can the concept of egalitarian, democratic citizenship operate as an organising concept for the diverse concerns of egalitarian theory and struggle? Can ideas and concerns expressed in debates on citizenship theory inform and advance egalitarian theory? And can egalitarian theory itself make a useful contribution to the theorisation of citizenship? I aim to examine all of these issues to varying degrees, but my guiding thread will be that citizenship does indeed represent a promising vehicle for egalitarian aspirations. In terms of equality, the guiding thread of the argument is that foregrounding the concept of citizenship within egalitarian debates brings distinct advantages, and allows us to avoid some of the pitfalls of the 'equality of what' debate. I do not aim to set out in any detail an account of what equality must entail, but – partly by drawing on the work of a number of prominent political theorists – I do want to show how the contours of a plausible account might be sketched.

The second set of issues concerns the connection between equality and citizenship in the work of contemporary theorists of justice and equality. How has citizenship been theorised by recent egalitarian thinkers? What resonances do contemporary egalitarian theories have with the actual social, political and economic practices of citizenship? What can a focus on discourses of citizenship tell us about the subject of egalitarian thought? Some of the chapters of this book examine what a focus on citizenship can tell us about dominant egalitarian theories, and in that sense their concern is analytical. They try to demonstrate that examining existing egalitarian theories through the lens of citizenship allows us to bring to light characteristics and assumptions of those theories that often go unremarked. One of the advantages of foregrounding citizenship is precisely that this makes the link between the political theory of justice and subjectivity explicit. One of the foundational myths of political theory was Rousseau's declaration that we could 'take men as they are and institutions as they should be' ([1762] 1978). To the contrary, political theories, and powerful political actors such as states, constitute their subjects in all sorts of ways – and a focus on citizenship provides a useful window onto some of these processes. In this sense, to misquote de Beauvoir ([1953] 1997), one is not born, but rather becomes, a citizen. 'What is altogether missing' on many accounts, argues David Burchell, 'is a sense of the citizen as a social creation, as an historical *persona*, whose characteristics have been developed in particular times and places through the activities of social discipline, both externally on the part of governments, and "internally" by the disciplines of self-discipline and self-formation' (Burchell 1995: 549).

Thus citizenship is a specifically political subjectivity, which encapsulates particular 'historically inflected, cultural and social assumptions about similarity and difference', leading in different times and places to 'quite different sets of practices, institutional arrangements, modes of social interaction and future orientations' (Werbner and Yuval-Davis 1999: 3). A focus on citizenship therefore brings to light questions about subjectivity, social relations and the good society which are suppressed in more proceduralist accounts, but continue to work unannounced below the surface. Whilst the liberal egalitarianisms of Rawls, Dworkin *et al.* are often condemned for their abstraction and generality, I take a slightly different line. They are not abstract at all, if this means that they abstract from the preoccupations, assumptions and contradictions of political and economic life. Indeed it is a working assumption of the present account that the supposedly deontological and proceduralist accounts of many liberal theorists embed quite specific projections of subjectivity, community and the good life, and that an inspection of the ways in which they theorise citizenship provides an illuminating window onto this.

The structure of the argument is as follows: broadly speaking, Part I of this book represents a critique of liberal equality, and of the vision(s) of citizenship we find in liberal egalitarianism. In this first part of the book, I read these theories alongside the concrete practices of citizenship in the modern West, in order to help reveal the interconnections and tensions. Chapter 1 examines Rawls's theory of justice, and draw a comparison between Rawls's account and T.H. Marshall's account of social citizenship. Like Marshall (1950), Rawls (1971) tried to integrate a concern for economic equality into the framework of liberal citizenship. As such, both accounts represent attempts to heal the dualism of what Marx called bourgeois citizenship. There is much to celebrate in this basic ambition, and the idea of social citizenship can be tied to the very real achievements of post-war solidaristic welfarism, the social insurance state and partial social democracy. But ultimately, the central problematic of Marshall's account, as Turner (1994: 6) notes, was 'how to reconcile the formal framework of political democracy with the social consequences of capitalism as an economic system'. And Rawls, like Marshall, seemed to share the widespread hope of mid-century social welfare politics that 'political strategies could ameliorate the hardship of the worst off without destroying the principle of productive labour' (Rose 2000: 1400).

Despite its initial promise, the account also leaves a lot to be desired, and interestingly Rawls's account is vulnerable to exactly the same criticisms that have been advanced against Marshall. It significantly underplays and even displaces profound political conflict: Rawls's account recalls the aspirations of the post-war consensus, a corporatist dream where citizens would avoid conflict by accommodating themselves to the inevitable but essentially productive nature of inequality. A crucial aim of Marshall's scheme was to reduce the resentment which inequalities tend to produce, and hence, by fostering social cohesion, to ensure a system which functioned more smoothly over time (see Barbalet 1994), and we can make the same judgement of Rawls. Moreover, as has been widely noted, both theories offer wholly inadequate accounts of inequalities organised around race and sex, and both inexcusably neglect the global inequalities which sustained the social citizenship regime of the rich West.

The era of social citizenship was fairly short-lived. By the time Rawls published his theory of justice, the emergent project of neoliberalism had begun its attack on 'the social': the dismantling of the social welfare state and its replacement with an entrepreneurialist vision of 'active citizenship', where individual citizens would take responsibility for insulating themselves against the contingencies of fate. A hollowed-out notion of personal responsibility has been crucial in reconfiguring the relationship between individual and state, and inter-citizen relations have been redefined in terms of competition and consumerism rather than the (albeit limited) cooperation and interdependence embodied by the solidaristic welfare state. The political and economic impact of neoliberal politicians has been profound, and neoliberal ideas of opportunity and responsibility continue to define the political projects of contemporary centrist parties such as New Labour in the United Kingdom. As such the achievement of parties such as New Labour, as Stuart Hall (2003) puts it, has been to incorporate social democracy within neoliberalism. The core elements of neoliberal discourse have been increasingly 'normalized' by Western governments (Hay 2004), so that active citizenship is defined primarily in terms of the right to work (and therefore the right to education as training), and the responsibility to engage constructively with the flexible modern labour market.

The second chapter reads Ronald Dworkin's egalitarian theory alongside these developments. Dworkin's account of equality of resources is often taken as the point of departure for a hugely influential school of egalitarian thought, namely 'luck egalitarianism'. The most significant element of the luck egalitarian literature is the foregrounding of notions of personal responsibility and individual choice, which according to its advocates not only give shape and force to egalitarian concerns, but also allow it to meet head-on the most significant opponent of equality – the ideology of the New Right. By tailoring the distribution of scarce goods on the basis of effort and choice, Dworkin and his followers believe they provide an egalitarian account immune to the criticisms of the New Right (I tend to use the broader term neoliberalism).

To assess whether this claim holds, this chapter scrutinises Dworkin's advocacy of a hypothetical insurance market, which, it is shown, closely parallels many of the shifts within welfare provision that have taken place since the rebirth of neoliberalism. As Lacey (1998: 51) notes, the idea 'that citizens are entitled that the meeting of certain needs be guaranteed by communal provision' has 'dominated the development of welfare states', and what goes 'hand in hand with this is the idea that certain kinds of risk – such as those relating to disability, illness, poverty...should be socialised'. What distinguishes the approach of Dworkin from the practices of welfare states (and also, in a way, from the ideas of Rawls) is that the concept of the needs of citizens has more or less dropped out of the picture, to be replaced with the calculating self-interest of prudent individuals. Even the socialised element of Dworkin's scheme is justified on the basis of an individualised, entrepreneurial logic and demands rational prudence as a precondition. Dworkin may provide some kind of justification for the status quo, but it is not even a very secure justification, as it surrenders far too much to the neoliberal opponents of solidaristic welfarism. The vision of citizenship we find in Dworkin is just as hollowed-out as the neoliberal vision of active, consumerist citizenship. By way of conclusion, I argue that although Dworkin situates his work as part of a third way between the 'old' social democracy and the new right, his theory incorporates and reproduces much of the neoliberal project. As such Dworkin's achievement, at the level of political theory, has been precisely to incorporate liberal egalitarianism within a broadly neoliberal framework.

Chapter 3 draws a brief comparison between the liberal emphasis on equality of opportunity and New Labour's rhetoric on social inclusion, to show how both have normalised neoliberal concerns. Specifically, both liberal equality of opportunity and the third way ideal of social inclusion foreground the importance of labour market participation as a cure for a range of social ills. Equality itself, rather than being seen as a precondition of democratic citizenship, is increasingly repackaged in terms of a right of inclusion to the labour market. Considerations of economic opportunity strongly inform political rhetoric not only on class, but also on the equality of women, ethnic minorities and the disabled. Many of these moves have been justified in the language of 'choice', but the 'choice revolutions' promised by liberals, neoliberals and proponents of social inclusion have been defined in quite specific and limiting ways. Whilst the value of choice within both neoliberal and liberal luck egalitarian discourse has largely functioned as a category of economic life, this chapter draws on feminist and socialist arguments to re-emphasise an opposing conception of active citizenship that focuses on democratic participation in collective decision-making. The chapter concludes by drawing a further parallel between the politics of inclusion and liberal equality, highlighting the way in which both discourses concentrate overwhelmingly on the habits and propensities of the poor – ensuring that inclusion and liberal equality serve as integrationist rather than transformative discourses.

Against this background, the most pressing priority is to re-envisage egalitarian citizenship in such a way that it can pose a challenge to the neoliberal transformation of society and contest the substantial structural inequalities – economic, sexual and ethnic, to name a few – which that project conceals. As Petersen *et al.* (1999: 2) put it, the ideal of citizenship is of crucial importance as 'a site for exploring the meanings and limits of liberal democratic participation and for contesting the imperatives of neo-liberal rule'. Rather than rejecting the language of citizenship, Part II investigates the possibilities for rethinking the language of citizenship in more politically productive ways. Whereas the first three chapters of this book are largely critical, the final four chapters are in this sense reconstructive.

Chapter 4 considers the role(s) that responsibility might play in egalitarian theory and politics. Although it is admirable that luck egalitarians have engaged so directly with the neoliberal invocation of the value of responsibility, it is unfortunate that luck egalitarians have not been particularly circumspect about the notion of responsibility that they have absorbed. Luck egalitarians have operated under the assumption that the neoliberal conception of responsibility can be deployed for radical political ends, an aim which looks increasingly unlikely to yield much in the way of progress. As a result, they have largely ignored the possibilities for theorising responsibility differently, against the grain of neoliberal discourse. This chapter seeks to draw out the peculiarities and exclusions inherent in the neoliberal conception of responsibility and examine what a more critical theory of responsibility might look like. Any moralised account of responsibility is framed by the kind of 'irresponsibility' it seeks to discourage, and to a large extent the neoliberal and liberal luck egalitarian discourse on responsibility places an image of the work-shy, dependent and non-autonomous citizen centre-stage. In opposition to this, I employ the notion of 'privileged irresponsibility' that is more prevalent in feminist theory (see Tronto 1993), and which relates to those who disconnect from, or deny, responsibilities to vulnerable others. As such I examine three ways in which the notion of responsibility might operate differently in an account of egalitarian citizenship, which relate to economic life, ecological duties, and duties of care.

Chapter 5 turns to the role of opportunities within contemporary egalitarian thought. The hegemony of equality of opportunity of some kind is profound within the liberal literature, and even beyond. Insofar as this is true, the Marxist egalitarian John Roemer feels able to assert without fear of contradiction that 'Defensible egalitarianism *is* equality of opportunity' (Roemer 1994: 3, my italics). Liberal egalitarianism has focused overwhelmingly on equal opportunities to earn income within a market economy, and has offered an insufficient interrogation of the systematic inequalities that characterise contemporary societies. This chapter examines two responses to this. Specifically, it critically analyses Iris Young's and Anne Phillips's approaches to egalitarian politics. Both theorists want to challenge the methodological individualism of liberal egalitarian theory, to challenge its identification of inequality with choice, and to reinsert a concern with systematic inequalities based around, for instance, race and sex. Part of this project involves a critical interrogation of the role of the ideal of equal opportunities within liberal thought.

These two theorists agree on much, and it is notable that in their critiques of liberal egalitarian theory both theorists turn towards the value of democratic participation and communication. Nevertheless, they differ on the suitable role for the ideal of equal opportunities within a viable egalitarian theory. Essentially Young wants to broaden out the notion of opportunities, to include a much broader concern with opportunities for self-development and self-direction, and especially opportunities for meaningful democratic participation and communication. Phillips, on the other hand, wants to downscale the role of the ideal of opportunities, and uses a concern for the basic priority of our status as equal democratic citizens to assert the value of equality of outcomes, or condition. The claim that a certain level of material equality is necessary to safeguard genuine political equality is present in the work of Rawls and Rousseau, of course, but Phillips's position has a number of distinct features – not least that she extends the argument to equality of social roles and responsibilities, and employs a far more sophisticated account of group-mediated inequalities. In this chapter I side with Phillips, arguing that the commitment to equality is ill served by an exclusive focus on opportunities. Although my own argument emerges somewhat indirectly in this chapter, my primary concern is to draw out and endorse what I call a critical group-oriented principle of equality. I claim that the goal of a critical egalitarian politics should be to end substantial inequalities in incomes *and* social roles such as caring aggregating around hierarchical constructions of race or ethnicity and binary constructions of sex and sexuality. In addition a critical egalitarian politics should involve at least a continual scrutiny of established hierarchies of respect and reward within the major institutions of society. But there must be a *double* justification for such standards. Part of this justification may well refer to the likely outcomes if opportunities were genuinely equal, but such counterfactuals can only take us so far. Thus a substantial part of the justification must also refer to the equal status of citizens within a democratic polity.

In Chapter 6, we turn to an issue which has generated a great deal of discussion recently: the inter-relation of economic and cultural or symbolic inequalities. This chapter addresses these issues through a critical analysis of Nancy Fraser's work on 'recognition and redistribution'. Fraser's work initially suggested a limited role for the ideal of equality: whereas equality provided a crucial language for the advancement of claims for economic redistribution, such language seemed to be out of place in claims for cultural or symbolic recognition. In fact there are reasons for profound scepticism about this claim, and Fraser's position in her more recent work has indeed shifted on this question. For one thing, equality seems to have been rehabilitated as a vehicle of political claims for recognition. More importantly Fraser's assertion that diverse claims of justice can be best played out under the banner of what she calls parity of participation is to be welcomed. Such an ideal is clearly egalitarian, and also, or so I claim, gestures towards an account of egalitarian citizenship. This framework suggests that egalitarian commitments are best understood as struggles over the meaning of democratic citizenship, and this chapter links Fraser's arguments here to her earlier work on 'need interpretation', which gestures towards an open-ended and democratic contestation of the meaning of political membership. On the other hand, the usefulness of the recognition/redistribution framework is far from certain, and this signifies a failure, ultimately, to transcend the dualism between culture and economy. Instead, it is suggested here that a commitment to equal citizenship or parity of participation may be better served by a focus on oppression and hierarchy, categories which span these putative categories.

Chapter 7 concludes by examining the prospects for egalitarian citizenship at a global level. Opinion is divided on whether the immanent value of the ideal of citizenship has any force beyond the boundaries of the nation-state, with 'communitarian' theorists assuming (along with Rawls 1999b) that it has not. As such, both citizenship and the hopes of a substantive egalitarian politics are tied to the fate of the nation-state. In recent years an opposing narrative has gained momentum, which claims that the role of the nation-state as the 'container' of political identity and power – and as the locus of egalitarian struggle – has been eroded. Whereas the regime of citizenship based around the nation-state has been inherently exclusionary, this alternative narrative would have us believe that we are witnessing a trend towards a global regime of citizenship embodying a more cosmopolitan political ideal. In an influential formulation Linklater (2002) asserts that a nascent global citizenship regime is epitomised by the universal system of human rights, an ethic of global responsibility, and a worldwide public sphere or 'global civil society'. This chapter examines this latter narrative in order to investigate the potential of such a citizenship regime to serve as a vessel for democratic egalitarian politics. In fact, there are grounds for profound scepticism about some of the enthusiastic claims made on behalf of an emerging global citizenship, and if such a regime is developing it appears to be both broadly neoliberal in form and to possess dubious democratic credentials. In the global South and also in the rich West, neoliberalism has if anything widened and entrenched the dualism of liberal citizenship: whilst civil rights (and property rights in particular) are aggressively extended, there is serious resistance to the realisation of socio-economic rights, especially when this implies an attack on the property rights of more privileged participants in the world economy. At the same time, the role of global civil society as a conduit for a vigorous democratic politics is highly uncertain. This suggests that the prospects for an egalitarian, democratic form of global citizenship are more distant than some cosmopolitan theorists have suggested. Nevertheless, the final chapter draws to a close by pointing to some of the ways in which a putative regime of global citizenship is being contested to more radical ends, in an attempt to make 'global' citizenship a category of equality rather than one of hierarchy.

The Conclusion to this book, finally, draws together the most important arguments presented in the preceding chapters.

I

A CRITIQUE OF LIBERAL EQUALITY

1

The troubled life of social citizenship:

Rawls on equality

Introduction: social citizenship between Marshall and Rawls

IN THIS chapter, I examine John Rawls's account of citizenship in a just society. Rawls's account of justice has been hugely influential, although relatively little attention has been focused on Rawls's theory *as a theory of citizenship*. But this chapter addresses Rawls's work as precisely that: an attempt to ground a satisfactory version of free and equal citizenship, by drawing on ideas and values that are deeply embedded in Western liberal societies. Specifically, Rawls attempts to overcome the dualistic nature of liberal citizenship by drawing out the implications for social or economic equality of our status as equal citizens. This chapter seeks to examine and to evaluate that project, but first frames the argument by drawing out a comparison with a parallel attempt by the twentieth century's other great theorist of liberal citizenship, T.H. Marshall.

Overcoming the liberal dualism?

For the most part pre-modern conceptions of citizenship were intimately related to the ownership of property, and as such citizenship was always simultaneously a political and an economic category. In modern liberal societies, however, citizenship becomes detached from property qualifications. As Marx noted, this detachment has the effect of opening up the radical prospect of equal citizenship *for all*, regardless of wealth. But this radical prospect is not delivered on in practice; liberal citizens, as Marx ([1843] 1994: 28–50) claimed, are required to lead 'schizoid' lives, having secured political but not economic emancipation. The state claims to have dissolved divisions of rank and caste in public life, and yet the economic life of citizens is characterised precisely by division and brutal inequality. This schism also tends to be reproduced in liberal theory. Historically speaking, liberal discourse on citizenship tended to be narrowly focused on the political and civil rights of individuals, and not on any more substantive claims about, for instance, economic equality. But as Marx asserted, citizenship without an economic dimension is not citizenship at all. Or to be more precise, the rights of civil citizenship possessed by all were only meaningful for the few, since the primary aim of civil citizenship turned out to be the protection of their private property.

Marx's solution to this problem is well known: to abolish these divisions within economic life by socialising the means of production. In that sense, Marx's approach to equality and citizenship is 'postliberal'. But whereas this implies that citizenship must be an empty promise in a liberal state, liberal thinkers themselves have not been so sure. The twentieth century saw a much greater focus on the question of how liberal citizenship might be made more substantive whilst preserving the key liberal institutions of the 'free' market and 'neutral' state. How might we integrate a concern for economic justice into the framework of liberal citizenship? Could we avoid social disharmony by domesticating the inequalities inevitably produced by free markets, at the same time entrenching our status as political equals? Many theorists have answered these questions in the affirmative, but two accounts stand head and shoulders above the rest in terms of impact: those of John Rawls and T.H. Marshall. I will begin here by briefly outlining the first, highly influential attempt to elaborate the preconditions for genuine membership within a polity, which is presented in Marshall's discussion of 'social citizenship'. In his highly influential essay on *Citizenship and Social Class*, Marshall (1950) argued that the idea of equal citizenship was in a sense embedded in the ideas of Western democracies (and particularly Britain), though it had not been completely realised in practice. Most famously, Marshall suggested a gradual historical trajectory along which citizenship rights have been progressively realised. These rights should be seen as threefold in nature: a full version of citizenship requires, specifically, the satisfactory achievement of civil, political and social rights. Civil rights imply personal freedoms and equality before the law; political rights on the other hand principally involve the right to vote and hold public office. Such civil and political rights had been achieved in Britain during the seventeenth, and in the eighteenth/nineteenth centuries respectively. The development of the third, 'social' form of citizenship rights was a peculiarly twentieth-century phenomenon however, and can be associated with the great reforms of post-war Western liberal democracies.

For Marshall the achievement of these social citizenship rights has 'closed the circle' of citizenship. Adequate social citizenship, for Marshall, demanded a 'modicum of economic welfare and security', though the precise meaning of this demand was left notoriously open, not least since it necessarily varied, Marshall suggested, 'according to the standards prevailing in the society' (1950: 11). Certainly, though, it implied entitlement to a decent minimum provision of welfare and security. Later, Marshall pointed to public investment in education, housing, welfare and health, tied to a Keynesian economic system, as the chief achievements of social citizenship (Marshall 1964). Significantly the job of social citizenship was not to secure equality of condition, but to rein in otherwise productive inequalities sufficiently to protect the basic 'equality of status' of citizens (1950: 102–103). The central problematic, then, as Turner (1994: 6) notes, was 'how to reconcile the formal framework of political democracy with the social consequences of capitalism as an economic system'. Marshall – like Rawls – expressed the widespread hope of mid-century social welfare politics that 'political strategies could ameliorate the hardship of the worst off without destroying the principle of productive labour' (Rose 2000: 1400). A crucial aim of his scheme was to reduce the resentment which inequalities tend to produce, and hence, by fostering social cohesion, to ensure a system which functioned more smoothly over time (see Barbalet 1994).

Marshall's approach was hugely influential, and continues to structure sociological and philosophical debate on citizenship to a considerable extent. Nevertheless, the somewhat triumphalist teleology of Marshall's model notwithstanding, the 'closing of the circle' of citizenship has been revealed to be a forlorn hope. This is not just because of the latter ascendancy of neoliberalism, which radically scaled back the state's egalitarian ambitions, but also because Marshall's model itself contained a number of weaknesses. These problems have been set out many times, and I will briefly outline a few of the major lines of criticism.

The first line of criticism seeks to disrupt Marshall's assumptions about the relationship between the three forms of rights. The relationship between social and political rights in particular is far from straightforward. For one thing, in many 'developed' states there are large numbers of people, including immigrants, refugees and guest workers, who possess some 'social' rights whilst being politically disenfranchised and marginalised, a fact which disrupts Marshall's view of the historical expansion of citizenship rights (Brubaker 1989; Benhabib 2001; Soysal 2001). In fact Seyla Benhabib (2002: xiii) argues that we can observe a 'disaggregation effect' whereby the various components of modern social citizenship are increasingly being pulled apart in practice (see Chapter 7). For another thing, the delivery of universal health care, education and social welfare in practice has all too often led to the disempowerment of 'recipients' or 'claimants'. In this sense, the achievement of social rights actually comes at the *expense* of political engagement, not through it (Hindess 1994). It has been a longstanding and deserved criticism of Marshall that his account ignores the place of politics in the achievement (and later delivery) of social citizenship rights and is therefore ambiguous in terms of the debate between 'active' and 'passive' forms of citizenship.

Secondly, Marshall's account glosses over inequalities relating to 'race' and 'sex'. Far from resolving the major inequalities which characterise modern societies, the twentieth-century practice of citizenship as described by Marshall failed to address many issues of concern to feminists and critical theorists of race or ethnicity. The very welfare rights Marshall celebrated were after all closely related to the reproduction of the patriarchal nuclear family, and largely predicated on female economic dependency (Pateman 1988: 238; see also Longo 2001). More broadly, there is no doubt that historically 'citizenship has been made in the male image' (Pateman 1989: 14), and it is equally apparent that the Western citizen has been a free-born, usually white, national, prepared to bear arms for his state. In this sense, the 'modern' citizenship of Rousseau, for instance, does not depart as radically as we might like to think from the 'ancient', highly exclusionary citizenship of Athens and Rome. A key challenge then is whether the idea of citizenship can be sufficiently transformed so as to divest itself of its associations with belligerent masculinity, exclusion and racism. Here, Marshall provided us with few leads.

The final problems chiefly relate to economic justice. It has been frequently said that Marshall seriously underestimated the structural injustices of societies such as Britain, as if these were in the process of being smoothed out by the expansion of citizenship rights. But would the provision of limited welfare rights really settle the substantial social and economic conflicts of our time(s)? Marshall has been roundly criticised for the ambiguity of his position on economic justice, and particularly his view of the relationship between citizenship and capitalism. What exactly was the relationship? Does Marshallian citizenship fundamentally challenge the economic order, or does it merely repave the road of continued capital accumulation on behalf of the few? The latter appears more likely, especially given his implicit claim that the social rights of the poor will not challenge the civil (including property) rights of the rich. It is a pertinent question, in this context, why Marshall believed that social inequalities could be achieved primarily by the provision of *welfare* rights, and why he did not contemplate, for example, the development of a form of 'economic citizenship' implying substantive economic restructuring, or perhaps some form of industrial democracy. Finally, Marshall sadly neglected the fact that the very citizenship rights which were increasingly enjoyed in states like Britain were purchased to a significant extent by its place in a hugely unequal global economic system.

In the second half of the twentieth century, the defence of equal citizenship found its foremost expression in the political theory of John Rawls. Rawls's theory has generated an unprecedented wealth of critical literature, and has some claim to foundational status within the contemporary political theory of justice. But despite the recent resurgence of interest in the concept of citizenship, there has been little consideration of how the conception of citizenship suggested by Rawls bears on or relates to the conception suggested by Marshall. Clearly, the two accounts are different in many ways, not least since Rawls inhabited a much more self-consciously philosophical tradition. Nevertheless, there are significant points of similarity between the accounts of citizenship suggested by Marshall and Rawls. Both accounts argue that the ideal of equal citizenship is in some way inherent or immanent in the history and political culture of Western democracies, and that major political issues should be settled with reference to the logic of such a tradition. Indeed Rawls's defence of equal citizenship shares with Marshall's many of the same values of civility, solidarity, reciprocity, stability and social cohesion, as well as faith in the essential remediability of social conflict. And like Marshall, Rawls's account represents an attempt to integrate a concern for economic justice within a more conventionally liberal account of citizenship. More specifically, as Brian Barry (2001: 7) puts it, 'Rawls's first principle of justice, which called for equal civil and political rights, articulated the classical ideal of liberal citizenship, while his second principle gave recognition to the demands of social and economic citizenship.'

Given these similarities, it may be useful to ask how many of the criticisms levelled at Marshall's conception might also be levelled at Rawls's. In fact it will be argued that every one of the criticisms discussed above (the diminished role of political conflict, the neglect of inequalities organised around race and sex, the impoverished account of structural inequalities, a pervasive ambiguity on questions of economic justice, and a failure to adequately address global inequalities) has considerable bite when directed at Rawls. This much is to be demonstrated in any case. The job of this first chapter, then, is to present the main ideas of egalitarian citizenship as set out by Rawls, highlighting some of the controversies along the way. Section 1 outlines Rawls's account in brief. Sections 2 examines the charge that Rawls fails to adequately challenge economic inequalities, and analyses the shifting fortunes of the 'difference principle'. Section 3 then moves on to raise some critical questions about the inequalities Rawls's theory addresses. The most obvious elisions are inequalities organised around notions of sexual or racial difference, and this section examines the former in some detail. But the latter part of this section also discusses Rawls's position on global inequalities. Section 4 discusses the role of the values of stability, cohesion and community in Rawls's account of citizenship, and examines the place of political conflict in Rawls's account. Finally Section 5 sums up by drawing out the similarities between Marshall and Rawls, and indicating the challenges that Rawls's theory sets up for an adequate account of egalitarian citizenship.

1   Rawls on equal citizenship

The aims of *A Theory of Justice* (1971) were hugely ambitious, but first and foremost Rawls wanted to suggest a set of principles that should govern relations between free and equal citizens in a democratic polity. Explicitly following Rousseau's approach to equality, Rawls declares that 'the fundamental status in political society is to be equal citizenship, a status all have as free and equal citizens'

(Rawls 2001: 132). The primary intention was to model the relations between such citizens, and to identify the social and distributive preconditions necessary to sustain this ideal. Like Marshall, Rawls claimed that this conception of citizenship was in some way embedded or latent in the shared understandings common to the populations of Western liberal democracies, but in need of careful philosophical exposition. As Rawls has it, 'we look to the public political culture of a democratic society, and to the tradition of interpretation of its constitution and basic laws, for certain familiar ideas that can be worked up into a conception of political justice. It is assumed that citizens in a democratic society have at least an implicit understanding of these ideas' (2001: 5). Once worked up philosophically, these ideas provide 'a public basis in the light of which citizens can justify to one another their common institutions' (1980: 561).

The principles of justice

In elaborating the preconditions for equal citizenship, the main subject of Rawls's theory is the 'basic structure' of society – 'or more exactly, the way in which the major social institutions distribute fundamental rights and duties and determine the division of advantages from social cooperation' (Rawls 1971: 7, 2001: 10). This structure determines (or at least strongly influences) the way our lives go 'right from the start'. But key here is the way in which the basic structure influences the distribution of important social goods. The enjoyment of free and equal citizenship requires us to possess shares of these goods, which are defined simply as 'things needed and required by ... citizens who are fully cooperating members of society' (2001: 58).[1] These goods include 'rights and liberties, powers and opportunities, income and wealth' in addition to 'the social bases of self-respect' (1971: 62). So how should these 'primary' goods be distributed? One possibility would be strict equality: we could all get equal shares of each good. Rawls argues instead that the correct principles should be more complicated:

First principle
> Each person has an equal claim to a fully adequate scheme of equal basic rights and liberties, which scheme is compatible with the same scheme for all; and in this scheme the equal political liberties, and only those liberties, are to be guaranteed their fair value.

Second principle
> Social and economic inequalities are to satisfy two conditions: first, they are to be attached to positions and offices open to all under conditions of fair equality of opportunity; second, they are to be to the greatest benefit of the least advantaged members of society. (Rawls 1993: 5–6)

The content of the first principle, Rawls claimed, should be uncontroversial in a democracy: there can be no justification for allocating basic rights and liberties on anything other than a basis of equality. Indeed, in a just constitutional state, this principle should be placed beyond the reach of political debate. Everyone simply must have a substantial set of rights and freedoms; in this sense, the theory is notably more egalitarian about liberty than it is about the other primary goods (Nagel 1989: 3). Although the first principle directly concerns rights and liberties, it also has some implications for the allocation of material resources, which Rawls drew increasing attention to in his later work. In a Rousseauian vein, Rawls held that the basic political equality of citizens must inevitably be endangered by huge inequalities in wealth. In such conditions, the rich can easily 'capture' political power. For this reason, Rawls advocates a minimum set of conditions, including the public financing of elections, universal basic health care, and the role of 'society as an employer of last resort' (Rawls 1993: lvii–lxix), in order to guarantee the 'fair value' of political liberties. Partly for this reason, some commentators have argued that this is the really egalitarian principle: Norman Daniels, for instance, has said that 'it is the first principle, rather than the second, which carries the egalitarian punch' (Daniels 1989: 280; see also Estlund 1998). This may be true in a literal sense, but it is important to affirm that the freedom and equality of citizens as a whole is not to be produced by any one principle or subprinciple, but by the *interaction* of all of them – by the overall shape, that is, of the basic structure Rawls wants to suggest.

The second principle has two parts. The first guarantees that any jobs, public offices and so on will be filled by a scheme of fair equality of opportunity. This is 'a difficult and not altogether clear idea' (Rawls 2001: 43). Rawls actually equivocates between two versions of this principle. One is 'formal', and demands 'equality as careers open to talents' (1971: 65), plus a 'background of diverse opportunities' (1980: 526). At first, it seems that Rawls rejects this conception as far too narrow, in favour of a second conception. The second, though loosely defined, implies something much more radical, such as more or less identical wealth for all citizens with broadly similar ambitions. But the evidence suggests that, over time, Rawls came to favour something barely more demanding than the merely 'formal' idea of opportunity that he earlier appeared to reject. Pogge's argument that Rawls 'offers no tenable specification of fair equality of opportunity at all' (Pogge 1989: 196) is therefore hard to reject. The second part of the principle is usually called the 'difference principle' in its own right. This principle states that any tolerable inequalities must be to the greatest benefit of the 'least advantaged'. Rawls was prepared to countenance inequalities provided – and only provided – that they improved the position of the worst off. This is potentially a very demanding principle: we cannot justify inequalities according to any of the usual reasons we might expect, such as greater talent or greater effort expended in a particular activity. Inequalities correlating with effort or talent may be tolerated, but if – and only if – they are to the benefit of the least advantaged. If the benefit of the least advantaged requires that we do not reward either talent or effort, then so be it. In this sense, both are morally neutral; we can either reward them or not, according to the best interests of the worst off (see below).

It is also important to note that the principles of justice are governed by a 'priority rule' (Rawls 1971: 302–303), which states that, in cases of conflict, the first principle is to take precedence over the second.[2] This is because liberty is so fundamental, and because after a certain level of well-being, we are said by Rawls to prefer more liberty to greater shares of the other goods, such as income and wealth (which is certainly debatable, when more people in wealthy capitalist democracies protest over fuel prices than the curtailment of freedoms following 9/11, for example). A further priority rule applies within the second principle, stating that if fair equal opportunity conflicts with giving benefit to the least advantaged, equal opportunity is to take priority. Even if in some highly unlikely circumstances excluding women from certain jobs or positions would be for the best of the least advantaged, this would be impermissible. When the principles conflict, as they often will, Rawls seeks recourse to the overarching idea of equal democratic citizenship – to the idea of individuals interacting as free and equal citizens.[3] As he argued,

> As far as possible the basic structure should be appraised from the position of equal citizenship. This position is defined by the rights and liberties required by the principle of equal liberty and the principle of fair equality of opportunity. When the two principles are satisfied, all are equal citizens, and so everyone holds this position. In this sense, equal citizenship defines a general point of view. The problems of adjudicating among the fundamental liberties are settled by reference to it. (1971: 97)

So Rawls actually suggests a somewhat complex set of distributive principles, tailored to the nature of the goods in question. For basic liberties, the principle of distribution is strict equality: given our commitment to democracy, and the nature of these liberties, it would be illicit to distribute them in any other way. For jobs, positions of public authority and, we might suggest, university places, we have a principle of fair equality of opportunity. For income and wealth, the social bases of self-respect and so on, finally, we have the principle of giving priority to the worst-off. Out of all the available possibilities (excluding those that conflict with equal basic liberties and equality of opportunity), we should select whichever arrangement gives the greatest advantage to the worst-off in society.

Talent and effort
One of the most controversial parts of Rawls's argument, which I will briefly examine now, is the suggestion that it is morally arbitrary to reward talent. This

clearly offends the meritocratic belief, more or less firmly held by many people, that the talented deserve to be rewarded for their abilities. Rawls held that this kind of argument will not stand up to critical scrutiny. In essence, talents form a part of our natural circumstances, which we do not create and which it would be therefore unfair to either reward or punish us for directly. This idea is both simple and radical, and has accounted for much of Rawls's influence on the theory of liberal equality – and particularly what has come to be called luck egalitarianism. Luck egalitarians have argued that Rawls starts off (but does not complete) a train of thought which seeks to make distributions insensitive to any of the brute circumstances which influence our lives, such as talent, family background, class, race or sex, for instance. The logical extension of this project, luck egalitarians suggest, is that distribution should be sensitive to what *is* under our control – and the only plausible candidate must be our own conscious choices. The implication for the distribution of wealth and income is that we should be rewarded not for differential talent, but for differential effort or ambition (see Chapter 2).

But Rawls did not in fact argue that it would be unjust for the talented to benefit from their talents, as many luck egalitarians have gone on to do. What he actually argued is that 'No one deserves his greater natural capacity nor merits a more favourable starting position in society. But it does not follow that we should eliminate these distinctions' (1971: 101). Instead according to the difference principle the grounds for deciding this kind of issue are simply *different*. If the worst off also benefit when the talented benefit from their talents (regardless of whether we think they deserve to or not), we cannot object. To be sure, Rawls sought to limit such rewards, and specifically to ensure 'that the unequal rewards attached to equal opportunities are only those necessary as incentives to labor and those consistent with the public characterization of [citizens] as equal moral persons' (Gutmann 1980: 124). As such, Rawls stated that 'the disparities likely to result will be much less than the differences that men have often tolerated in the past' (Rawls 1971: 158). But these inequalities are not to be limited on the basis of whether they were 'earned' or not, or on the basis of whether they are the result of genuine choices.

So Rawls did not reject the idea of desert outright. Generally speaking, his attitude was that considerations of moral desert are so controversial that they cannot underpin a conception of justice that would be acceptable to all (2001: 73).[4] Building a theory on the basis of moral desert – for instance by constructing a system with the express intent that it should reward the hard-working – was for Rawls an unlikely project. To be sure, individuals in Rawls's scheme might well be 'entitled' to certain rewards, but that entitlement could only arise from a positive agreement of citizens about their mutual benefit, and not from any more metaphysical source. He was duly cautious about the prospects of tying equality too closely to responsibility, and his general strategy was therefore to 'bypass' these issues (Smilansky 2001). Scheffler (2003: 11) is therefore correct in arguing that 'it is a mistake to construe Rawls as appealing to a general distinction between circumstances and choices … he simply does not regard the distinction as having the kind of fundamental importance that it has for luck egalitarians'.[5] The starting point for Rawls's project was not any metaphysical claim to extinguish the influence of 'chance' on distribution, then, but an investigation into how the equal status of citizens might be made concrete. The rest of this chapter examines the prospects for such a project.

Interrogating Rawlsian citizenship

From the 1970s onwards, Rawls's defence of equality had a good deal of impact on academic debates about justice. The primary aim of what follows is to examine how Rawls's theory impacts on issues concerning the concrete inequalities that characterise modern societies, including sexism, the inequalities that accompany a broadly capitalist economic system, and global inequalities. What kind of challenge does Rawls's theory represent to these inequalities? Is it radically transformative or essentially conservative in orientation? To begin with, it is important to recognise that Rawls's theory has generated a whole host of conflicting opinions. Some have called it 'revolutionary' (Callinicos 2000: 48), or at least declared that it has more radical implications than has often been realised (Gutmann 1980: 3). Others have charged that it is essentially conservative (MacPherson 1973), with still others claiming that it has no political implications whatsoever (Barber 1989), or that in any case liberal egalitarians have shown no interest in implementing them. It is certainly disconcerting to observe even defenders of the radicalism of Rawls's project, such as Thomas Pogge, arguing that Rawls resisted the 'progressive power' of his core ideas 'every step of the way', and that he was 'bent on ensuring that these conclusions would be as bland, traditional, and mainstream American as possible' (1989: 9–10).

An unavoidable problem here is that the theory is indeterminate at a number of crucial points, making it very difficult to pin down. It is undoubtedly true that many find Rawls's philosophical style both alienating and infuriating, and understandably so. Rawls is certainly, as Honderich (1999) has caustically remarked, 'doctrinally burdened', whilst Benjamin Barber considers the theory 'extravagantly formalistic to the point of utter irrelevance' (Barber 1989: 309, 313). Despite the intricacy of the account a number of general – but significant – ambiguities linger in the theory. For instance, who are the least advantaged or worst off? The difference principle is supposed to apply to 'representative persons' for the sake of comparisons. But what does this mean? Rawls equivocated about what the 'representative person' is representative *of*. Is she representative of a class, such as an 'unskilled worker', or an income-defined group – e.g. everyone who earns less than half of the average? Rawls only says that either measure will do (Rawls 1971: 98). This is a remarkable elision, since it does not take much imagination to see that the definition of the worst off will be hugely important in selecting appropriate policies. For this reason, Ronald Dworkin (2000: 330) has justifiably declared that 'the concept of the worst-off group is too malleable to generate any detailed welfare scheme'. On these as on many other issues, 'His silence facilitates a consensus of sorts': many can endorse his theory, 'interpreting it broadly or narrowly according to taste' (Pogge 1989: 7). But the question is whether, politically speaking, this represents a consensus worth having.[6]

It would be a hopeless task to cover the extensive literature on Rawlsian justice, and the remaining sections will only examine some of the more salient issues. Each of these relates (though not always directly) to the criticisms commonly aimed at Marshall's model which were outlined in the introduction to this chapter. To begin with I will examine the charge that Rawls fails to adequately challenge economic inequalities, and analyse the shifting fortunes of the difference principle.

2 Capitalism and the marginalisation of the difference principle

It is no exaggeration to observe that the implications of Rawls's theory for economic life are hotly contested. Rawls suggested that the choice between private property and socialism was left deliberately open (1971: 258), though he did attempt to at least narrow the field of possibilities. In particular, he suggested a distinction between the idea of a 'property-owning democracy' and a 'welfare state'. In a welfare state, a basic minimum or safety-net is provided for all citizens, but 'large and inheritable inequalities of wealth' are still permitted which are incompatible with our political equality as citizens (1999a: 419). By contrast, the institutions of property-owning democracy are much more compatible with his theory of justice: 'the background institutions of property-owning democracy', he argued, 'try to disperse the ownership of wealth and capital, and thus to prevent a small part of society from controlling the economy and indirectly political life itself'. This is not to be achieved by ameliorative redistribution, but by initially ensuring a broad distribution of the means of production (1999a: 419), to be secured in part by some form of progressive inheritance tax (2001: 161).

Rawls conceded that his ideas here were both 'rough and intuitive', and 'highly tentative' (2001: 135–136). This is undoubtedly true: it is certainly curious, for instance, that even in his discussion of property-owning democracy, Rawls seems happy to talk of the relative fates of an 'entrepreneurial class', as opposed to a 'class of unskilled labourers' (1971: 78). Whilst acknowledging that the distinction between the two types of system was inadequately drawn in *A Theory of Justice*, Rawls unfortunately undercut the distinction further by suggesting that the difference principle, for instance, might be compatible with either a 'property-owning democracy' or a form of 'liberal socialism' (1999a: 420). But he did not explain what 'liberal socialism' – which could mean a whole host of things – actually implies. The low level of specification here – and, we might add, the lack of integration of these already sketchy ideas into his theory as a whole – means that Rawls did not give definitive grounds for refuting the common charge that he uncritically accepted capitalist institutions (see e.g. Wolff 1977; Simpson 1980; Doppelt 1981; Young 1981a). Lessnoff concludes that Rawls developed an elaborate justification for 'a set of social institutions consisting of liberal democracy, the market economy and the welfare state' (Lessnoff 1999: 243) which exist already. As such, Rawls's theory essentially functions as a complex justification of something like the post-war settlement in Western welfarist democracies. Iris Young argues that the strange pseudo-abstraction of the theory makes little sense otherwise – the theory 'must have some substantive premises if it is to ground substantive conclusions', she argues, 'and these premises implicitly derive from the experience of people in modern liberal capitalist societies' (Young 1990: 4).

Such conclusions are indeed hard to resist. But we will move on to discuss, now, a far more specific question, which has generated much recent debate in egalitarian theory. Specifically, it is instructive to look a little further into the operation of the difference principle and the assumptions Rawls is said to make about individual behaviour in an egalitarian society. We saw earlier that the difference principle, so long as the principles of equal liberty and equal opportunity are satisfied first, rules out any inequalities which do not benefit the worst-off group (whoever they are). The flip side of this is that any inequalities that do benefit the worst-off are potentially ruled *in*: though it remains an open question whether such inequalities are required in practice, any such inequalities are permitted in theory (see the discussion below). As Lessnoff (1999: 246) concisely puts it, 'the Rawlsian contract stipulates that everyone starts equal, then seeks to show how far away from equal we may move without injustice'. But what does this mean in practice? The idea has generally been taken to imply an acceptance of productive incentives. Indeed such incentives, as noted above, do not even need to be *deserved* in any morally significant sense (contrary to what luck egalitarians argue); they are justified if, and only if, they are useful for improving the condition of the worst off.

Julian Lamont notes that one of the reason economists have been so interested in the theory was that they found in it a justification for 'incentive effects' (Lamont 1997: 26). Rawls's account subsumes equality to 'empirical claims about the way in which markets operate, about the size of incentives that are needed to make entrepreneurial types maximally productive, and so on'. Thus *if* 'the Thatcherite claim that deregulating the market and privatising the welfare state would in the long run maximise the economic prospects of the worst-off could be shown to be true, then these policies would be chosen by the Rawlsian difference principle' (Miller 1997: 87). In this way, equality in income and wealth becomes conditional on the 'rational' behaviour of individuals in the economy (see Armstrong 2003a). Different rewards for different jobs, for example, may (only) be justified if they lead to a net improvement of the living standards of the worst off (presumably by generating increases in total productivity). The *eventual* equality of the account depends on how incentives work and are likely to work in the economy, and in particular it becomes conditional on the rational 'utility preferences' of high earners and the owners of capital. If disincentives really bite (i.e. if higher levels of taxation on the rich really lead to a decline in enterprise, effort and hence productivity), Rawls's theory of justice will rule such disincentives out, and thus it will be compatible with a good degree of inequality of incomes. Similarly if socialist policies at the national level looked likely to trigger international capital flight, the difference principle would rule such policies out. Thus, Rawls's account can lead to either great equality or great inequality, depending on the assumptions we make about 'economic behaviour'.

It is not, in the end, particularly clear whether Rawls considered such productive incentives necessary, and to what extent. Nevertheless, there are several dangers with establishing the argument in this way. One is that Rawls reproduces the weaknesses of the utilitarian defence of equality, so that what we find is at best 'egalitarianism by serendipity: just the accidental result of the marginal tail wagging the total dog' (Sen 2000: 163). My own judgement, along with many commentators, is that the difference principle can only be safely discussed at a very high level of generality, and that whilst it gives some shape to a broad intuition, it does not provide enough shape to securely generate a specific policy programme. As such, it seems *at first sight* to be deployable in defence of more or less any policy position between socialism and neoliberalism. Rawls disarmingly conceded in his later work that it might not even be *clear* in practice whether the aims of the difference principle have been met in any given situation (Rawls 2001: 162). But there is a deeper issue at stake: whilst 'knowledge' of the likely shape of economic processes may be important, it is also highly suspect. And this is not only because we disagree about the nature of the processes at work. It is also because economic theories strongly influence economic reality: they are in that sense performative. As Marx saw it, the line between description and prescription of profit-seeking behaviour is comprehensively blurred. Waiting for an authoritative, pre-political conclusion to debates about likely economic behaviour is not an option, and claims about the incentives 'necessary' to trigger 'rational' behaviour are inescapably ideological. Indeed states continually act on economic life, often constructing their own smokescreens of 'necessity' as they do so. Although it is untenable to describe the state as omnipotent, it is also untenable to buy into the myth that the state is powerless and merely responsive to economic forces. Since the 1970s reform of corporate taxation, in addition to privatisation and deregulation, has meant that in many places the state has engaged in a process of substantial upwards redistribution of wealth accounting for much of the growth in economic inequality (see Duggan 2003; Levitas 2004). And this upwards redistribution has been justified precisely by invoking the possibility of international capital flight (see Callinicos 2001a), by politicians who present the dictates of the 'new global economy' as inevitable and irresistible. Sure enough, the possibility of concerted, international resistance to business interests fall out of the picture on Rawls's account too, although for somewhat different reasons (see Section 3).

These kinds of concern come clearly onto the horizon in the philosophical literature when Rawls's defence of productive incentives is scrutinised further. Despite the uncertainty surrounding the difference principle, controversy has continued to revolve around its apparent acceptance of incentive effects. Some critics, and most notably G.A. Cohen, have objected to the assumptions Rawls seems to make about individual behaviour. Cohen (2000) considers it unjustifiable that Rawls's account of equality seems to make demands of social institutions but not of the behaviour of individuals. Rawls's difference principle is sometimes taken to imply that if wealth-producing, talented people demand more money to work hard and contribute to the 'creation' of wealth, they apparently should get it. But Cohen rightly points out that this represents a form of blackmail, whereby the successful can threaten to withhold their efforts if asked to contribute – a form of blackmail, moreover, that is rarely open to the poor. Common assumptions about incentives are often deeply problematic, and there is a pernicious double standard at work in conventional views about incentivisation within the economy. Negative incentives (reducing welfare benefits, rather than providing better benefits for workers) are seen as necessary to get the poor to work (including by some liberal egalitarians), whereas to get bosses to work harder, we apparently need to pay them more, rather than less (Baker 1987: 94; see also Gutmann 1980: 225–226). There is surely something suspect about the deeply ingrained idea that big bosses need huge 'performance incentives', because otherwise they won't bother raising shareholder value, whilst the poor are apparently content with their meagre lot unless they can be catalysed into productive activity. More broadly Cohen challenges the idea that we can produce an equal society by all becoming more individualist and acquisitive, and by vetoing any policy which does not maximise our self-interest. He believes, on the contrary, that structures need to be filled by people prepared to make sacrifices and to think of others (Cohen 2000: 134–147).[7]

Cohen's critique of Rawls has received a good degree of critical attention, but it is important to be clear what is at stake in the debate here, which may be both far more and far less than we would assume. Rawls repeatedly indicates that in a just society individuals will act with an eye towards just principles (although his account here is not entirely clear). He also argues (though again without much explicit support) that necessary incentives will be severely diminished in a just society, and that as such the difference principle will not tolerate much inequality. By contrast Cohen is not arguing that a just society is incompatible with individuals behaving selfishly 'to some reasonable extent', whatever this means (1992: 302; 2000: 206). Neither is he arguing that incentives to get people to perform certain types of work are illegitimate (2000: 207–208). On the other hand, Cohen has actually argued that the difference principle is not *sufficiently* ambition-sensitive (2000: 206), that it does not appropriately reward differential choices, and hence that, on this dimension at least, it is inappropriately egalitarian. Any substantive comparison is difficult to make on this point, and it is certainly possible that Rawls's system would be as egalitarian in its results as Cohen's alternative; the point is simply that in the absence of clearer specification we don't know.

Philosophically Cohen wants to make a somewhat deeper point, though. This is that Rawls's system, in order to be truly just, requires our behaviour to be more strongly informed by an *ethos* of equality than Rawls acknowledges. Such an ethos would lead us to see certain forms of rent-seeking behaviour (seeking higher rewards for not especially unpleasant work, just because we can) as an act of moral bad faith. Cohen therefore argues that for a theory of justice to be properly just, it must have 'comprehensive justification'. This means that not only must its principles be just, but any assumptions about likely behaviour which underpin those principles must be assumptions about just behaviour alone. Thus '*both* rules *and* just personal choice within the framework set by just rules are necessary for distributive justice' (Cohen 2000: 2). We must not only conform to political rules, but we must each do so for the right reasons. Two issues divide supporters and critics of Rawls here. Firstly, much of what Cohen suggests would almost certainly be ruled out by the equal opportunities principle (which clearly requires freedom of occupational choice), and even, perhaps, by the liberty principle. At present the implications of Cohen's demands here are unclear. Are we really prepared for people to be impelled to perform jobs against their will, or work harder, because they think the rewards are insufficient, or because they just don't feel like it? If not, what is the point of the intervention? Secondly, what especially concerns some commentators is that Cohen's position appears to be motivated by a Christian moral underpinning (see Callinicos 2001b: 178; Stevens 2001), and especially the idea of spiritual self-sacrifice. It must be said, in a diverse, multicultural society Cohen's demands therefore seem to represent a very steep requirement. In view of the resort to religious justification, Rawls's claim that some moral positions are too controversial to gain support in anything like our diverse, pluralistic societies begins to appear more attractive to many critics (see Daniels 2003; Meckled-Garcia 2002; Estlund 1998; see also Van Parijs 1993). Nevertheless, Cohen's broader point appears highly salient within an increasingly marketised society. There is much to be said for the assertion that our citizenly duties cannot be limited to pursuing our own self-interest within the bounds of civility, and further work on the meaning of an egalitarian ethos would therefore be welcome (see also Chapter 4).

These debates over the meaning of the difference principle, though inconclusive in themselves, have led many supporters of Rawls to try a different tack. In response to the potential inegalitarianism of the difference principle, Rawlsians sometimes claim that the great inequalities which characterised the era of Thatcher and Reagan, and which continue to characterise the era of Blair and Bush, would be ruled out by other components of the theory of justice. In particular doubts about the power of the difference principle have led some, including Rawls, to place their faith in the power of the liberty principle. Surely if the difference principle will not condemn the great inequalities in society, the liberty principle might? Rawls certainly leaves open the possibility of outlawing excessive inequalities on the basis of the fair value of political liberty. Is political equality, the argument goes, really compatible with great social and economic inequalities? If we took political participation really seriously, would this not provide a further argument for *relative* equality? (see e.g. Gutmann 1980: 190; Daniels 1989: 256; Estlund 1998: 110). There were already some leads for this in *A Theory of Justice* (Rawls 1971: 81, 226), where Rawls suggested taxation and some adjustment in property rights as means to equalise the value of political liberty (1971: 225–226). As Gutmann notes, 'his argument for the fair value of [political] liberty suggests that a minimum level of primary-good distribution must be achieved before equal liberty is recognized' (Gutmann 1980: 258). The idea that the fair value of liberties has economic preconditions is refigured in Rawls's later work too: 'what should be a constitutional essential', we are told, 'is the assurance of a social minimum covering at least the basic needs' (Rawls 2001: 162).

This resort to a basic social minimum is not entirely promising in itself, and seems highly redolent of liberal welfarism. Nevertheless, the argument that political equality makes demands on economic equality is plausible, and capable of more radical interpretation (indeed I consider attempts to deliver on its potential in Chapter 5). This possibility certainly seems to crystallise many of the remaining hopes of Rawlsian theorists. But this move has the interesting effect of further marginalising the difference principle within Rawls's theory. More precisely, it sets up an unfortunate dilemma. Rawlsians can either defend the significance of the difference principle, despite its vagueness and potential inegalitarianism. Or they can seek to entrench the equality of Rawls's account by using the liberty principle to override it. There is no obvious answer, and the debate even raises tensions about whether the two principles are compatible. Thus, although the difference principle has generated an enormous amount of discussion, it turns out to be the most problematic, and arguably least significant, element of Rawls's theory. In his later writings Rawls confessed increasing doubts about the likely success of the difference principle as an argument, and its prospects for acceptance as a political principle (see e.g. Rawls 2001: 133). It was certainly not seen as a constitutional essential for a just polity (2001: 162). Indeed, Pogge (1989: 161) cites evidence that he came to view it as 'all but dispensable'. As a highly ambiguous principle, which already sits at the bottom of Rawls's pecking-order, its utility as a tool for social and political criticism comes under serious question. But it has to be said that, without such a principle, the distinctiveness of Rawls's scheme is largely lost. The novelty and value of Rawls's account of citizenship lies, if anywhere, in his attempt to integrate a concern for substantive economic inequalities into the previously narrow and formal liberal account of the equality of citizens. But there are serious questions, as with Marshall, about whether Rawls was able to integrate a satisfactory approach to material inequalities into a broadly liberal account of citizenship.

3   Which inequalities matter?

I want to move on to another question now, which concerns the specific inequalities which Rawls's account considers insignificant. There are two broad sets of issues here. One concerns the boundaries of Rawls's account of citizenship, and particularly his claim that the proper domain of such an account is the modern nation-state. Another set of issues concerns inequalities organised around group 'identities' such as 'sex' and 'race'.

I will deal with global inequalities in due course, but for now will concentrate on this second set of issues. It has been a longstanding point of debate whether Rawls's account is either too focused on, or is warped by its focus on, material goods such as wealth and income. Rawls makes the troubling assumption that income and wealth can be treated as stand-ins for the other social goods in working through the implications of his account. He takes income and wealth as standard cases, that is, in fleshing out his principles of justice, and assumes that his scheme will work in broadly similar ways for the other goods. Income and wealth can be taken to correlate with other goods when defining the worst off, it is assumed, and in working through the implications of the principles of justice. But the assumption that the 'worst off', for example, can be straightforwardly identified with the poor is highly dubious. There are many disadvantages in contemporary societies, based not only on class, but also on (what is defined as) ability or disability, race, religion, nationality, locality, culture, language, sex and sexuality. And these inequalities never neatly map onto each other. As Barber (1989: 303) asks, 'who then is to be regarded as the least advantaged: the prosperous black or the poor white?' Indeed, there are a number of groups – most notably gay and lesbian citizens – who suffer disadvantage in ways that will often not clearly correlate with income and wealth at all (though this is not to say that this disadvantage is not also economic in character – see Chapter 6). Samuel Freeman (1998) happily concludes that 'there is no major problem of practical implementation' in this regard, but Rawls's theory looks like a crude tool when faced with the complex nature of these inequalities.[8]

As shown by the debate on capitalism, there has been a suspicion that Rawls's theory is unable to get at some of the more enduring inequalities of modern societies. But we need to work with this suspicion a little further. Rawls does at least provide us with some tools with which to address economic inequalities – though these tools may not be particularly effective. But there are many sweeping and hugely important inequalities which Rawls engaged in little or no discussion of. Nevertheless these inequalities surely do, to adopt the Rawlsian language, affect our lives right from the start. For instance, although Rawls did discuss issues of religion and of religious freedom, he did not address inequalities linked to race or ethnicity. To be sure, Rawls wrote within, and was no doubt influenced by, the context of the civil rights era in the USA, and we can safely assume that he was deeply concerned about the lack of access to various primary social goods for many black Americans. Rawls may be right to argue that inequalities in the possession of primary goods was an important part of the injustices suffered by various ethnic groups. A form of socialist redistribution may therefore ameliorate many of these problems. But this is a very long way from being the whole of the issue.

Rawls's final response to the criticism that he neglected race and sex (Rawls 2001) was ambiguous, and difficult to unpick. As I read it, though, his point was that since the injustices suffered by women and ethnic groups was not primarily a matter of access to primary goods, it would not be considered in his theory of justice. Rather, we could assume that in any more or less just society, such issues would be settled. This is a hugely problematic argument, for two reasons. On the one hand, it could be argued that if his theory didn't consider any kind of inequalities other than in the possession of social goods, then the theory itself is inadequate. A theory has to answer to the nature of concrete injustices, not the other way around. Secondly, we cannot simply assume, without further specification, that issues of sexual and racial inequalities will in some way be 'settled' in the near future, if only for the reason that there is a huge amount of debate over what such a settlement could possibly be. Would a just society be one 'beyond' race and sex, for instance, or one in which all 'identity groups' are equally valued? Such a lack of connection with the intricacies of group-based injustices may in turn have influenced the literature that has built up around Rawls's ideas (Laden 2003: 369–70, for instance, observes a relative lack of African–American scholarship on Rawls, and notes the possibility that such scholars find Rawls's work 'unengaged' with the pressing issues they face). In Chapters 5 and 6, I consider the work of some contemporary theorists who take seriously the need to respond directly to issues of sexual, 'racial' and cultural injustice. There has at least been a substantial literature on Rawls and gender, and for now we will briefly examine this more prolific controversy.

Sexual inequalities

Modern societies are characterised by large inequalities in the division(s) of labour, by widespread 'domestic' violence, increasing levels of sexual violence, a globalised sex trade linked to organised crime, and pervasive inequalities in the political representation of women, just to start with. Any persuasive theory of justice must explicitly recognise these facts, and at least begin to specify what appropriate remedies might be. On these issues, there are a number of reasons for doubt about Rawls's position. The most serious attention has focused on whether the institution of the family is considered a part of the basic structure of society or not, and whether it is therefore to be regulated by Rawls's principles of justice.[9] Susan Moller Okin (1994) showed that, over time, Rawls's account actually equivocated about whether the family was a subject of justice or not. But the evidence is that even when the family *was* considered as a part of the basic structure, it was assumed to be essentially non-political in character. The internal order of the family is simply assumed not to conflict with the demands of justice (O'Neill 1997: 41).

Rawls addressed these concerns to some degree in later writings, where he finally affirmed that 'The family is part of the basic structure, since one of its main roles is to be the basis of the orderly production and reproduction of society and its culture from one generation to the next' (Rawls 1999b: 595; cf. Okin 1989). Therefore, he argued, the principles of justice must apply there (Rawls 1999b: 596). Nevertheless, his final position is still not wholly satisfactory, not least since Rawls remained ambiguous about whether his theory would radically transform the division of labour and wealth within the family, as feminists such as Okin have demanded. On the one hand, he argued that 'principles of justice ... can plainly be invoked to reform the family' (Rawls 1999b: 598). On the other hand, there is still an odd theoretical division of labour in operation, since although Rawls argued that principles of justice should *constrain* what happens in the family (e.g., protect basic liberties: 1999b: 597, 599), he maintained that they should not directly *regulate* it (1999b: 598). For instance, he argued that the state can seek to prevent 'involuntary' inequalities in the division of labour, but ultimately any 'voluntary' inequalities must be tolerated (1999b: 600). If Rawls had been more familiar with the nuances of feminist critiques of the public/private division, he would surely have considered this theoretical option a weak one. The notion of a modern state constraining but not substantially influencing what goes on within families is a fiction. For one thing, the family as a legal institution is of course *defined* by the state, and given definitions are defended through family law, immigration law and so on. For another, any policy a government may pursue or fail to pursue in the fields of law and order, economic and welfare policy will directly shape the options available to individual men and women, and hence the balance of power between them (thus notably the social citizenship described by Marshall is widely acknowledged to have underpinned – if not legally enforced – a specific gender order in terms of family life: specifically one organised around the 'family wage' and an assumption of women's formal economic dependency). In the aftermath on the feminist critique, refusing to take a position on the division of labour is not a viable option. Instead Rawls undercuts much feminist theory by asserting that arguing for changes in the division of labour is not the job of political philosophy (Rawls 1999b: 600).

As such, Shane O'Neill (1997: 45) is justified in concluding, after carefully examining the evidence, that 'It would appear that Rawls is unwilling to consider seriously justice in the family in any sense.' Whilst Rawls (1999b) glibly asserted that he believed the issues of sexual inequality had been solved by John Stuart Mill and did not require further comment, for feminists unconvinced by Mill's own strategies for sexual equality this is unlikely to provide much reassurance. More broadly Rawls offers us no insights into the gendering of citizenship, or the way in which the nature, rationalities and responsibilities of citizenship have been constructed in relation to sexist assumptions about public and private life. Far from it, Rawls reproduces one of the least informative images of liberal theory: that of the state as umpire of pre-existing difference, rather than as an institution that is, in many different ways, implicated in struggles to define individual subjects. As Jacqueline Stevens (1999: 4) puts it, 'Rawls understands political society as the location that settles differences, rather than the form that gives rise to them.' In terms of uncovering, degendering or democratising the covertly gendered narratives of liberal citizenship, Rawls does not even provide us with the beginnings of a helpful response.

Global inequalities

Rawls's position on global inequalities has been roundly and severely criticised, even by many of his supporters. The principal reason for this is Rawls's view that the nation-state is the primary arena of justice and equality. Thus whilst Rawls clearly took a *position on* global justice (see below), he did not set out – and did not intend to present – anything that could be recognised as a 'theory of global justice'. Despite some early interpretations to the contrary, this intention should have been evident in *A Theory of Justice*, where Rawls makes it clear that he considers societies as 'self-contained' (1971: 457), 'more or less self-sufficient' (1971: 4), and therefore as 'closed system[s] isolated from other societies' (1971: 8). The only principles of international justice he considers in *A Theory of Justice* (and then extremely briefly) are those relating to war, non-intervention and national self-determination (1971: 378–379); the over-riding sense is therefore of a resolutely Westphalian approach to justice.

In a world of global economic, cultural and political inter-penetration, such a view should be seen as highly problematic (see e.g. Benhabib 2002: 168). Nevertheless, it is only in his *The Law of Peoples* (Rawls 1999b) – by far Rawls's least well-accepted book – that he cashes these ideas out further. The question he sought to answer in this book is essentially that of what the foreign policy of a just liberal state – as described in more or less detail in *A Theory of Justice* – should be. The main argument Rawls presents here is that, in the interests of toleration of diversity, liberal states should not impose their values on non-liberal states, so long as these respect fundamental values such as basic human rights, for instance (1999b: 59–60, 63–67). What is especially significant here is that, when transposed onto the international context, the idea of free and equal citizenship ceases to perform the key role in Rawls's approach to justice (1999b: 69). There is no common political culture of citizenship at the international level; no overarching arsenal of ideas on citizenship which the political theorist can work up into a plausible conception of justice at the global level. All that remains is the value of basic humanity, which can only provide a fairly thin set of global principles.

As such, Rawls's primary emphasis is on the equality of 'peoples' rather than of individuals or citizens. In the absence of common conventions on liberal and democratic values, states – being concerned only with power and wealth – are entitled to pursue their self-interest no matter what the impact on non-citizens, and to treat their 'own' subjects as they see fit (1999b: 25–35). Although the position advocated in *The Law of Peoples* does reflect some development over the isolationism and autarchy depicted in *A Theory of Justice*, the only genuinely significant change is a new stress on the obligations of liberal states to assist the reform of 'poorly ordered' ones. This obligation, though, is an obligation to offer *political* rather than economic assistance (there is no recognition, here, that the political equality of states might benefit from some albeit basic economic equality; see Beitz 2000). What is particularly puzzling to Rawls's many critics is his insistence that the fate of poorly ordered states is to be seen as rooted in domestic rather than international factors: that the poverty of nations, we might say, has more to do with bad management than it has to do with colonialism and neo-colonialism, or the vicious exploitation by richer states of their superior economic bargaining power (see e.g. Pogge 2002). In shifting the emphasis from the domestic to global levels, any concern for material privilege and oppression largely disappears from Rawls's radar (Young 1995).

Rawls's position on global justice has been roundly criticised. Pogge (2002: 108) considers it 'a rationalization of double standards', whilst Nussbaum (2002: 285) considers it 'inadequate and half-hearted'. There are a number of serious problems with his position, but perhaps the most important one is expressed early on by Charles Beitz (1979). If we are concerned with the effects of the basic structure of society on the life-chances of individuals, Beitz asks, should we not be directly concerned with the consequences of, for instance, global capitalism? Even critics with impeccably liberal credentials have found Rawls's assertion that the fortunes of nations depend on intra-and not inter-national factors incredibly naïve. In fact, as Pogge (1989: 11) argues, 'we are advantaged participants in an institutional scheme that produces extreme poverty on a massive scale so that many persons are born with no realistic prospects of a life without hunger, malnutrition and oppression'. Moreover national borders are global institutions, and 'local' economic decisions have global effects. In environmental terms, the freedom of the free American citizen to cruise down the highway in his or her gas-guzzling car is not an abstract freedom, but a concrete one, which 'always already' affects other people in distant parts of the planet (see Dobson 2003: 18–19).

There are many ways in which we can interpret the consequences of these facts, and some of the possibilities are discussed in Chapter 7. Not to pre-empt that discussion, some would want to extrapolate from the facts of global economic and ecological interconnection to suggest a global form of citizenship. But for now, it is merely worth asserting that any citizenship regime is a regime with a history, and even parochial, national citizenship has a global history. Even if we consider the normative resources for a form of global citizenship to be absent, acknowledging this fact will already imply profound consequences for debates on equality and citizenship. If most commentators have considered Rawls's position on global inequalities wholly inadequate, they are right to do so.

4 Equality, community and political struggle

There must be an agreed scheme of conduct in which the excellences and enjoyments of each are complementary to the good of all. Each then can take pleasure in the actions of the other as they jointly execute a plan acceptable to everyone. (Rawls 1971: 576)

This chapter has steered clear of Rawls's famous account of how his principles of justice might be derived from (or at least bolstered by) a hypothetical Original Position, for two reasons. Firstly I believe that this account is wholly unsuccessful; here I agree with Thomas Nagel ([1975] 1989: 15), who argued early on that 'Rawls's conclusions can be more persuasively defended by direct moral arguments for liberty and equality' (see also Roemer 1996: 176).[10] Rawls (1971: 15) himself indicated that readers could accept the account of justice with or without its foundation in the Original Position, an option that this chapter has taken him up on. Secondly, the suppositions embodied in the Original

Position have often led Rawls – wrongly – to be associated with atomistic individualism, thus provoking a largely unilluminating reprise of some very old themes in the new guise of the so-called 'liberal-communitarian debate'. In fact as Laden (2003: 376) points out, in many ways 'Rawls was a singularly bad choice for demonstrating the flaws that communitarians saw within liberalism.'

Despite Rawls's frequent association with atomistic individualism, the values underpinning his scheme are often strongly opposed to self-interested rationality: they involve fair cooperation, mutual reciprocity, symmetry and solidarity. Specifically, his defence of equality is underpinned by his idea of the 'social union of social unions', which refers to 'a community of individuals who have developed and coordinated their different and complementary powers'. Rawls asserted in no uncertain terms that 'Only in the activities of social union can the individual be complete' (1993: 321). Through social union citizens can be a part of a larger good, reaching across time and generations (1971: 528). The idea of the social union of social unions in fact puts many 'communitarian' and republican visions of social cooperation to shame. As Roberto Alejandro has pointedly observed, it 'presupposes a harmony among all members which not even the most passionate ruminations of communitarians have ever proposed' (Alejandro 1998: 31). It is very instructive to examine the kinds of metaphor Rawls employs to illustrate his vision of social union, as Nancy Love (2003) suggests. The first, intriguingly, refers to Adam Smith's idea of the 'invisible hand' which guides the economy. Thus Rawls compares the demands of social union to the way in which an efficient division of labour is achieved in economic life (see e.g. Rawls 1971: 525). Secondly, Rawls often uses the metaphor of a game, in which each agree to abide by rules for mutual benefit. Thirdly, Rawls repeatedly uses the metaphor of an orchestra to illustrate the 'democratic resolution of individual and society' (Love 2003: 129; see e.g. the metaphor in Rawls 2001: 76). Part of citizens' identity is 'the shared final end of giving one another justice' (Rawls 2001: 199), much as the job of a violinist or clarinettist is to contribute to a musical experience that is greater than the sum of its parts.

So where does this harmony of interests come from? Given their concern to produce a system which will possess long-term *stability*, Rawls argues that prudent individuals (including those reasoning within the Original Position) will be concerned to design a basic structure which will *engender* the long-term allegiance of citizens. Rawls requires his deliberating citizens to favour 'a basic structure that has a strong tendency to engender a normally overriding moral allegiance to itself' (Pogge 1989: 102). The basic structure must be designed to elicit long-term allegiance, for it is only such allegiance that can produce the long-term stability that Rawls requires. As such, Rawls's basic structure *produces* the free and equal citizens whom until now had been purely hypothetical. Rawls's scheme thus becomes partly circular, since far from depending on, and building up from, our shared conceptions about justice, the scheme is supposed to 'encourage the cooperative political virtues' (Rawls 2001: 194) of our putative citizens. Far from being able to presume such virtues in practice, Rawls's deliberating citizens are supposed to set out to *create* them (and they are forced to do so because Rawls requires them to construct a system that will have long-term stability).

There can be no doubt about Rawls's 'communitarian' attachment to a 'realistically utopian' harmony of interests. But this does beg the question of whether Rawls had an understanding of society as essentially non-conflictual. Roberto Alejandro (1998) persuasively takes Rawls to task for assuming a basically fair world of cooperation and inherently remediable conflict, where the achievement of justice resembles something like a problem of management or coordination. Either way, one thing which progressively moves out of focus in this cosy vision is the need for substantive democratic control over social institutions. Indeed, the only way to create a just social order which is stable over time, and commands the allegiance of its happy cogs, it seems, is to ensure that the biggest political questions are 'taken off the political agenda' (Rawls 1987: 14). As Alejandro (1996, 1998) observes, citizens are to be present at the founding of the just Rawlsian constitution, but thereafter are shuffled off to work for its continued existence, and not to engage in continual and destructive questioning of core institutions. This was obviously the case in the Original Position, where some positions are simply removed without comment from the theoretical menu (Marxism, it seems, is off today). Any real diversity or disagreement threatens to disappear, and in fact famously the principles could be produced by any one rational person, with no debate whatsoever. Rawls states that 'I shall not even ask whether the principles that characterize one person's considered judgements are the same as those that characterize another's' (1971: 50). But even in Rawls's later work, which sought precisely to recognise and accommodate profound moral conflict, such harmony was still to be achieved by depoliticising contentious issues and marginalising 'unreasonable' views. Rawls certainly devoted much more time in his later career to questions about how his vision of harmonious social union was to be sustained in a diverse society, but the suspicion remains that he saw society as essentially non-conflictual, and such problems as did exist as essentially remediable given the reasonableness of citizens.

These criticisms are now common, and Bonnie Honig argues with some justification that Rawls replaces politics with administration (Honig 1993; see also Connolly 1991). For Alejandro, 'Rawls's political liberalism is an arena of public deliberation where legal arguments, lawyers, and judges, have the final say in settling controversies' (Alejandro 1996: 22). The most notable characteristic of Rawls's 'political liberalism', then, is its squeezing out of many issues of political debate, its narrowing of political boundaries, and its privatisation of conflict. William Connolly does well to bring out the theme of noise and silence at work here. He argues that Rawls asks for the silence of citizens precisely where their disagreements are most intense; as such his theory is 'tone-deaf to multiple modes of suffering and subordination currently subsisting below the public register of justice' (Connolly 1999: 10). Jürgen Habermas employs a somewhat different metaphor to Connolly, but is surely right to argue that citizens in a Rawlsian state would find it hard to 'reignite the radical democratic embers ... for from their perspective all of the *essential* discourses of legitimation have already taken place within the theory' (Habermas 1995: 128). An astonishing early example of this squeezing of the political arises with Rawls's call for 'a cooperative, political alliance of minorities to regulate the overall level of dissent' (Rawls 1971: 374). Such a 'political understanding among the minorities suffering from injustice' can be attained with 'perceptive leadership', and can thereby place a limit on civil disobedience (1971: 375). If the competing demands of oppositional movements represented merely a problem of practical coordination, the lives of political theorists would be much easier – or, indeed, completely irrelevant. But there are scarcely such reasons for optimism.

Inequality, community and citizenship

Rawls's account of the just society as a whole is redolent of organicism and functionalism. Even in the works of authors such as Talcott Parsons, it is hard to find more functionalist language than this:

> It is a feature of human sociability that we are by ourselves but parts of what we might be. We must look to others to attain the excellences that we must leave aside, or lack altogether ... the good attained from common culture far exceeds our work in the sense that we cease to be mere fragments: that part of ourselves that we directly realize is joined to a wider and just arrangement the aims of which we affirm. The division of labor is overcome not by each becoming complete in himself, but by willing and meaningful work within a just social union of social unions. (Rawls 1971: 529)

We are to be content, then, to be part of a larger system, contributing in our own ways to the health of our community. This contentment bears directly on the inequalities we are prepared to accept. Because the system is based on the mutual giving of justice from each to each, any actual inequalities between individuals in fact become easier to swallow. As Rawls puts it, in his just republic 'The disparities between [the least advantaged] and others, whether absolute or relative, should be easier for them to accept than in other forms of polity', not least since they are 'probably' less than have often prevailed (1971: 536). This is important given that 'envy' is so 'troublesome' and destructive (1971: 537). Such envy may in any case be minimised, since the happy citizen will tend to compare himself only with those close to him: Rawls makes the astonishing assertion that, given that individuals tend to participate in relatively separate institutions and organisations, inequalities will not attract 'the kind of attention which unsettles the lives of those less well placed [thus] ignoring ... differences in wealth and circumstance is made easier' (1971: 537). In a just polity, the wealthy, obeying the dictates of civility, will not be so ostentatious with their wealth as to deliberately engender the humiliation of the poor (1971: 537).

At this point the armed inequalities of Rio, and the gated communities of the West loom disturbingly on the horizon. Are we, then, required to accept inequalities so long as the consumption of the rich remains inconspicuous? The answer is unclear, but brings to light one of the apparent contradictions of Rawls's account. Whereas Rawls seems to recommend harmony and community, at other times – see the discussion of the difference principle, above – he seems ready to accept systematic inequalities, whether they are deserved or not. How are the two to be squared with each other? The suspicion is that, like Marshall, Rawls is simply arguing for *community despite inequality*. As reasonable individuals we are to accept inequalities as basically functional and continue to act as reasonable and civil citizens in the face of them. As Barbalet (1994) argues of Marshall, Rawls's scheme is clearly designed to reduce the resentment which inequalities tend to produce, and hence, by fostering social cohesion, to ensure a system which functioned more smoothly over time. So long as inequality is domesticated, and the rich do not 'grind the faces of the poor', as Walzer (1983) puts it, it seems that citizens have a duty to accept and adjust themselves to the inherent and necessary inequalities of Western societies. As with Marshall (1950), citizenship may have been transformed into 'the architect of legitimate social inequality', whilst some of the most profound inequalities that characterise contemporary societies are rendered immune to critique.

5 Rawlsian citizenship in question

There has been a great deal of discussion of equality and citizenship in recent years, and to a great extent the approaches of both Rawls and Marshall continue to structure debate. To be sure, Rawls has had a more overt influence on egalitarian theory, whilst Marshall has had a greater influence on contemporary discussions of citizenship, particularly within sociology. But it has been argued in this chapter that the two accounts have a great deal in common. Both present attempts to remedy the dualistic nature of liberal equality – its claim to endorse the political and civil equality of citizens in the presence of substantial material inequalities – by inserting into liberal theory a concern with the social or material prerequisites of equal citizenship. Both reject the 'extremes' of socialism and the untempered free market, and seek to render compatible the claims of citizenship and the productive imperatives of the market.

This goal of overcoming the dualism of liberal citizenship is an important one, and the social citizenship models of Marshall and Rawls clearly had something significant to contribute. There is much to be said for Rawls's basic orientation in particular, which maintains that if we claim to stand in relation to one another as free and equal citizens, then we need to pay attention to the material prerequisites of such freedom and equality. It is highly unfortunate that within the subsequent 'equality of what?' debate Rawls's focus on substantive citizenship as a guiding thread for egalitarian politics often went by the wayside in the drive to determine a single 'super-principle' of equality, and to an extent the chapters included in Part II of this book represent attempts to recover that kind of focus.

In a sense, Rawls's approach reproduces in a highly complex form the message of many traditional socialist critiques of liberalism, which point out that formal freedoms and formal equalities have little meaning unless accompanied by material redistribution, and caps on future inequalities. Although Rawls's approach to economic equality is highly ambiguous, it is not unreasonable to claim that if a Rawlsian scheme was implemented in an inegalitarian state such as the UK or the USA, it might generate considerable improvements in terms of economic equality. Indeed, within an American context the much-vaunted achievements of social citizenship were scarcely even partially realised (Nancy Fraser and Linda Gordon 1992 offer a sobering perspective here by arguing precisely for the displacement of the dominant discourse of civil citizenship within the USA by an ideal of social citizenship). In most European countries the practice of social citizenship came under considerable attack during the 1970s and 1980s, an attack that continues to varying degrees, with huge implications for gender politics (Pettman 1999, Siim 2000). In the British context, the post-war experiment in social citizenship may have represented something of a high-water mark, for as Ruth Lister (2002) notes, the UK is in many ways now moving towards a residual 'poverty relief' model of social security long typical of the USA. Sceptical as we might be about the partial achievements of the model of social citizenship, they were indeed achievements, and worth fighting to defend and deepen. It is possible, then, to feel nostalgic for the ideal of social citizenship which Rawls's theory seems to offer some kind of justification for, albeit an esoteric and often infuriating justification. But this should not blind us to its profound problems. Though Rawls attempted to overcome the dualism and contradictions of liberal discourses on citizenship, his remained a resolutely liberal account. In this sense, it is a pertinent question whether many of the seeds of the neoliberal doctrine of active citizenship were already contained within Rawls's account. For our present purposes, the object is to reiterate that Rawls's account exhibits serious problems which mirror the weaknesses of the Marshallian model. To sum up here, we can say that:

- Like Marshall, Rawls gave every impression of seriously underestimating the structural injustices of societies such as the UK and USA. As Hindess (1994) puts it, although Marshall and Rawls may be right to claim that the principle of citizenship and its attendant equalities are 'embedded' in the political cultures of the modern West, there is much less reason to support their claim that those principles have been substantially *realised* in practice. To begin with, the assumption that contemporary societies are 'nearly just' is not an auspicious beginning, and denotes a failure to connect with the complex nature of contemporary inequality.

- Like Marshall, Rawls glosses over issues relating to race and sex. Rawls provided a weak response to the many issues of concern to feminists in particular, and appeared resolutely opposed to thinking through the consequences of the feminist critique for the theorisation of justice, equality and citizenship.

- Rawls has rightly been criticised for the ambiguity of his position on economic justice, and particularly the implications of the difference principle. Rawls attempted to remedy the peculiar hollowness of modern liberal citizenship, but in his later work he seemed content, like Marshall, that citizenship could be rounded off by integrating rights to an adequate level of welfare provision. Rawls seemed prepared to abandon any strong claims for the difference principle, so that the economic egalitarianism of his account rested on a fairly weak set of preconditions for satisfying the fair value of political liberties: chiefly among them, the kind of adequate social minimum that Marshall himself suggested. Ultimately what we are left with, then, is a rather ambiguous attempt to 'limit the negative impact of class differences on individual life-chances, thereby enhancing the individual's commitment to the system' (as Turner 1994: 6 says of Marshall). For Marshall this was in no small part a defensive exercise, by which 'the market [is] civilised, and therefore saved from those who would overturn it in favour of common ownership and equality of outcome' (Faulks 1998: 41), and it is difficult ultimately to resist the same conclusion for Rawls. As such, the attempt to extract the radical potential of democratic citizenship is at best a partial success.

- Rawls's response to global justice is widely and fairly rejected for being essentially conservative. The claim that the ideal of citizenship ceases to make demands at the international level means that injustices of economics, ecology and political voice across borders are not adequately interrogated. Again like Marshall, Rawls showed a severe lack of attention to the fact that the very citizenship rights which are enjoyed in wealthy Western democracies are purchased to a large extent by such nations' place in a hugely unequal global system. Historically, much of the critical force of the ideal of citizenship has rested in its opposition to hierarchy, and the (at least potentially) transformative struggles of those (including slaves, women, ethnic minorities and 'colonial peoples') who have made citizenship possible for some only at the cost of their own exclusion. In an 'interconnected' world, to use a common euphemism, the claim that the immanent force of citizenship must cease at the borders of the nation-state may preserve such hierarchy, and radically curtail the critical force of the ideal of citizenship.

- Issues surrounding political struggle and democratic participation were in many ways merely deferred and displaced by Rawls. Marshall has been widely criticised for conceiving of citizenship in an essentially passive sense, with little focus on the importance of political participation in contesting and negotiating the terms of citizenship. Rawls's appears above all to be a 'managerialist' position, seeking a harmonious reconciliation of the opposed forces of society, to be enshrined in a constitution, and interpreted by a judicial elite. Like Marshall, Rawls downplays the place of concrete political struggle in the achievement and delivery of social citizenship rights, and can therefore be seen to support overwhelmingly 'passive' rights to material goods.

Each of these problems sets up distinct challenges for any adequate theory of egalitarian citizenship within a democratic community. As I take it, the most significant of these questions are:

- Can an egalitarian view of citizenship take serious account of the pervasive inequalities organised around race and sex which are a feature of all contemporary societies?
- Might we develop an account of egalitarian citizenship that took seriously the structural economic inequalities that characterise modern societies, as well as the hierarchies of labour, power and social roles that divide contemporary citizens?
- Could, or should an account of equal citizenship foreground democratic political struggle as a means of achieving positive social change?
- Must the immanent power of the ideal of equal citizenship cease at state boundaries, or might we deploy the ideal of equal citizenship as a critical tool for advancing global economic, political and ecological justice?

Whether answers to these questions are available is a question to be addressed in the rest of this book. For now, we turn to consider the work of the most influential of Rawls's successors, Ronald Dworkin.

Notes

1 As Rawls put it, primary goods 'are characterized as what persons need in their status as free and equal citizens, and as normal and fully cooperating members of society

over a complete life ... these goods are seen answering their needs as citizens' (1999a: 417).

2 On Rawls's priority rules, and especially for critical views on Rawls's defence of the priority of liberty, see Barry (1973), Hart (1989) and Taylor (2003).

3 It has often been thought that the priority rule – which gives priority to the liberty principle over the second principle (and equal opportunities over the difference principle) – thereby prioritises liberty over equality per se. This is not necessarily the case. Any equality resulting from the account arises, in fact, from the interaction of all of the principles, rather than being produced or constrained by one in particular. Indeed it could even be argued that the liberty principle actually *protects* the eventual equality of the account from the potential inegalitarianism of the difference principle. The reason why this is at least logically true is that the difference principle acknowledges no limits on legitimate inequalities, other than the interests of the worst off. In certain circumstances, this might conceivably recommend very substantial inequalities, at which point it would actually be over-ruled by the liberty principle (since, simply speaking, basic political equality is incompatible with huge economic inequalities). This reaffirms the basic point that any equality inherent in the account is not located in any one principle or subprinciple, but in the whole taken as a coherent system.

4 Rawls certainly did not adopt a luck egalitarian position, then; and in fact there are powerful reasons why, on his theory, he was unlikely to. Most significantly, Rawls considered effort itself to be morally arbitrary in much the same way as talent (Barry 1989: 225 makes this point well). Rawls makes the very telling point that reliably isolating talent from effort is likely to prove inoperable in practice. As he puts it, 'it seems clear that the effort a person is willing to make is influenced by his natural abilities and skills and the alternatives open to him. The better endowed are more likely, other things equal, to strive conscientiously, and there seems to be no way to discount for their greater good fortune. The idea of rewarding desert is impracticable' (Rawls 1971: 312). Rawls also points out that making distribution genuinely insensitive to such brute facts would require us to neutralise the influence of, for example, family background (1971: 74).

5 Rawls's Original Position did, of course, famously seek to prevent factors which are 'arbitrary from a moral point of view' affecting *how we choose principles of justice* (Rawls 1971: 12, 15). But Rawls did not seek to prevent such factors affecting the distribution of resources per se. Rawls was clear, therefore, that 'The difference principle is not of course the principle of redress. It does not require society to try to even out handicaps as if all were expected to compete on a fair basis in the same race' (Rawls 1971: 101). He argued that 'the idea is not simply to assist those who lose out through accident or misfortune (although this must be done), but instead to put all citizens in a position to manage their own affairs and to take part in social cooperation in a footing of mutual respect under appropriately equal conditions' (1999a: 419; see also 2001: 139). Certainly, he asserted that 'one follows the idea that the two principles attempt to mitigate the arbitrariness of natural contingency and social fortune' (1971: 96). But note the term *mitigate*, as opposed to correct or compensate for. Thomas Pogge makes this point clearly: 'this does not mean that endowments are to be equalized or that an economic scheme must not offer greater rewards to those better endowed. The point is that the better endowed have no special claims upon the construction of the criteria of social justice'. This means two things: firstly, that 'it is morally inappropriate for endowments to be a factor in the participants' bargaining position', and secondly that 'natural endowments do not reflect an intrinsic moral worth that would set bounds on the terms an economic scheme may offer' (Pogge

1989: 73). As Pogge (2000) puts it elsewhere, the drive to eliminate the influence of contingency does not serve as a 'mastergoal' for Rawls in the same ways as it does for luck egalitarians. Any reference to the moral arbitrariness of social and natural chance is only one among several egalitarian ideals underlying Rawls's account (see also Daniels 2003).

6 Just as surprising for some is the assertion that the principles of justice will only work in what is already a 'nearly just society' (Rawls 1971: 387). Does the theory assume a society that is essentially un-oppressive to begin with? Rawls (2001: 34–5) states that he derives his conception of justice from 'the political culture of a democratic society that has worked reasonably well over a considerable period of time'. But surely this hardly describes a society like the USA, which as Rawls was developing his theory was still characterised by widespread racial segregation and the de facto disenfranchisement of many black Americans. It is just as questionable whether it describes wealthy Western democracies now, given that they are still riven by political marginalisation, pervasive racism and sexism, and characterised by everyday acts of violence, discrimination and cultural prejudice. Moreover describing nations such as the USA as reasonably just requires us to arbitrarily ignore the external dimensions of justice – that is, the often negative, not to say hugely destructive role such a nation plays in global economic, military and ecological processes.

7 This specific critique obviously recalls traditional Marxist critiques of liberalism. As Estlund (1998: 99) notes, 'Marx argued that liberal politics, by insulating certain areas of life from political intervention, gave primacy to a non-political, non-communal conception of the person, and thereby condoned and encouraged egoistic behaviour within the constraints of the law'. And as Estlund correctly observes, what Cohen does is mount 'a new version of the Marxian charge that liberalism takes egoism as a fact of nature and condones it' (1998: 100).

8 Moreover it is possible that if we took other social goods as starting points we might well come up with very different conclusions. It has been argued that Rawls arbitrarily excludes some goods from the index of social goods, and that if these were integrated we would be led to different political conclusions. One example is health. Kymlicka (2002: 71) argues that Rawls is unjustified in restricting the index of well-being to primary social goods, and should have considered the role of primary natural goods such as health and physical ability in influencing our life-chances. Rawls initially excluded health as a social good by assuming that all people are 'fully functional' over a 'normal life'. In his later work, he acknowledged the importance of addressing those who fall outside of the 'normal range', but argued that the resulting issues could be dealt with at a later 'legislative stage', and hence must not detain designers of a putative theory of justice (Rawls 1993: 184; 2001: 173). This is very doubtful, but there have been some relatively harmonious suggestions for adding health to the metric of social goods. Norman Daniels (2003) and Fabienne Peter (2001) argue that Rawls's account could and should be extended to deal with disease. One implication of this approach for the USA would be a renewed call for at least a full and free health care system, but such a move would also turn our attention towards the 'social determinants of health'. Given that class correlates so strongly and straightforwardly with health and with life expectancy, such an argument provides a further argument for a more substantial equalisation of material resources.

9 Some attention has focused on Rawls's description of the parties to the Original Position (OP) as 'heads of families' (Rawls 1971: 128, 146; see e.g. Okin 1989). In line with my approach in the chapter as a whole, I consider debates surrounding what precisely the nature of the OP tells us about Rawls's view of the individual to be

...as important as the actual principles Rawls suggested.

...ogy has been discussed at length by numerous authors. His account ...the device called the Original Position (OP). This invoked a version ...act theory: a procedure for deriving principles which, though hypothetically ...could be used by the philosopher to demonstrate that the resulting ...re both fair and just. Despite its apparent elegance, there are ongoing ...ies about the role of the OP. It should be clear that the OP is not to be ...od as the source of Rawls's principles of justice, but as a means of expounding ...defending it (Kymlicka 2002: 64; Miller 1999a: 58; Talisse 2001: 32). It is, as ...says, an 'expository device' (Rawls 1971: 21), which seeks to demonstrate the procedural fairness of his theory. Indeed Rawls readily admitted that the OP had been ...signed specifically to yield the conclusions he wanted to argue for (1971: 141, 155). As Nagel (1989: 1) argued, the OP is essentially a heuristic or 'proxy', a 'specially constructed parallel problem of individual choice, which can be solved by the more reliable institutions and decision procedures of rational prudence'. Its success, then, depends entirely on our acceptance that the problem Rawls sets up is suitably 'parallel', and that the terms of 'rational prudence' are indeed capable of 'reliable' resolution. There are in fact many reasons to be deeply sceptical about this, and many critics have given good reasons for doubting that the OP would regularly and consistently deliver the results Rawls said that it would – see John Harsanyi (1975), Benjamin Barber (1989), Richard Norman (1987: 67), and John Roemer (1996: 181). Will Kymlicka (2002: 69) has argued with considerable justification that in the final analysis, the entire social contract method is more or less extraneous to Rawls's account of equality, and does little to forward it.

2

Equality, risk and responsibility:

Dworkin on the insurance market

Introduction

IN THE FIRST chapter of this book, it was claimed that Rawls's account of equality runs close to the vision of social citizenship espoused by Marshall, and at least partly implemented within Western liberal democracies from the 1950s onwards. Though the development of social citizenship involved many admirable achievements (such as free health care and welfare rights), and at least partly succeeded in re-establishing a link between economic and political equality, this was also a vision with its own set of unresolved problems. Nevertheless, these problems were to be intensified rather than resolved in subsequent decades. From the 1970s and 1980s onwards, social citizenship as a practice and as an identity was attacked – and at least partially dismantled – as a result of the neoliberal critique. Neoliberalism as an ideology or strategy of government has espoused a much thinner conception of 'active' citizenship, where equality, rights and obligations are overwhelmingly defined in relation to the wealth-creating free market, and welfare institutions based on principles of solidarity or community have come under sustained assault.[1]

The aim of this chapter is to read the work of Rawls's most prominent successor within liberal egalitarianism – Ronald Dworkin – alongside these developments. At the same time as the neoliberal critique was gaining momentum, the 'luck egalitarians', beginning with Dworkin, started to adapt and refine what they took as the core advances achieved by Rawls's theory. Specifically, they drew on a theme only partially revealed in Rawls's work: the ideal that equality implies eradicating any influences on distribution other than the effort or ambition of individuals (see Chapter 1). As such, liberal egalitarians from Dworkin onwards have taken seriously the neoliberal assertion that distribution must be tailored, above all, to *choice*. Whilst the New Right or neoliberal influence on their ideas has been pointed out by luck egalitarians themselves, no sustained analysis has been made of the resonances between liberal equality and the neoliberal conception of active citizenship. This chapter attempts just such an analysis.

1   Risk, insurance and neoliberalism

> Poverty, in any sense implying suffering, may be completely extinguished by the wisdom of society, combined with the good sense and providence of individuals. (Mill [1863] 1991: 146)

In recent decades, the concept of risk has come to occupy centre-stage in the debate about individual and social responsibilities. A 'new emphasis on risk and reward' (Baker and Simon 2002: 5) has seen political leaders defining their platforms on the basis of a division between those risks they would lift from the shoulders of citizens (such as crime, security or ignorance) and those they would place on them (such as poverty, health care, or old age) (see Giddens 1999). We find an accompanying emphasis on 'risk management', which is simultaneously prudential – a responsibility of cautious, forward-planning individuals – and entrepreneurial – an opportunity for speculation and accumulation, which is to be encouraged in the interests of wealth creation. As Giddens (1999: 8) argues, risk is at once something we have responsibility for limiting, and an 'energising principle' within capitalist markets: where there is risk, there is profit.

The notion of risk plays a role in all sorts of debates, including those surrounding crime and order on the one hand, and internal or external security on the other hand. In terms of the fields of welfare, social security and wealth production the paradigmatic form of risk management is that of insurance, which rationalises the contingencies of fate and insulates the wise against their effects. Such insurance may be either public or private in character, with the practice of social citizenship embodying a highly socialised, public form of insurance provision. Nevertheless, the significant point to note here is that contemporary welfare states have seen the insurance system undergo two parallel shifts towards policies that embrace risk as an incentive. Firstly governments have encouraged a proliferation of private insurance provision as an alternative or supplement to state insurance schemes, in order to 'reduce individual claims on collective resources'. Secondly, they have increasingly introduced risk as an incentive into *public* insurance schemes (Baker and Simon 2002: 4): 'reformist' centre-left parties, just as much as their conservative counterparts, have declaimed the need to incentivise the welfare system to reduce the 'moral hazard' of dependency. As O'Malley (1996) suggests, the responsible individual is increasingly called upon to remove himself from dependency on socialised provision, and adopt a prudential attitude to the vicissitudes of ill-health, unemployment, old age and disability. This redefinition of the terms of citizenship is partly rhetorical (in the UK, Unemployment Benefit has been renamed a Job-Seekers' Allowance; in Canada Unemployment Insurance has been renamed Employment Insurance; and in the USA the Social Security Act has been replaced by the Personal Responsibility Act), but it is also often accompanied by 'authoritarianism about the social obligations of welfare claimants' (Jordan 1996: 12).

Despite the fact that this process has been justified through the language of choice, control and individual autonomy, the increasing focus on the governance of risks has ensured that 'within a regime of liberal governance, insurance is one of the greatest sources of regulatory authority over private life' (Baker and Simon 2002: 13). Seen from this perspective, ceasing to govern may entail an extension of government by other means (Ericson *et al.* 2000). This is often explained in turn by reference to the character of neoliberalism as a set of practices or a mentality of government. Firstly, neoliberalism involves a continual self-interrogation of government: it enacts a continuous liberal critique of liberalism, centred on the question of whether it is possible to govern less, and yet at the same time more economically. Secondly, whilst neoliberalism seeks to roll back the frontiers of the state, it also seeks 'to extend the rationality of the market ... and the decision-making criteria it suggests' to diverse areas such as criminal policy, the regulation of families and delinquency (Foucault 1994: 79), as well as the regulation of welfare, education and health. Thirdly, neoliberalism pursues the 'autonomisation' of society: it seeks to achieve the unmediated government *of* individuals *by* individuals. The objective of neoliberal government in any formal sense is to repeal itself, and set in its place microgovernment by rational and responsible individuals. The reason this 'autonomisation' is an ambiguous process is that the construction of individual citizens as autonomous and rationally self-governing is paradoxically a highly ambitious project. Indeed, governments of many hues have since the 1980s preached a gospel of liberation from 'old-style' government, whilst in fact increasing regulation of various 'quasi-non-governmental' forms.

Within political discourse on welfare policy, individuals are increasingly portrayed as having untapped potential, and the goal of government is to facilitate its self-expression, chiefly by removing obstacles (but also by providing incentives where necessary). As Tony Blair (1992) has argued, 'People are held back; by lack of decent education, poverty, immobility, vested interests. From these they must be released. The idea of empowerment is stronger than that of liberty.' Neoliberal government aims at 'encouraging or compelling citizens to act on their own behalf' in predicting and minimising the effects of misfortune (Petersen *et al.* 1999: 38–39). 'A "new paternalism" arises in which insurance against eventualities such as unemployment, ill-health and old age becomes a private choice rather than a communal responsibility, with the insured person construed as a rational and autonomous agent' (Petersen *et al.* 1999: 45; see also O'Malley 1996). As Nikolas Rose argues, 'social insurance, as a principle of social solidarity, gives way to a privatisation of risk management' (Rose 1996: 58). The connections between responsibilities and risks proliferate as modern governments insist that we cannot possess unconditional rights to, for example, medical services when risks are clearly related to 'lifestyle practices' (Giddens 1999) and even our 'genetic gambles'.

The analysis seems persuasive as an explanation of recent shifts in welfare politics, but it appears curiously disconnected from the dominant trends of normative political theorising within the academic world. On the one hand, the rise of the phenomena of 'insurance as government' and 'risk management as responsibility and opportunity' have not obviously been addressed even by prominent liberal political theorists, and these concepts seem neither to be defended nor even acknowledged in their work. This is perhaps not surprising given that although liberal political theorists 'can accommodate the welfare state' as a whole, they have 'actually had relatively little to say about it' (Lacey 1998: 56). On the other hand, the analysts of neoliberalism cited above have devoted little attention to tracing the patterns of neoliberal concepts within the academic literature on political theory. This chapter is an attempt to begin to remedy this disconnection. It will show how Ronald Dworkin – perhaps the foremost liberal theorist writing today – offers us an account of egalitarian justice which foregrounds the apparatus of insurance, and represents the management of risk within the welfare system as both an opportunity and a responsibility. Although Dworkin suggests that the broad approach can be applied to a whole range of problems (including genetic testing, criminal law and even liberties, to name a few), we will concentrate on his arguments about welfare provision, and to a lesser extent health care. Far from representing a challenge to the neoliberal shift in contemporary politics, Dworkin provides a close analogue of the neoliberal incitement of the individual to take on responsibility for managing and capitalising on risk. The impulse of Dworkin, as of the neoliberal, is captured well by Rose: the rational, responsible citizen 'is to add to his or her obligations the need to adopt a calculative prudent personal relation to fate now conceived in terms of calculable dangers and avertable risks' (Rose 1996: 58). Furthermore Ericson *et al.* (2000: 554) suggest that a core element of neoliberalism in practice is the portrayal of inequality as choice: 'Within a neoliberal regime of responsible risk taking all difference, and the inequalities that result from it, is seen as a matter of choice. If one ends up poor, unemployed, and unfulfilled, it is because of poorly thought-out risk decisions.' As I will show Dworkin's approach, too, seems peculiarly incapable of providing satisfactory responses to many of the inequalities that do characterise contemporary societies other than by presenting them as the product of autonomous choices. This is not to say that Dworkin's scheme is without its advantages, but it is to say that the concessions it makes to the neoliberal model of risk management are so profound that it seems incapable of mounting any serious opposition to the neoliberal transformation of society.

2   Equality and individual agency

The starting point of Dworkin's theory is his notion of treatment as equals, which he defines as the fundamental value of liberalism (Dworkin 1985). Governments should show equal concern for all individuals, and should respect their integrity and dignity *as* individuals. Liberals do not mean by this that we should all be treated *in the same way* all of the time – for example, that we should all receive the same benefits, or pay the same taxes. On the contrary, treating individuals *as equals* means treating them on the basis of what is distinctively individual about them, and this may require treating different individuals differently. On this account, equality comes to be conceived as a 'sorting' concept: this is to say that equality represents a way of *dividing* all sorts of moral and political 'facts' – the environment we live in, our individual actions, or inclinations, our identity, a multitude of social forces – into those which should influence any just distribution, and those which should not. Crucially, this contention seeks to shift the burden of political argument: it presumes that equality is the default position, and demands that departures from it need to be justified with a good reason. As Benn and Peters stated, we 'presume equality until there is reason to presume otherwise ... What we really demand, when we say that all men are equal, is that *none shall be held to have a claim to better treatment than another, in advance of good grounds being produced*' (1959: 111, 110, italics in original). If we extend the anti-discrimination argument far enough, egalitarian theory reverses its polarity. If individuals are treated equally unless and until we establish good reasons for treating them otherwise, the debate effectively turns into a philosophical inquiry into the question: once we have cleared away the detritus of arguments based on rank, caste or identity, how *can* we justify legitimate *inequalities*?

Pursuing a similar logic, Dworkin suggests that some kind of 'cut' needs to be made between the sphere of individual choice or preferences on the one hand, and our 'circumstances' or 'environment' on the other. This echoes many hugely important distinctions which have pervaded the social sciences (and which have also been highly gendered): 'nature' versus 'nurture', nature versus culture, virtue versus fortune, free will versus determinism, structure versus agency, individual versus society, and so on. For theorists from Machiavelli to Mill and through to Dworkin, it is the sphere of action or choice (culture/virtue/free will/agency) which should influence the way our lives go, whereas the influence of the sphere of contingency and chance (nature/fortune/determinism/structure) should be either neutralised or compensated for. What is distinctive about Dworkin's argument is exactly where, and the persistence with which, the distinction gets drawn. If it is unfair to treat people on the basis of factors outside of their control, such as sex, or class, or race, it must therefore be fair to treat individuals on the basis of what *is*

A critique of liberal equality

in their control. As such Andrew Levine (1999: 404) argues, such 'liberal egalitarians are committed to the view that only differences arising in consequence
of individuals' free choices can be defended by appeal to the idea of equality'. In
its simplest form the linking of equality to choice has some initial plausibility,
since it seems to chime with many common intuitions, and, perhaps more
significantly, many of the political sentiments of the 1980s and 1990s. Liberal
egalitarians have in recent decades understood their major opponent to be not
Marxism, but the anti-egalitarian New Right – a movement which as expressed
by Hayek witnessed invectives against both redistribution *and* the notion of
meritocracy, which threatens to meddle in the business of the wealth-creating
market. Within liberal egalitarianism there has been a belief that the best way to
deal with the New Right challenge is to co-opt some of its core arguments. As
such, Cohen celebrates Dworkin's version of equality on the basis that he 'has,
in effect, performed for egalitarianism the considerable service of incorporating
within it the most powerful idea in the arsenal of the anti-egalitarian right: the
idea of choice and responsibility' (Cohen 1989: 933). John Roemer, similarly,
argues that 'this new articulation of responsibility in the theory of distributive
justice, and of egalitarian theory in particular, is the signal achievement in the
field of the last fifteen years' (Roemer 1996: 309). For Richard Arneson, this
development makes it possible to assert that 'egalitarianism and responsibility
are comrades, not adversaries' (Arneson 1997b: 329). As Levine suggests,
'Liberal egalitarianism has become a dominant position within contemporary
political philosophy in part because its defining conviction appears to be incon-
trovertible. What persons freely do is normatively significant, if anything is'
(Levine 1999: 407).

Dworkin's approach is peculiarly monological, then, insofar as it dictates that
for the realm of distributive justice there can only be one relevant reason for
treating individuals differently, and that this reason must be individual choice –
and especially the exercise of effort or ambition. As such, his theory constitutes
itself to a great extent through its rejection of meritocracy (conceived as the
rewarding of talent). Rawls's attack on 'formal' equality of opportunity is widely
taken to be the defining moment of the resurgent liberal egalitarianism.
Dworkin (2000) agrees that from the perspective of justice, talent is morally
arbitrary, and therefore argues that no one should have less income simply
because they possess less natural talent. The problem with rewarding talent, for
both Rawls and Dworkin, is that it is a morally neutral artefact which whether it
is conceived as a natural artefact *or* as a social product, has only a dubious relationship with individual choice. Where the two theories depart is that Rawls
wants to downscale the role claimed for the idea of meritocracy, whereas
Dworkin wants to *reformulate* it and in so doing provide a sweeping basis for a
theory of justice. His theory rejects what we can call 'narrow' equality of opportunity in favour of a 'deep' equality of opportunity (Callinicos 2000: 39–57), or,

I might add, a 'new' meritocracy.[2] If rewarding talent is to perform the wrong 'cut' between the individual and his or her circumstances, we need to reject and replace it with *effort* as the generator of legitimate inequalities. If we link rewards to effort and ambition, we can genuinely isolate those decisions which are the result of free choice, and for which individuals can therefore be held account- able (see Armstrong 2003a). Meritocracy thereby shifts from the rewarding of talent, to the rewarding of effort or choice itself. We can now turn to a closer analysis of Dworkin's proposals.

3   Dworkin on equality of resources

Dworkin considers his theory of equality to be the correct distributive expres- sion of the ideal of treating individuals as equals. His theory, originally published in 1981, has been taken as the main point of departure by the major- ity of the so-called 'luck egalitarians', including Arneson (1989), Cohen (1989), Rakowski (1991) and Roemer (1996), and certainly his theory represents the first concerted attempt to integrate considerations of choice and personal responsibility into egalitarian theory. Dworkin argues that sensitivity to our individual *choices* or preferences is a crucial test for any fair distribution, and one which other theories of equality have always failed to meet. By contrast, any just distribution must simultaneously be insensitive to our *circumstances*, such as the talents we possess, or the environment we happen to be born into.[3] I will deal with the goal of choice-sensitivity first. To establish this sensitivity, any truly fair distribution must satisfy a device Dworkin calls the *envy test*. This test dictates that a fair distribution of resources should be one which is tailored to our own choices in the sense that, standing back from it, we wouldn't swap our bundle of resources for those of anyone else. If you and I both start off with a hundred pounds and you spend yours on avant-garde cinema whereas I spend mine on chocolate, there is nothing unequal about the end results so long as cinema and chocolate are really what we respectively value in life: the resources we buy have equal value *to us*. Dworkin develops this idea by asking us to imagine a hypothetical auction, in which we all want various goods, and in which we each have an equal number of bargaining chips with which to satisfy our wants: as such, the auction displays the features of a perfectly competitive market in which all participants have equal purchasing power. The auction grants each lot of goods to the highest bidder, and finishes when all goods have been allocated. Dworkin's contention is that any outcomes of this imaginary auction represent a distribution of resources which is both fair, and responsive to individual choices, and to a large extent Dworkin's goal is to discover how such an ideal (equal and yet completely choice-sensitive) distribution might be best approximated in practice.

There is, however, one problem. As Dworkin argues, the resulting outcomes won't quite do, because they cancel out inequalities in *external* circumstances like money, but not inequalities in *internal* circumstances such as ability. For physical reasons, we may not all be able to make the same *use* of a given set of resources. Because of the 'natural lottery' of life, we all have different levels and types of talent, and some of us suffer from various disabilities. For reasons outside of our control, we may still be disadvantaged, and for that reason we might still envy others' bundles of resources. This inequality of internal resources obviously cannot be rectified directly, and yet is clearly arbitrary from a moral point of view. As such, it seems to require some kind of compensation. This generates its own dilemma, for Dworkin points out that in a world with finite resources, disabilities or a lack of talents can never be so fully compensated for that a disabled or untalented individual will truly not envy the lives of anyone else. The only option in the real world is for such people to receive what we think is a *fair* amount of compensation. But how do we decide how much is 'fair'? To solve this problem, Dworkin introduces the second key innovation of his theory: the *hypothetical insurance market*. Individuals in his auction, in a state of ignorance about their own abilities or talents, should be given the opportunity to purchase packages of insurance against disability or illness or other such contingencies. They may either choose to adopt expensive packages or cheap packages, depending on how risk-averse they are. If I am particularly risk-averse, for example, I might choose to spend half of my resources on a package offering me generous compensation in the event of such contingencies. What is crucial about this is that it *restores* the link between choice (or, as Dworkin puts it, 'option luck') and the 'brute luck' of ill-health or disability. To be more precise, it at least partly brings these brute facts under the domain of human agency, by linking how we will be compensated for such brute luck with the option luck of our purchases of insurance cover. In this sense, the eventual worth of what we end up with is once more responsive to our choices, and is in large part once more a product of our own decisions. Though not perfect this auction and insurance model is the best available method of making distribution genuinely sensitive to choice, and yet insensitive to arbitrary contingency.

So far, so hypothetical. But how could Dworkin's analysis be used to generate specific policy conclusions? The (contentious) step which Dworkin takes is to argue that a representative, average, and most importantly 'rational' decision about how much insurance to purchase in the hypothetical auction can be taken as both fair and just for actual societies. This obviously requires illustration, and the best example of Dworkin's method in practice comes with his discussion of a hypothetical insurance market for health care. He argues that 'A just distribution [of health care] is one that well-informed people create for themselves by individual choices, provided that the economic system and the distribution of wealth in the community in which these choices are made are themselves just' (2000: 313). Specifically, he suggests we look at life through the eyes of a prudent and rational 25-year-old individual. Such a rational individual, if choosing how to insure himself against ill-health, would opt, Dworkin asserts, for moderate but not excessively expensive medical cover. Thinking rationally about how to spend the resources available to him, he wouldn't see it as sensible to choose an expensive policy which provided for free cosmetic surgery, or for expensive life-prolonging care in hopeless medical circumstances. Rather, he would choose a somewhat cheaper policy which concentrated more on provisions for his younger, more 'vigorous' life. Dworkin therefore argues that something like the policy outlined above should be institutionalised for *all* citizens (not just 25-year olds), and financed through taxation. This implies a free, universal basic health care system, which would be necessary for the goal of circumstance-insensitivity. He also argues for a second element of provision, however: we should also encourage private companies to provide a range of schemes for top-up cover, which individuals could sign up to on a voluntary basis. This latter addition is necessary to make the account more choice-sensitive, since those with greater aversions to risk could then freely purchase more cover. Dworkin believes that the hypothetical insurance model can be applied in many other cases, though he has not spelled out the precise implications for all such cases. He does argue, though, that in terms of socio-economic reforms more broadly, reasonable individuals in the auction would opt for moderate welfare provision and the guarantee of a basic minimum (2000: 334–8).

It is interesting to note that what Dworkin actually recommends is very close to the present scheme of a basic welfare system and a two-tier health system (albeit one perhaps closer to the UK model than to the present US one). Most welfare states now operate similar two-tier (contributory plus non-contributory) schemes of provision. There are, then, two distinct approaches to insurance in Dworkin's scheme. First, we have a strategy of *socialising* insurance, under which individuals still face risks, but society (via state taxation) endeavours to pick up the tab for some of the negative consequences of such risks. Such a strategy is particularly associated with the post-war settlement within Western welfare democracies, which 'incarnate[d] social solidarity in collectivising the management of the individual and collective dangers posed by the economic riskiness of a capricious system of wage labour, and the corporeal riskiness of a body subject to sickness and injury, under the stewardship of a "social" state' (Rose 1996: 48). Secondly, though, we have a strategy of *individualising* insurance, under which individuals again still face risks, but are enabled or encouraged to directly manage the consequences of such risks through rational calculation, theoretically without state mediation. This implies what we could call a *prudentialisation* (see O'Malley 1996) or an *entrepreneurialisation* of risk management. The first, socialised strategy is necessary to insulate us against the consequences of the natural lottery of talents, abilities and health. The second is necessary to inject choice-sensitivity into the scheme: to ensure, in short, that the bundle of resources we end up with is in some way influenced by our own rational decisions about and attitudes towards the contingencies of life. We will address the political implications of Dworkin's scheme further later on, but for now I want to raise two theoretical questions about the account.

Firstly, it is instructive to examine the criteria for determining that particular outcomes are just on the theory of equality of resources, and which Dworkin suggests in setting up the hypothetical auction. There are three of these criteria: firstly, resources must be shared as nearly equally as possible; secondly, all relevant state of the art information must be widely known; and, thirdly, no one must know 'how likely any particular person' is to suffer any negative consequences of the natural lottery (Dworkin 2000: 311–12). Although Dworkin calmly asserts that 'they are not, I think, beyond the reach of the imagination' (2000: 312), these criteria are extremely exacting. None of them are true now, and neither are they likely to be achieved in the near future. This raises serious questions about the applicability of Dworkin's theory, because by hypothesis *any* policy proposal in the absence of (for instance) equal resources would be unjust. Despite this it seems that even in the very marked absence of Dworkin's preconditions, he is prepared to make numerous policy proposals for the here and now. In the case of health care, for instance, Dworkin is arguing for a specific position on the delivery of health care in American society. But this is really remarkable, since the system he recommends, by his own logic, would be unfair in the present circumstances, unless preceded by a drastic equalisation of resources. For instance, top-up schemes of private provision for health (the individualised or *entrepreneurialised* element of the account) would, on Dworkin's theory, only be fair if we all had equal money to spend or not spend on this option. On the contrary, in reality such schemes are usually associated with 'middle class flight': they are used by the wealthy to opt out of common institutions, which frequently suffer decline as a result. Not only does Dworkin have no praxis of the social or political change required to equalise resources, but he seems content to view current, actual decisions about health insurance in the USA as a rough guide to what would actually be a fair system.[4] On this point, Ian Shapiro quite rightly states that 'it is hard to see why Dworkin attaches any normative weight to market behaviour in a society he has already stipulated to be unjust' (Shapiro 1999: 214).

Secondly, it is difficult to know what to make of the declaration that 'it seems fair to construct a mandatory coverage scheme on the basis of assumptions about what all but a small number of people would think appropriate' (Dworkin 2000: 315), because we simply do not know what individuals in the hypothetical auction would decide about health care, or even if they would coalesce around one position. Indeed, Dworkin's account becomes ineffable precisely because – just as Nagel (1989: 1) says of Rawls – he actually works on the basis of a 'proxy', or a 'specially constructed parallel problem of individual choice'.

Dworkin believes that practical problems can thereby be more 'reliably' solved given certain conditions of ignorance and assumptions about rational choices, which as with Rawls provides us with a 'rational' or 'prudent' solution. The authority placed on the 'results' of the hypothetical auction renders highly dubious Dworkin's claim that his theory 'makes no use of any social contract [and that] it hopes to find whatever support its political claims may claim not in any unanimous agreement or consent, even hypothetical' (2000: 5), and as such Dworkin's account is vulnerable to many of the problems engendered by Rawls's recourse to an Original Position. In particular his method opens Dworkin up to Fleurbaey's criticism that 'The fact that an ideal individual would be ready to sacrifice her own welfare in a particular (uncertain) state of nature gives no argument in favour of sacrificing the fate of a surely existing subpopulation' (Fleurbaey 2002: 90; this certainly calls to mind the kind of criticism Dworkin himself levelled at Rawls). As with the Original Position, the method immediately provokes the charge that the auction is somehow an inadequate or at least a skewed device: has Dworkin rigged the auction?[5] We have to consider the possibility that genuine resource equality would require provision beyond what individuals might choose in the auction. Obviously, as is the case with Rawls, it is possible to argue that Dworkin has taken one particular notion of (what he thinks would be) a rational choice, and tried to render it inevitable. Any rival choice beyond the average is therefore labelled 'imprudent' or 'irrational', despite the fact that it could be quite plausible to some (Van der Veen 2002: 73). For this kind of reason, Fleurbaey (2002: 83) argues that the auction is 'a very poor device'.

We can develop the analogy with Rawls a little further, because Dworkin, like Rawls, does not use his proxy to *actually derive* principles of justice (indeed, like Rawls, he *couldn't*, because the auction, like Rawls's Original Position, requires impossible knowledge conditions). Like Rawls, Dworkin in fact has a preconceived idea of what constitutes a rational, reasonable and prudent approach to risk, which he uses the auction to illustrate. When the auction approach becomes too ineffable, Dworkin simply refers directly to claims about prudence and rationality. But as Colin MacLeod correctly observes, this 'actually constitutes an abandonment of the hypothetical market as a theoretical device for gauging the demands of justice. Once the focus shifts directly to the question of what constitutes reasonable compensation for a disability or a prudent amount of health care, the insurance market apparatus becomes superfluous' (MacLeod 1998: 95–96). It is interesting enough that Dworkin exaggerates the gulf between his reasonable persons approach and that of Rawls, but there is a more important issue at stake, which is that the method seriously undermines the pretensions of the scheme to defend the value of individual responsibility, for it now turns out that rather than individuals making choices, one particular idea of a responsible choice is to be 'enforced' (Dworkin 2000: 319). The schemes

Dworkin suggests actually enforce what he takes to be 'prudent' outcomes of 'informed' choice, and in practice therefore bypass *actual* individual choice.[6] The only significant difference here between Rawls and Dworkin is that whilst both produce a rationalist, individualistic defence of equality which crumbles under closer scrutiny, Rawls at least can fall back on a deeply 'communitarian' vision of the values of individuals committed to solidarity and cooperation. Dworkin, on the other hand, though he has attempted to defend the value of community in his work, has done so in a very ambiguous way (see Frazer and Lacey 1993: 68, 114), and more to the point he does not resort to values of community and solidarity *even* in defending the socialised element of his insurance scheme. If we reject his rationalised defence of equality of resources, as we should, it is not clear what he has to fall back on.

4 Implementing equality of resources

Assessing the concrete implications of Dworkin's scheme is not easy. One major problem is that given the level of abstraction at which it operates – as with Rawls – it is not obvious how we would even know if equality of resources had been achieved, as even his most ardent supporters concede.[7] But it is interesting that despite having no praxis of how to achieve equality of resources, Dworkin seems content to recommend concrete policy positions which could only be justified if it, or something like it, existed already, and it is tempting to read this as a clue of some significance. It is important to recognise the partial successes in tackling entrenched injustices that Dworkin's scheme would achieve, and even a basic universal health service for the USA would mark real progress in a time of general retreat from collectivism. Nevertheless, it is difficult to construe many of Dworkin's other policy proposals (including state encouragement of private health top-ups, a defence of private funding of political parties, a welfare system designed to make seeking even low-paid jobs an attractive option[8]) as radical in intent. Dworkin (2000: 7) himself relates them to the 'Third Way' between conservatism and the 'old' egalitarianism, and Alex Callinicos considers him a 'right-wing social democrat' (2001b: 184).

Whilst Callinicos's assessment looks about right, it has frequently been argued that making society genuinely insensitive to the brute luck of our 'circumstances' would require far more radical changes than Dworkin ever contemplates. It might require substantial inroads into the way in which parents raise, nurture and educate their children, for instance, or substantial redistributions of wealth, allied with a ban on inheritance, and other great interventions into the minutiae of individual lives. Nevertheless, it is important to be clear that Dworkin frequently rejects such radical transformations for the exact reasons that they would interfere with the family, with personal freedom, or with some wider notion of 'efficiency', for instance. As with Rawls, the rejection of 'formal' in favour of 'deep' (or 'fair') equality of opportunity is not clearly carried through. This leaves his defenders with a distinct quandary. Thus Kymlicka (2001) bemoans the fact that Dworkin has spent far too much time discussing how we might make distributions much more choice-sensitive, but far too little time considering how we might make distributions genuinely insensitive to our circumstances. Kymlicka appears to consider this a forgetful elision, giving Dworkin's work 'a (perhaps unintended) conservative cast' (2001: 5). Kymlicka concedes that

> Dworkin's policy suggestions are surprisingly modest. They are primarily focused on *ex post* corrections to the inequalities generated by the market – i.e. they take the existing level of inequality in market income as a given, and ask how best to tax some of the unequal income of the advantaged and transfer it to the disadvantaged. But these proposals leave unaddressed an important plank of his theory – namely that people should have equal *ex ante* endowments when they enter the market ... Of course, any attempt to achieve this sort of *ex ante* equality would require a major attack on entrenched economic divisions in our society. Dworkin himself offers no concrete policy suggestions about how to achieve this. (2002: 82)

This, for Kymlicka, is 'disappointing'.

I agree with Kymlicka's analysis here, but suggest that we explain it with reference to the logic of Dworkin's own theory. Specifically, we can learn from Van der Veen's (2002) careful analysis, which suggests that the two goals of choice-sensitivity and circumstance-insensitivity pull us towards quite different practical policy implications. If this sets up two horns of a dilemma, all the evidence Kymlicka cites suggests that Dworkin is content to prioritise the goal of choice-sensitivity. Whilst Dworkin's position may not be coherent, prioritising the other goal, of circumstance-insensitivity is surely no more coherent either, and clearly requires stronger support than Dworkin's theory of equality of resources can give it. Indeed, Kymlicka lets the cat out of the bag somewhat in raising the question of whether choice-sensitivity and endowment-insensitivity are *compatible*. On the one hand, the logic of choice-sensitivity surely suggests a completely voluntary, individualised scheme – and might also suggest means-tested benefits conditional on willingness to work, deregulated economic policies and privatisation. But these measures would fail, however, to be insensitive to circumstance. On the other hand, for distribution to be genuinely insensitive to circumstance would require a much more generous welfare system than Dworkin allows us to contemplate,[9] and might imply unconditional health provision, a guaranteed income scheme, universal pension rights, or restrictions on capital mobility. But these measures would be insensitive to choice, or might even restrict choice – at least for some.[10] Although directly contrary to the logic of Dworkin's account, one of the most promising ways of blocking the monotonous regularity of elite reproduction might actually be to increase the influence of *genuine* chance. For instance, in educational selection, the best way of breaking the power of elites to reproduce themselves over time might be to make greater use of lotteries in allocating places between suitably qualified candidates. Such a proposal would be anathema to luck egalitarians, but deserves serious attention.[11]

By the same token, if we really want to insulate people from the brute luck of their circumstances, the establishment of a citizen's or basic income appears a particularly promising possibility. A number of justifications have been suggested for such a scheme (see Van Parijs 1992): that it would increase workers' bargaining power vis-à-vis employers; that it would enable citizens genuine choice to pursue the kinds of lives they consider important; that it would prevent carers being disadvantaged by their social roles; or that it would open the doors for a more fundamental challenge to capitalism and/or liberal welfarism (see Gorz 1999; Levitas 2001). Some feminists, to be sure, have been wary of this idea,[12] and some of these have instead endorsed a 'participation income' conditional on some kind of work, be it paid work, caring work or voluntary citizens' work (see Young 1997b; Lister 2003). But either way, the approach does seem to provide a way of challenging the ascendancy of paid work within liberal egalitarian discourse (see Chapter 4). Whilst luck egalitarians have sometimes been sceptical of the idea precisely because it seems detached from the exercise of choice and responsibility, defenders of the scheme often point to the very 'liberal' justification that it would secure the grounds for genuine freedom and diversity (see e.g. Van Parijs 1995), whilst perhaps providing a foothold for more radical reform.[13]

In the end, the dilemma Dworkin faces turns us back to the very thorny question of whether we can in fact separate talents from ambition, as Rawls (1971) doubted we could.[14] Philosophically speaking, Dworkin has never satisfactorily grounded the ideas of choice and responsibility that his theory so clearly relies upon; he has instead adopted what Fleurbaey calls an 'institutional' approach, which declares that some things simply *have* to be our responsibility, since 'individuals, as moral agents, cannot but assume responsibility for our ends' (Fleurbaey 2002: 84). I will not develop this point here, but it is indeed interesting to inquire what the disembodied ambitions and preferences Dworkin seems to suppose might look like. If we really strip all forms of (arbitrary) talent from the individual, the basis for distribution that remains is presumably something like pure will: the abstract desire to possess, undifferentiated and unrefined. Meritocracy is thus replaced with willocracy – distribution to the ambitious, those who want resources the most. Despite Dworkin's earlier (1989) assertion that egalitarianism should be 'metaphysically unambitious' the problems which he saddles himself with are profound. The debate about the nature of choice is notoriously imponderable, and in the end Dworkin makes no serious contribution to it. Rather than providing a theory of choice itself, choice is used as a rhetorical device to justify what Dworkin believes is demanded by rationality and prudence. Despite his reticence about specifying choice in any way, the theme of choice and responsibility resonates throughout his work. In the next section, we will examine the extent to which Dworkin, like the neoliberals, presents inequality as a quandary about individual choice.

5 Equality and individual choice

Within Dworkin's account, equality is to be achieved by ensuring that the right characteristics of individuals get rewarded, with possible candidates being industry, effort, ambition or taste/preference. As with neoliberal rhetoric, it may well transpire that this serves to deflect attention away from the institutions and processes that produce relations of inequality. It has always been questionable whether strictly liberal defenders of equality have ever drawn on any significant theory of *inequality*, aside from pointing to the brute irrationality of individual acts of discrimination or poor judgement. The literature characteristically works through hypothetical examples of the fate of Adams and Bettys, who differ in terms of their histories, abilities or tastes. Although such comparisons do well to reveal differences in the possession of various goods, they typically tell us little about the *relationships* between such hypothetical individuals, still less social groups. In this abstract world oppression, domination, sexism, racism, are therefore factored out. As a consequence, as Phillips (2004) notes, if we discern variations of achievement between groups, the first place we should look for an explanation is towards different preferences or predispositions towards lucrative work. When considering whether a given distribution is just or unjust, we simply have to perform the egalitarian 'cut': we either label it as a (just) consequence of preference or choice, or an (unjust) result of brute luck. But the division of everything into either 'choices' or 'circumstances' ignores the fact that *relationships* are often what matter, and detracts our attention from the processes that produce injustice (see Chapter 5).

Dworkin's position on preferences or beliefs is actually slightly more sophisticated than this. As observed above, Dworkin avoids the minefield of analysing what our preferences or beliefs are caused by, and asserts that we must be held responsible for them so long as we *identify* with them (2000: 7). But this does not solve matters at all. In fact in Dworkin's case we can see that the envy freedom, insurance auction-led approach gives wholly unsatisfactory answers to many of the pervasive inequalities that characterise contemporary societies. Dworkin had been widely criticised for simply not taking any position on sexual inequalities (Iorns 1993; Schwartzman 2000; Kim 2001), but the account he finally does present is revealing. In response to the suggestion that many women suffer disadvantage because, for instance, of the gendered nature of the division of labour, Dworkin has asserted that this issue is to be addressed like any other on his account: as policy-makers, we need to tackle such sexual inequalities only if women fail the envy test – if, on reflection, they would prefer the position of men. Specifically, Dworkin resorts to a rhetorical strategy he uses elsewhere (2000: 292), that of a hypothetical magic pill. If women would not take a pill that would turn them into men, with all of the distributive implications, then neither should they be compensated in any way (cited in Robeyns 2003: 541). Many feminists would rightly consider this insulting, but surely this 'choice' tells us little about the actual position of women. Is pride in one's 'identity', in these circumstances, to be considered an 'expensive taste'? Even referring us back to an idea of rational prudence doesn't help matters, because this strategy generates conclusions just as baldly impossible (does prudence require that we do identify with our 'identity', and claim nothing in the way of 'compensation', or does prudence require that we renounce our 'identity' in return for 'compensation'?). The point to make about the insurance/auction approach, then, is that it is insufficiently conscious of the intersubjective nature of social or cultural forms of inequality, so that instead of focussing on the ways in which identities are formed in hierarchy, our adherence to 'identity' itself becomes the problem (and in this sense, identity itself is prudentialised). Dworkin's theory either neglects, or insults oppressed groups,[15] and presents them with 'choices' which are never faced by those whose identities are dominant and normalised.

Similar points have been repeatedly levelled at Dworkin with regard to his treatment of disability. Effectively, by individualising the issue (would I choose to be disabled, in an abstract world?), the theory again requires a brutal choice between valuing our own identity and achieving valuable resources. The issues at stake in terms of disability have been discussed most comprehensively and persuasively by Colin MacLeod (but see also Tremain 1996), who argues that 'because Dworkin's theory views compensation as mainly a matter of adjusting individual ownership of resources, it is insensitive to broader concerns about the complexion of the social environment in which persons with disabilities must live' (MacLeod 1998: 14). The primary problem in practice is that Dworkin 'locates the problem of disability in the "qualities of mind and body" of persons. The physiological and psychological attributes which some persons have (either as a matter of natural endowment or as the consequence of calamity) create obstacles to the living of a satisfactory life which are not faced by others who are more fortunate' (1998: 84). This ignores the fact that the disadvantages faced by disabled persons are at least partly 'creations of the discriminatory practices which dominate the social environment in which they conduct their lives' (1998: 85). Or more precisely, we might add, Dworkin merely assumes such discrimination and prejudice away to begin with, and as with the material equality required for his theory to materialise, it never reappears (see e.g. Dworkin 2000: 158–61; see Robeyns 2003). In effect, what MacLeod does is to bring in the lessons of what has come to be known as the social model of disability: the marginalisation of 'the disabled' cannot be reme-died merely by transferring resources to compensate them (and the weakness of this strategy is not, as Dworkin suggests, simply that there is not enough money to go around). Rather, the social model of disability suggests that 'disability' is at least partly a reflection of the way in which the social and physical environ-ment is more hospitable to the needs of some people than it is to others. As such, Ingrid Robeyns is surely right to suggest that the theory is 'structurally unable to account for the cultural aspects of gender, race, and other dimensions of human diversity that create unjust inequalities between people' (Robeyns 2003: 541). To be more precise, it is unable to cope with them without shoe-horning us into certain repugnant 'choices'. This reification of identity reflects a broader problem, which is a neglect of the fact that circumstances are shaped by other people's choices. In the next section, it will be argued that rather than heading off the New Right, the wholesale and uncritical incorporation of ideas of choice and responsibility has been debilitating for his egalitarianism.

6   Making plans for justice: choice, responsibility and prudence

If winners were made to share their winnings with losers, then no-one would gamble. (Dworkin 2000: 185)

As noted at the outset, one of the major attractions of Dworkin's theory is often said to be that it presents a serious challenge to the New Right (I will hereafter use the broader term neoliberalism) – precisely because it co-opts the core idea of that tradition: 'the idea of choice and responsibility' (Cohen 1989: 933). Serious doubt will be cast on this idea in this final section. Although neoliberal-ism managed to transform the landscape of political debate in most Western countries, one of its many problems – or perhaps, in practice, strengths – is that it exhibits a constant slippage between the concepts of choice and responsibil-ity. Despite Cohen's (1989) implication that they are, in fact, a single idea, they are clearly not. One of the problems of Dworkin's theory – and one of the reasons why it does not, after all, pose a serious challenge to such neoliberal thought – is that it imports this ambiguity wholesale. The relationship between choice and responsibility has remained unelaborated. I suggest that there are three major arguments about choice and responsibility present in neoliberalism:

- *The freedom argument*: people should have a range of choices open to them, so that they can exercise some control over the way their lives go.
- *The rewards argument*: justice demands that we link (chiefly economic) rewards to the exercise of ambition, effort or prudent choice.[16]
- *The responsibility argument*: people should be encouraged to act responsibly and prudently; as such, it may be necessary to deter people from making imprudent choices.

The key point to make here is that these ideas are analytically distinct: we can accept the first without accepting the second and third (or, we can accept the first two without accepting the last). In fact, neoliberal rhetoric draws most of its legitimacy from the first idea, which seems broadly acceptable to many people – as such, the neoliberalism has always constituted itself as a creed of liberation and empowerment. By contrast, the second and third ideas frequently function to actually undermine the first idea, as political practice incentivises and disincentivises certain 'choices'. It is in any case crucial to neoliberalism in theory and practice that it shows a constant slippage between the three ideas. Rather than drawing any broader connection between Dworkin and neoliberal thought, the present argument holds that his theory has tended to work in much the same way in the case of choice and responsibility. Dworkin presents versions of the three arguments about choice and responsibility at various points, and does not draw any analytical distinction between them. Again, although his theory draws most of its force from the rhetorical strength of the first idea, in advancing the second and third arguments he ultimately undermines it.

I will draw attention only to some of these slippages. To begin with, Dworkin has all the ingredients for a paternalist account of distributive justice, but seems unsure about whether to use them. He argues that individuals have objective (or 'critical') interests, which can be distinguished from what they actually want (their 'volitional' interests). He believes, further, that individuals can be mistaken about those critical interests, of which governments may have more objective knowledge. Similarly, he makes continued reference to his 'challenge model of ethics', which dictates that a 'successful' life is one in which we endeavour to meet worthwhile challenges. Indeed, in the most remarkable turn of phrase in *Sovereign Virtue*, Dworkin states that we have 'equal importance' as citizens not because our lives are 'equally valuable' but because they must not be 'wasted' (2000: 5). Nevertheless, he accepts that choices cannot have any value for individuals unless they personally identify with them (see MacLeod 2003: 139). Thus whilst some of the liberal egalitarians he has influenced use similar arguments to argue for 'quasi-paternalist' policies such as workfare schemes (see e.g. Arneson 1997a), Dworkin seems to reject paternalism in principle.

But whilst Dworkin is officially concerned to avoid paternalism, his insurance model does clearly take him all the way towards a 'new'-paternalist position. Indeed, many of Dworkin's proposals are not defended at all by the choices people tend to make, but by assertions about what it would be prudent for us to choose, as he admits (2000: 492). Despite his avowed intention to avoid the excesses of neoliberal moralising (2000: 320–1), he largely reproduces the familiar neoliberal litanies of social reform: for Dworkin, hypothetical insurers 'would be alive to the commercial importance of discouraging poor and unmarried women from becoming pregnant' (2000: 339). For Dworkin (2000:2)

'There is nothing to be said for a world in which those who choose leisure though they could work are rewarded with the produce of the industrious.' He argues that insurers must be able to require claimants to take any job they suggest, or be able to take away benefits altogether (Dworkin 2000: 336; 2002: 114). Often, impoverished but work-shy individuals claim benefits they simply have no entitlement to (and Dworkin particularly feels sympathy for the 'hard-working middle classes', who have to 'subsidize fraud' (2000: 331)). Insurers would be concerned to minimise this 'moral hazard' by making unemployment significantly less attractive than employment (2000: 335).

The role of the market in Dworkin's scheme, similarly, is highly conflicted. At some moments, Dworkin is perceptive about the problems of market fundamentalism. Dworkin quite astutely points out that 'there is no such thing as a "natural" market: we use "market" to designate a range of economic mechanisms, all of them regulated ... in some way' 2000: 327). Defending policies on the basis that they would replicate the 'natural' outcomes of an 'ideal' insurance market therefore should not be an option. But this is exactly what Dworkin does do. Most if not all of his proposals are justified as the likely outcomes of an ideal insurance market in which individuals did not make significant errors in their reasoning about risk. It's worth quoting Dworkin at length here: 'mandatory regulation – forced choices [sic] – is sometimes the most effective way of mimicking free market choices when the actual market is corrupted by externalities ... In such cases we force people to choose in certain ways, making assumptions about how they would have chosen if the imperfections had been cured, and to bear the costs of those forced choices' (2002: 111). This fetishisation of the 'perfect', 'uncorrupted' market is absolutely key to Dworkin's policy recommendations, but seems to be ruled out by his erstwhile admission about its fictional nature.

Even Dworkin's defence of collective provision for health and unemployment cover looks highly unstable, to say the least. The general logic of Dworkin's theory is that if people have the ability to insure on fair terms, then the ensuing outcomes are fair, whatever they happen to be: 'equality of resources means that people should be equally situated with respect to risk rather than that they be equally situated after the uncertainties of risk had been resolved' (2002: 121). The notion of individual responsibility for risk, carried to its extreme, suggests the privatisation of justice altogether. If we could only reason about risk adequately, we could surely achieve an end to any kind of common provision. And surely enough Dworkin often observes that if we could obtain the necessary information to establish a system of purely individual insurance, that would be preferable (see e.g. 2000: 478). Any insurance system should 'leave scope for the play of personal choice, the influence of character, and the attraction and utility of gambles' (2000: 334), and in such a case 'corrective' interventions by the state could be minimised. Nevertheless he does make recourse to such 'correctives': as he argues, some 'limited' paternalism may be needed as a 'correction' of bad choices (2002: 114). Given that genuine choice is supposed to legitimise otherwise unacceptable inequalities, it is not obvious how these corrective measures are justified. This is not to deny that insulating us from the contingencies of life is in many ways an important goal: this idea is neither particularly debatable nor in any way novel. But it is to point out that Dworkin does not justify such interventions on the basis of the needs of citizens *qua* citizens, or the requirements of self-respect, the demands of community or the merits of relative equality. Such considerations have been crowded out of the picture.

Dworkin may provide some kind of justification for the status quo, then, but it is a very insecure justification, and it surrenders far too much to the neoliberal opponents of solidaristic welfarism. We need to balance the possible gains from a Dworkinian system with the costs of Dworkin's concessions to neoliberalism. It is important to remember that in practice the individualisation of insurance has been profoundly inegalitarian, leading to subclasses of the uninsured who are ill protected from the whims of the employment market (Heimer 2002). As Ericson *et al.* (2000: 533) observe, 'the contemporary private insurance industry is characterized by increasing risk segmentation or the unpooling of risks'. This ironically means that although insurance is supposed to spread risks evenly, in practice it increasingly fragments into smaller, less risky pools which are more advantageous for some, but exclude others, producing 'the deselected insurance poor, who cannot afford the premiums necessary to buy their way into social and economic networks of risk-taking' (Ericson *et al.* 2000: 555). At the same time, the middle classes have increasingly opted out of public institutions, and according to Giddens they are quite right to do so because they face a different situation of risk (Giddens 1999: 7). And Dworkin follows suit: there can be no justification for ruling out insurance schemes which are only available to 'the rich' (2000: 437), or indeed 'the very rich': we cannot interfere with personal freedoms for the sake of relative equality (2000: 440). In this context, a model which both defends the expansion of choice-sensitive insurance and which seeks to make social provision more conditional and incentivised is profoundly unhelpful. If the 'achievement' of New Labour, as Stuart Hall (2003) suggests, has been to incorporate social democracy within neoliberalism, Dworkin has clearly performed the same 'service' at the level of political theory.

Notes

1 A note on terminology: I use neoliberalism in this chapter to refer to a set of ideas which seeks to expand the logic of the free market within social life. The movement towards privatisation in the delivery of public services in areas such as welfare, education, health and crime is in that sense a neoliberal movement. Neoliberalism is also

the economic creed which has preached free markets and structural adjustment in the 'developing' and post-communist worlds, often with catastrophic consequences. Neoliberalism is a broad phenomenon, and along with many other commentators (see e.g. Hall 2003) I consider that reformist parties such as New Labour have achieved the incorporation of some vestigial social democracy into a broadly neoliberal framework. By contrast the New Right, a political movement including Thatcherism and Reaganism, was a somewhat unstable amalgam of neoliberal economic doctrine and social conservatism, which also mobilised markers of race and gender in a form of authoritarian populism (see e.g. Smith 1994). What is now called 'neoconservatism' in the USA exhibits similar features. This chapter also draws on the Foucauldian analysis of neoliberalism as a 'governmentality' or mentality of government, an analysis discussed at greater length later on in the introduction to this chapter.

2 I am aware that my description of Dworkin's position as 'meritocratic' is contentious. For some defenders of Dworkin, and of luck equality more broadly, the drive to factor out the influence of brute luck or circumstance on distribution presents a radical challenge to traditional meritocratic views which claim that talent can and should be rewarded. This much may be true, but the luck egalitarian position still holds that if we can factor out the influence of unequal circumstances, distribution should quite rightly be tailored towards rewarding greater effort or ambition. I would argue that this can be seen as a revised or 'new' version of meritocracy rather than a rejection of it.

3 Dworkin in fact uses a variety of terms at various points, including ambitions, choices, preferences or option luck versus endowments, circumstances or brute luck. I will use the terms choice and circumstances alone, in the interests of clarity, and because I think they best epitomise the cut that Dworkin is making. However, in the case of expensive tastes Dworkin seeks to hold us accountable for those preferences we identify with *whether chosen or not*, an argument that is examined further in Section 5.

4 Dworkin's position on campaign financing is broadly parallel. For a critique of Dworkin on this see Armstrong 2003b.

5 One particular issue concerns the fact that insurance provision is assumed to be private in the auction. Insurance agencies will therefore seek profit, and overall this will have the effect of making insurance relatively more expensive, and therefore less attractive to Dworkin's hypothetical individuals. Dworkin concedes that 'insurance is always a bad buy judged solely financially, by comparing the premium with the expected return' (Dworkin 2002: 139), but perplexingly maintains that 'nothing much turns on whether we count insurance company profits in the hypothetical calculation of premiums' (Dworkin 2002: 110). This is surely false, as Van der Veen (2002) suggests.

6 Dworkin, in his response to various critics, addresses the point that his device 'rewards people not for the choices they have actually made, but for choices the community assumes they would have made in stipulated but imagined circumstances' (2002: 111), but somehow ends up addressing his own much more limited version of the charge, from the perspective of the free rider (why should I pay in to a system I didn't choose?) The broader question is how Dworkin can construct a theory that claims to reward our individual choices (about how to protect ourselves against contingency), but which actually doesn't give us a choice about how to protect ourselves. Although the argument for a range of optional top-up schemes makes the system more choice-sensitive, it is still a substantially mandatory system. The more

logical conclusion from the point of choice-sensitivity would be a completely free market, though this in turn would be circumstance-sensitive.

7 Despite his general appreciation for his theory, Will Kymlicka has argued that 'The hypothetical calculations Dworkin's theory requires are so complex, and their institutional application so difficult, that its theoretical advantages cannot be translated into practice' (2002: 82). As Dworkin concedes for instance, 'It is impossible to say, a priori, whether the difference principle or equality of resources will work to achieve greater absolute equality in what Rawls calls primary goods. That would depend upon circumstances' (2000: 203).

8 Dworkin's approach to welfare is firmly opposed even by some fellow left-liberal egalitarians. Whilst Dworkin (2003b) bemoans the culture of 'dependency' created by modern states, Michael Walzer argues to the contrary that it is a 'sign of the success of a contemporary welfare state that its beneficiaries develop increased self-respect and are unwilling to take available menial jobs that are below some minimal level of dignity'. At its best, welfare policy has often been about insulating people from certain 'desperate choices' (Walzer 1983: 166–7), and not necessarily multiplying the quantity of choices per se.

9 Dworkin actually suggests that considerations of efficiency might mitigate against any strong insurance provision, even though this undermines the resulting equality (2000: 106).

10 Despite the general thrust of luck egalitarian argument, it seems inevitable that a serious attack on structural inequalities would involve concerted inroads on the choices of the already privileged, and particularly on their ability to transmit that privilege across generations (inroads which have been resisted by theorists such as Dworkin). Even a consistent defence of equality of opportunity would have to stage a serious confrontation with the phenomenon of elite reproduction, as Rawls (1971) recognised (see also Baker, Lynch *et al.* 2004). An attack on inheritance would only be the first step, but would be a crucial one. In particular, as well as ensuring opportunities for children of poor families to succeed 'against the odds' of class, a satisfactory policy of equality of opportunity would have to eradicate the ability of wealthy families to secure successful positions even for their less talented or less hardworking offspring. The ability of wealthy families to prevent less able offspring from 'falling down' the class structure is profound, especially for male offspring (for comprehensive illustrations of this, see Marshall *et al.* 1997). Serious responses to this are often lacking from liberal egalitarian argument.

11 Educational lotteries are already established (though not uncontentious) practice in some countries, for cases where the number of highly qualified candidates for popular university courses such as medicine and dental or veterinary practice enormously exceeds the number of available places. The usefulness of the lottery as a way of allocating scarce resources, and at the same time minimising structural inequalities, has gained some recent favour in theoretical circles, but remains perhaps underexplored (Duxbury 1999).

12 This wariness relates to the fact that it remains to be seen quite what effect such a scheme would have on the gendered division of labour (see e.g. Lister 2003: 189). Would the scheme help to equalise caring responsibilities, or would it in fact entrench the gendered division of caring labour? As Ailsa McKay (2001) argues, the literature on Citizen's Income and its benefits displays an 'androcentric bias' by concentrating overwhelmingly on likely effects on the formal labour market, and neglects issues relating to informal sectors or considerations outside of work. Nevertheless McKay is right, I think, to argue that these problems are not irresolvable; it appears that feminists should still give Citizen's Income further attention. Carole Pateman (2004) has

argued forcefully for such a citizen's income as a strategy for a feminist, radical and democratic form of citizenship.

13 On a much more limited level, the UK government is currently examining the prospects for a 'Citizen's Pension', which would at least partially delink pension entitlements from the performance of paid work. This change is seen as desirable because many people (overwhelmingly women) who take breaks from paid work to care for children, or who do unpaid work for the sick or elderly, are thereby deprived of adequate pension rights. At present, only 13 per cent of women of pensionable age in the UK receive a full state pension (see Wintour and White 2005). Such a move to a Citizen's Pension would represent a small but positive advance.

14 Ian Shapiro also notes this problem, in arguing that 'the volitions we are able to form, the ambitions it occurs to us to develop – these are greatly influenced, perhaps even determined, by our powers and capacities ... Different people have different capacities to form different ambitions, and those different capacities must be as morally arbitrary from Dworkin's point of view as any other capacities' (Shapiro 1999: 157–8).

15 It is questionable whether we can extend this point to racial inequality. Dworkin (2000) has defended policies of affirmative action for black students, though it's not clear how this now fits in with his theory of equality of resources, or whether we would need sweeping rectification of past injustices before his theory of equality could work justly. See Frazer and Lacey (1993: 87), Lacey (1998: 42).

16 As has been frequently noted, neoliberalism as a broader phenomenon represents not so much a coherent set of ideas, as an uneasy melange of authoritarian, moralistic conservatism and neoliberal freemarket economics, as well as being supplemented by authoritarian populist positions on race, sexuality and nation (Hall 1983; Smith 1994). Some theorists (such as Hayek) distance themselves – though not wholly consistently – from any idea of just reward. Nevertheless some kind of meritocratic argument is a recurring theme in party-political debate, as I note in Chapter 4.

3

Equality versus social inclusion?

Introduction

FROM THE 1980s onwards, the doctrine of social citizenship came under sustained attack from neoliberal and New Right politicians. In theory, the equality of bureaucratic welfare regimes was depicted as suppressing choice and responsibility; in practice, the (albeit limited) equality delivered by the social rights advocated by Marshall were progressively revoked or circumscribed by politicians such as Thatcher and Reagan who instead asserted the values of individual self-reliance, enterprise and personal responsibility. As noted in the last chapter, in place of the social citizenship of the post-war consensus, neoliberal politicians promoted an ideal of 'active citizenship', whereby the responsibilities of citizens were primarily couched in terms of the duty to be economically self-supporting, to make responsible choices for oneself and one's family. These trends have had a significant impact on most Western societies, marking as they did a substantial rhetorical readjustment of the relationship between the individual and the state, a privatisation of previously publicly owned institutions and a thorough-going expansion of the logic of the free market and individual choice. Indeed, even non-rightist governments such as New Labour continue to be marked by much the same preoccupations and compulsions, and have largely 'normalised' neoliberal ideas (Hay 2004; see also Arestis and Sawyer 2005). Despite promoting grand policies of 'social inclusion', such parties have been now widely criticised for substituting a desire to tackle economic inequalities with an incitement for us to become obedient, productive citizens, and for their substitution of a fairly narrow conception of equal opportunities for any more substantial attack on the reproduction of inequality across generations.

This chapter examines how theories of liberal equality bear on these issues. It has been argued recently that liberal equality represents a much more radical alternative to the heavily diluted version of social democracy associated with exponents of the Third Way, and that liberal egalitarians are now the last real torchbearers for the principles of egalitarian reform. This chapter counsels against such a view, and instead draws a parallel between the way in which the 'problem' of inequality has been framed within the discourses of social inclusion and liberal equality. Specifically, Section 1 draws a comparison between the theory of luck equality and the discourse of social inclusion popularised by political parties such as New Labour in the United Kingdom. Section 2 indicates that there are good grounds for scepticism about any critical difference between the two accounts, and demonstrates that many of the barbs aimed at New Labour's discourse of social inclusion are often highly applicable to academic luck egalitarianism too. In particular, this section draws several strands from Ruth Levitas's critique of New Labour's rhetoric on social inclusion, in order to show how these also tend to hit the target when directed at much of the literature on luck equality. Section 3 demonstrates how the celebration of 'choice' that is central to the liberal egalitarian account turns out, like the discourse of social inclusion, to imply the choices of rational consumers and producers within marketised institutions, rather than the political choices of citizens engaged in determining the nature of those institutions. As such, it becomes possible to draw a distinction between a neoliberal and an oppositional conception of active citizenship, with the latter emphasising the centrality of democracy to the egalitarian project, and the former obscuring it. Finally, Section 4 suggests that the New Labour repackaging of equality as the equal opportunity (and responsibility) to insert oneself into the labour market, and to be rewarded for rational, prudent choice has echoes throughout the luck egalitarian literature, and examines some of the political consequences. Whilst it is *not* the goal of this chapter to argue that the various doctrines of New Labour and luck egalitarian theory are exactly the same or even substantially equivalent – which is clearly not the case – the underlying intention *is* to highlight how both New Labour discourse and luck egalitarian theory have subtly accommodated themselves to neoliberalism in many of the same ways. The point of this intervention is that, by bringing to light the quite specific moves that have been made within luck egalitarian theory the costs and benefits might be evaluated more clearly, and alternative possibilities might present themselves. The chapter concludes, then, by briefly returning to the divergent ways in which the 'problem' of inequality has been – and might be – framed, and introduces some of the alternative questions that the second half of this book will seek to address.

1 Equality and inclusion

Not a society where all succeed equally – that is utopia; but an opportunity society where all have an equal chance to succeed; that could and should be twenty-first century Britain under a Labour Government ... Where hard working families who play by the rules are not going to see their opportunities blighted by those that don't ... the reality of life has changed. The relationship between state and citizen has changed. People ... want to make their own life choices. Their expectations, their ambitions, their hopes are all different and higher. The twentieth-century traditional welfare state that did so much for so many has to be re-shaped as the opportunity society. (Tony Blair, Labour Annual Conference speech, 28 September 2004)

Many political parties once considered to be on the left – from New Labour and Schroeder's Social Democrats in Europe to the Democrats in the USA, as well as centrist parties in Canada, Australia and New Zealand – have recently drawn withering criticism for abandoning any socialist values they may once have had. In Britain, for instance, Alex Callinicos (2000) has railed against New Labour's retreat from a politics of redistribution, and charged its leaders with a failure to comprehend that substantive equality cannot be delivered under a capitalist economic system. As an indicator of this lack of radical intent, Callinicos charges that New Labour has taken only shallow readings of liberal equality; whilst it has sought to garner legitimacy by making reference to liberal theorists like Rawls and Dworkin, it has just as surely retreated from fully supporting their proposals (2000: 40–1).

Callinicos's point only makes sense, of course, if by contrast to New Labour the liberal egalitarians in question really do promise a much more consistent and attractive version of equality which demands radical reform of the capital- ist system – and Callinicos is in no doubt that they do (2000: 132). The view that liberal egalitarians are now the real torchbearers for radical reform is at first sight surprising, but is not as unusual as we might think (see also Warren 1997; Brighouse and Wright 2002). At least one critic of liberal equality, Kenneth Minogue, agrees from the other side of the fence, arguing that this disjuncture is so profound as to detach liberal equality from the political and philosophical mainstream. He asserts that as a result 'the entire theoretical literature on equal- ity ... is at best on the very margins of philosophy' (Minogue 1990: 101). Indeed Will Kymlicka (2001) provocatively claims that liberal equality has transformed the traditional terms of political debate, and destabilised the old spectrum of libertarianism, liberalism and Marxism: as a result liberalism seriously chal- lenges for a position to the left of the Marxist tradition. If radical thinking is what we want, liberal equality is where the action is.

The arguments of the first two chapters would recommend caution about such enthusiastic endorsements of the radicalism of theorists such as Rawls and Dworkin. The pertinent issue here is not Callinicos's ambitions for liberal egal- itarianism, though, which in any case seem to have been scaled back more recently.[1] Instead, the argument will focus on the claim that liberal egalitarians pose a progressive alternative to the kind of thinking attributed to New Labour and its close cousins. Far from it: in this chapter it will be shown that many of the criticisms levelled at New Labour are highly relevant to the liberal egalitar- ian literature too. Indeed such a comparison helps to draw out what is most distinctive about contemporary liberal egalitarian theory, the way in which it frames the 'problem' of inequality, and the remedies it proposes to address it. Therefore the apparent disjuncture pointed to by Callinicos (and indeed Kymlicka *et al.*) should be taken with a pinch of salt, as should the notion that we can use liberal egalitarian theories to get somewhere genuinely interesting and novel. To the contrary, it will be argued that the language of liberal egalitarianism closely resembles the sort of language with which parties such as New Labour operate.

The rise of inclusion

Many criticisms have been levelled at the New Labour government in the United Kingdom (see e.g. Finlayson 2003; Hall 2003; Callinicos 2001a). Indeed, even one former minister of Blair's government has charged him with being 'a complete convert to the neo-conservative view of the world' (Short 2003), an assessment which looks increasingly accurate. Here, though, I want to concentrate on one of the earliest and most cogent critiques, put forward by Ruth Levitas (1998). Levitas's primary focus is on the much-heralded discourse of 'social inclusion', a buzz-term which has come to the forefront of political debate in Britain and further afield. As Giddens (1998: 102) observes, 'the new politics defines equality as inclusion and inequality as exclusion': on this discourse, the 'problem' we should be concerned with is the marginalisation, powerlessness and alienation of those who are less economically fortunate, or disabled, or from disadvantaged minority communities. The 'solution' is inclusion: their reinsertion into the 'mainstream' of economic, political and social life.

Levitas maintains that talk of exclusion and inclusion can be positive, and can bring in train welcome redistributive measures (Levitas 1998: 14). But despite its promise, the rhetoric usually masks a real timidity in addressing economic inequalities; indeed New Labour's 'inclusive' agenda turns out to imply little more than an incitement for us to work and to become flexible, productive citizens. In New Labour's usage the idea usually degenerates into one or both of two particularly pernicious lines of discourse. In the first, the poor (or the 'underclass') are stigmatised for being morally deficient and insufficiently invested with a healthy work ethic – in this sense the project borrows heavily from the moralistic conservatism of the New Right. In the second line of discourse, social inclusion is collapsed into the right – and more significantly the responsibility – to develop marketable skills and to perform paid work, and in this way social inclusion appears only as a cipher for the interests of the modern 'flexible' employment market. Whilst the problem of exclusion may take various forms, the solution in each case is the same: a somewhat thin notion of equal economic opportunity. Thus the former focus in leftist thought on 'substantive' equality has disappeared and been replaced by a shadow of its former self, content merely to deliver equal opportunities to be subjected to the whims of an unequal employment market. This is an idea aimed, in Blair's words, at 'true equality: equal status and opportunity rather than equality of outcome' (Blair 2002). Citizenship has been pared down to encompass only our role as consumers of goods, services and those public provisions that remain unprivatised, and our common 'status' as active choosers within economic and political life. For Levitas, what the discourse of social inclusion promises above all is 'a transition across the boundary to become an insider rather than an outsider in a society whose structural inequalities remain largely uninterrogated' (1998: 7).

2   If liberal equality is the answer, what was the question?

Within the rhetoric of centrist politicians from Clinton through to Blair and Schroeder, then, equality has been depicted primarily in terms of the universality of labour-market opportunity. The 'problem' the Third Way and its variants try to solve is to ensure labour market entry on behalf of previously 'marginalised' groups. As Gordon Brown has argued, 'the answer to social exclusion is economic opportunity' (quoted in Levitas 1998: 5). Nevertheless we might expect a different story within liberal egalitarian theory, not least since if this theory has a foundational moment, it surely arises with Rawls's critique of meritocracy. For Rawls narrow versions of equality of opportunity merely present an 'equal chance to leave the less fortunate behind in a personal quest for influence and social position' (Rawls 1971: 108). Many of the criticisms levelled at equality of opportunity hark back to Michael Young's vision of *The Rise of the Meritocracy*, in which he described a future society dominated by a talented elite. Such a meritocratic system would be compatible with huge disparities in incomes and status, and with a polarised society (Young 1961; see also Tawney 2000). This depiction seems to sum up life under New Labour well, since the 'opportunity society' has been made compatible with *increasing* polarisation of wealth and income and the 'two-tierisation' of public institutions. But this should not suffice for liberal egalitarians. The only advantage such a talent-based meritocratic system would have over aristocratic regimes, for Rawls, would be the 'consolation' that the disadvantaged would know that they had genuinely failed because of their own personal deficiencies. Ronald Dworkin (2000) also has problems with narrow versions of meritocracy, chiefly since he agrees that from the perspective of justice, talent is morally arbitrary, and as noted in Chapter 2 goes on to argue that no one should have less income simply because of less native talent.

But this apparently intense aversion to meritocracy conceals more than it reveals, at least in terms of the luck egalitarian literature. The aversion certainly does not mean that the black sheep of the egalitarian family – equality of outcome – has been rehabilitated, as Phillips (2004) shows. What has really happened is that 'narrow' ideals of equality of opportunity have been rejected in favour of 'deep' equality of opportunity (Callinicos 2000: 39–57); or, as Chapter 2 put it, the 'old' meritocracy has been replaced with a 'new' meritocracy. In post-Rawlsian liberal theory, talent, which is morally arbitrary, and makes the wrong 'cut' between the individual and his or her circumstances, has been rejected and replaced by effort or ambition as the legitimator of inequality. By linking rewards to effort and ambition, it is argued, we can genuinely isolate those decisions which are the result of free choice, and for which individuals can therefore be held responsible. This theoretical move can be associated most closely with Ronald Dworkin. As we have seen Dworkin suggests that outcomes are fair if we start with equal 'resources', since equality must be, not talent- but ambition-sensitive (Dworkin 2000: 199). Eric Rakowski (1991) has been Dworkin's closest disciple, but such an approach has been widely taken up in an attempt to refine its core intuition. Richard Arneson has advocated what he calls 'equality of opportunity for welfare' (Arneson 1989): we should be provided with the means to secure welfare, but to actually secure it we must exercise effort and ambition. Amartya Sen on the other hand recommends equal 'capabilities to function', rather than equal end-results (Sen 1992).[2]

In fact, not one of the major liberal egalitarians believes justice to be primarily bound up in what we actually end up with. Whilst it would be a misrepresentation to claim these theorists believe that the demands of egalitarian justice end after any initial distributions, they are also strongly averse to continual attempts to restore an initially egalitarian position. John Roemer comments approvingly that 'All these proposals attempt to equalize opportunities, not outcomes' (1994: 179). Intriguingly, many avowedly (or formerly) Marxist egalitarians have made very similar moves, and now work forward from the premises of Dworkin's account. Thus Roemer himself is now happy to accept that 'Defensible egalitarianism is equality of opportunity' (Roemer 1994: 3). G.A. Cohen, on the other hand, advocates 'equal access to advantage', which he admits is very close to the proposals of Dworkin, Arneson and Sen (Cohen 1989: 907). Indeed Callinicos (2001b) argues that despite their minor theoretical differences, these theories are so close as to be indistinguishable in terms of practical application: each seeks to tailor end-results to the exercise of effort and choice, and not circumstance.[3]

The theoretical move from 'narrow' to 'deep' equality of opportunity raises several difficult questions, not least the difficultly of distinguishing effort from talent, and genuine from constrained choices. Moreover, it is quite possible that many, if not all of the criticisms of 'narrow' equality of opportunity are just as applicable to the 'deep' version. Sitting at his desk every morning, is it really going to be any consolation to an office junior if the rise of his more successful bosses had nothing to do with talent, and everything to do with their ambition? It might be, but several theorists – most notably Elizabeth Anderson (1999a) and Jo Wolff (1998) – have shown that the luck egalitarian position requires us to make judgements which are patronising, demeaning, and corrosive of the self-respect that they have claimed should be a key concern of egalitarians. According to luck egalitarian doctrine, on their view, those who succeed on their own efforts are able to enjoy the product of their labour, but those the egalitarian seeks to help are viewed as lacking in effort, ambition or personal capacities. Anderson has provided the most penetrating analysis of the rhetoric of luck equality here. She argues that the luck egalitarian vision 'abandons those disadvantaged through their own choices to their miserable fates, and defines the deserving disadvantaged in terms of their innate inferiority of talent, intelligence, ability or social appeal' (1999a: 311); plus presumably lack of effort or ambition. She therefore condemns luck egalitarians for reproducing 'the cramped vision of the Poor Laws, where unfortunates breathe words of supplication and submit to the humiliating moral judgements of the state' (1999a: 308). Minogue (1990: 103) earlier argued along similar lines that within liberal egalitarianism more broadly 'the conception is of people suffering from lack of material resources, education and other conditions commonly thought of, abstractly, as "advantages". The egalitarian project thus envisages active helpers of sad and pathetic sufferers ... it is a despotism mitigated by suburban values'.

It is a moot point whether luck egalitarians can accommodate or rebuff these concerns about the possible corrosion of self-respect, but in the meantime many of the judgements made by liberal egalitarians do seem peculiarly unforgiving. For instance, a crucial reason behind Dworkin's rejection of Rawls's theory of justice is that it is excessively egalitarian in the sense that it might reward those who choose not to work (Dworkin 2003b: 139). By the same token the doctrine of equality of welfare, which seeks to provide equal happiness or well-being to all, has largely given way to equality of opportunity to acquire resources – because welfare equality takes insufficient account of our expensive tastes and unequal propensities to work. Because it rewards, in sum, the spoilt and the feckless (Rawls too rejects welfare equality on the basis that the hard-working should not bear the costs incurred by people who have a 'lack of foresight or self-discipline'; Rawls 1982: 169). Similarly, Cohen, perhaps the most left-inclined of the luck egalitarians, says it is wrong that 'other people pay for [an individual's] readily avoidable wastefulness' (Cohen 1989: 911), along the way rejecting the claims of 'people whose inefficiency in turning resources into welfare is clearly their own fault' (1989: 911).[4] The end result of all of this is that 'genuine choice excuses otherwise unacceptable inequalities' (1989: 931). As these judgements stack up, they appear eerily familiar. The suspicion is that, as with New Labour in practice, the chief 'problem' liberal equality seems determined to solve is the inability or unwillingness of some among us to work, to produce and to consume rationally. Some of the political implications of this will be discussed in Section 4. The next section, though, seeks to delve a little deeper into the role the ideal of free choice plays in the arguments of luck equality and of New Labour – for if genuine choice excuses otherwise unacceptable inequalities, it is worth investigating how such choice comes to be defined.

3   Equality, inclusion and the revolution of choice

Within the discourse of the Third Way, within neoliberalism more broadly, and within the luck egalitarian literature, the notion of choice occupies an almost sacred position. In a sense there is nothing unusual about this: in the modern West, as Nikolas Rose suggests, we are increasingly called upon to see ourselves as independent, choosing individuals, and to understand our lives in terms of choices made, ambitions fulfilled or unfulfilled: 'modern individuals are not merely "free to choose", but obliged to be free, to understand and enact their lives in terms of choice. They must interpret their past and dream their future as outcomes of choices made or choices still to make' (Rose 1999: 87). Although this vision is undoubtedly linked to the development of industrial and post-industrial capitalism, it is not an entirely negative development by any means. To be sure, many feminist theorists in particular have argued that the aspiration to free choice may make limited sense of the actual experiences of our lives (see e.g. Mendus 2000) – but still, the achievement of independence and of choice have been hard-fought accomplishments for some, whose dependence has long underpinned the autonomy of wealthy, white, 'First World' men. And when contrasted with subjection to the will of others, free choice clearly has a lot to recommend it.

Nevertheless, the precise *nature* of the logic of choice that characterizes luck egalitarian discourse is in need of interrogation. And here, again, we can draw a parallel with the discourse of inclusion. Within neoliberal discourse more broadly, the focus on active citizenship has been almost wholly 'concerned with personal responsibility and individual choice in the marketplace rather than political participation'. Thus 'The "active citizen" is really a social entrepreneur; an individual who is empowered, not by democracy, but by property ownership' (Faulks 1998: 138, 131; see also Kantola 2003: 208). In the discourse of social inclusion, too, inclusion is taken to imply inclusion within the *market*, rather than meaningful *political* inclusion (indeed the 'imperatives' of the global market play such a powerful determining role within New Labour rhetoric that the space of 'the political' as an arena for popular control itself shrinks notice-ably). Even within the public service sector, choice implies not democratic reform, but marketisation or pseudo-marketisation of service provision. As such, for New Labour the goal of free choice within public services is largely to be advanced by means of privatisation, deregulation, the establishment of inter-nal markets, and our steady transformation from patients, students or claimants into service consumers. The role of the state itself undergoes a subtle transfor-mation here: since innovations such as the Citizen's Charter in Britain, citizens have been encouraged to side *with* the state *against* public institutions, to criticise and reject such institutions when they fail to meet the targets set for them by states, on behalf of service consumers. This odd alliance of citizen and state serves to delegitimise public services, to reduce the accountability of the state itself, and assists states in the complex project of blurring the boundaries between public and private provision. At each stage, substantive democratic control over service provision is also attenuated by the accompanying dilution of clear lines of accountability.

Things may be somewhat different within the liberal luck egalitarian literature, but choice does seem to play a similar role in at least three respects. Firstly, the role of choice is primarily to tailor distributions to our ambition, industry, preferences or differing aversions to risk (and for Dworkin at least this implies precisely the same blurring of public and private provision). Secondly, the exercise of choice and responsibility is frequently expressed by liberal luck egalitarians in terms of the responsibility to perform paid work (see Section 4). Thirdly, it is striking that throughout the extensive theoretical discussion on the role of choice in egalitarian argument, the spectre of democracy fails to rear its head at all. Instead it is straightforwardly assumed that the role of choice in egalitarian argument must relate to the drive to tailor end-results to decisions to consume, to produce, to save or to work. This reflects, perhaps, an instance of the bifurcation of liberal egalitarian theory from parallel defences of democracy (Gutmann 1980; Levine 1998), so that the latter seems to play little appreciable role in securing the goals of the former. Even for a theorist such as Dworkin, who attacks the choice-insensitivity of European welfare states, with their bureaucratic welfare institutions and universal benefits (see Dworkin 2003b), the potential for democratic reform, or citizens' control, of welfare institutions does not enter the discussion as a possible solution.

Active citizenship, democracy and the market

Both New Labour and the liberal luck egalitarian literature resonate, then, with the neoliberal discourse of 'active citizenship', where the rights and responsibilities of citizens revolve first and foremost around the institutions of the free market and paid work. As such a central dichotomy is that between the (bad) 'dependent' and the (good) 'independent' citizen, where dependency is defined as failure to support yourself economically, and independence is defined in terms of being economically self-supporting and suitably ambitious. I want to suggest, of course, that other paths could be taken, and one of the best leads here is provided by Iris Young's work on citizenship and independence. Young has argued persuasively against interpreting the ideal of independence in terms of self-sufficiency. For 'Normatively privileging independence in this sense, and making it a primary virtue of citizenship, implies judging a huge number of people in liberal societies as less than full citizens' (Young 1997b: 125). In particular, 'Dependent people and their caretakers come to be defined outside public social relations, marginalized to a private realm beyond the interaction of free and full citizens with each other' (1997b: 125). Indeed it is worth asking whether, in a complex marketised society, any of us is ever independent in the sense of self-sufficiency, or whether this should be an aspiration after all.

Nevertheless, demands for independence and for choice continue to characterise the claims of social movements arguing for institutional reform in Western societies, and not just those on the 'right' of the political spectrum. But here Young (1997b) is absolutely correct in arguing that, insofar as independence and choice-making *are* important values, the core aspiration is often better framed in terms of self-direction and political voice rather than a sociologically and economically naïve ideal of self-sufficiency.[5] Whilst in a complex society none of us will ever be truly self-sufficient, and while this is of dubious value anyway, the goal of many disabled activists, feminists, socialists and radical democrats has been to place decision-making power in the hands of citizens. As a result it is not, in fact, necessary to deny the neoliberal charge that institutions such as welfare states, national health services and educational establishments have often suppressed choice, and marginalised 'recipients' and 'claimants'. Indeed this charge has often been levelled by leftists too, who have argued that these institutions disempower individuals, and turn them into passive recipients of manna from the state (a version of this criticism was mentioned in Chapter 1, of course – a longstanding objection to Marshall's account of citizenship has been that it ignored the way in which the social rights of citizenship have been achieved without, or sometimes at the expense of, meaningful political rights within modern liberal bureaucracies).

But it is important to affirm that there are two possible solutions to this problem of the elitism and bureaucracy of public institutions. One is marketisation, and the other is democratisation. It is clear that neoliberals show a strong preference for the first option, but this strategy has two defects. Firstly, it tends to be inegalitarian in effects – not least because both privatisation and the two-tierisation of public services tend to disproportionately reward those with more resources and time to begin with, whilst doing little for those with lower mobility, or less time and resources. Secondly, it has actually tended to result in a decline in popular political control (Eriksen and Weigard 2000). There is no reason why egalitarians have to replicate this focus, though. Rather than commending bureaucracy and apathy, socialist and feminist critics have often emphasised instead the importance of democratic participation in establishing and delivering on citizenship rights (Dean 2003: 698). Crucially, whereas privatisation is predictably inegalitarian in its effects, democratisation appears much more promising from an egalitarian point of view. Fiona Williams (1999) observes that, by contrast to both neoliberal and New Labour constructions of citizenship, many oppositional groups have themselves suggested an oppositional definition of the active citizen as someone engaged in political decision-making and self-determination (see also Voet 1998; Siim 2000; Lister 2001). The notion of active citizenship that this suggests implies that participation in a wide variety of political arenas is central to the hope of an egalitarian society. Christopher Kutz therefore calls for an interpretation of equality that 'stresses political inclusion and collective agency, in particular acts of collective agency through which we as citizens together define the terms of equality ... we are political agents before we are recipients, and the terms of equality must be set together' (Kutz 2003: 10, 15). This commitment to the democratisation of both the conception and delivery of egalitarian change betokens a growing resistance to the ways in which the importance of democratic participation in setting the terms of, and achieving, equality has been downplayed in the work of liberal theorists such as Rawls and Dworkin, and reflects a belief that the goals of equality and democracy cannot so easily be detached (see Squires 2006). Even given the contemporary emphasis on 'active' citizenship, there is a clear and fundamental divide between those who understand the ever-expanding 'sphere' of the market as the proper arena for the exercise of choice and responsibility, and those who would seek to defend the values of equality and citizenship through a widening of what Mouffe (1996) calls the 'democratic revolution'. The arguments of this book would suggest support for the second strategy. In particular Part II of this book moves on to address the work of a number of theorists – including Anne Phillips, Iris Young and Nancy Fraser – who may help to move such a project forwards.

4   Equality of whom?

> Exclusion codes a way of thinking that paradoxically ... is more concerned with describing the damaging and dangerous effects of ... fragmentations on the individual and the community than with seeking to grasp the political and economic processes that generate such phenomena ... The excluded are characterized as failures, lacking personal skills and competencies. In the Third Way, these are to be addressed through practices of control targeted at the excluded themselves ... what is at stake here is actually the work ethic. (Rose 2000: 1406)

A primary goal of New Labour policy has been the absorption of the economically inactive into the employment market. Rather than being a an interactive concept (who oppresses or enables whom), equality hereby becomes a concept of inclusion and exclusion (who lives within the circuit of basic economic opportunities and who doesn't). In this context, it is worth asking questions about which inclusions and exclusions matter – about precisely *who* is going to be included, and whose exclusion we are concerned about. In fact, in an age of huge executive rewards for success (and failure) and the increasing tendency of the super-rich to opt out of participation in public institutions (what Giddens 1998: 103 has called 'the revolt of the elites'), 'new' centre-left parties such as New Labour have been attacked for their reluctance to address inequalities at the 'top' of the social scale. As Levitas notes, there is little political will to tackle this voluntary social exclusion of the rich (Levitas 1998: 21). One problem with this is that the position of the rich is thereby naturalised. Inequalities at the 'top end' are presented as a fact which governments might try to ameliorate (though they will always, we are reminded, be subject to the contingencies of finance and electoral politics), not something governments are actively involved in sustaining. To the contrary, the substantial increases in economic inequality that have occurred in states such as the USA and Britain since the 1970s have been driven by cuts in corporation tax, privatisation and deregulation, representing a substantial, government-directed upward redistribution of wealth. In this case markets have not functioned as 'neutral distributive mechanisms [but] mechanisms that are embedded in social and legal structures that sanction and support the redistribution of the social product away from workers and towards capital' (Levitas 2004: 68; see also Duggan 2003).

The neglect of such processes confirms that inequality is defined not as a problem of relative distribution of wealth and power, but as a problem of the economic underactivity of the poor. In the absence of the will to address relative inequalities properly, the focus of New Labour policy is almost exclusively on the poor, and so the drive for social inclusion increasingly looks like the co-option of the poor into the (by now largely mythical) 'mainstream' of society, and the eradication of their more disreputable and wasteful habits. The poor have ceased to be the oppressed, and have instead become, in Peter Mandelson's words, 'the inefficient who let the community down and impede its success', and 'the irresponsible who fall down on their obligations to their families and therefore to their community' (quoted in Levitas 1998: 122).

Perhaps partly because of a desire to avoid New Right accusations of 'levelling', the liberal luck egalitarian literature also largely steers clear of addressing itself to the status of the wealthy, who are more or less absent from the accounts of Dworkin, Arneson, *et al.* In any case, as Dworkin (2000: 440) argues, we cannot interfere with the personal freedoms of the rich merely in the interests of relative equality. Unfortunately, the same courtesy is not extended to the poor – as with New Labour, Arneson and Dworkin appear prepared to countenance coercive measures for those who make poorly thought-out or 'imprudent' decisions. The last chapter detailed Dworkin's neo-paternalist injunctions on workfare policy, but it is not only Dworkin who is willing to defend compulsory welfare-to-work schemes, for instance. Richard Arneson is even more adamant that paid employment, not guaranteed welfare, must be the default option for modern-day legislators (for another, slightly different liberal egalitarian defence of the responsibility to work, see White 2001).[6] As Arneson argues, 'the basis of the "paid employment only" transfer policy is the judgment that for most poor people, having a job is good for you whether you think so or not'. As with Dworkin, such policies are justified with reference not to what individuals actually tend to choose, but with reference to what individuals would choose if they really were rational or prudent. Since 'impoverished members of society tend to be cursed with choice-making and choice-following deficits' (Arneson 1997a: 332), their choices are quietly displaced. Thus Arneson is able to assert that 'the policy I am recommending would be quasi-paternalistic in that policy designed to benefit an adult individual who is neither feeble-minded nor crazy would not be guided by that individual's judgment of where her good lies. A policy that overrides the judgment of the individual about her own good when benefit to her is the aim of the policy is, let us say, quasi-paternalistic' (1997a: 348).

Echoing the rhetoric of Third Way politicians, Arneson justifies this 'quasi' paternalism on the basis that 'assiduously seeking employment, taking it when it is available, and standing fast by the best job one can get even when it is from the dregs of labor market opportunities are in the self-interest of almost any individual in the long-run' (1997a: 348). This may be all too true, of course, so long as we take great care not to question the system that throws up the options from which we choose. In the absence of any such scrutiny, the degree to which liberal egalitarians have paralleled New Labour's link between equality (in the form of the provision of welfare benefits) and responsibility (understood as willingness to work) leaves at least one friendly critic uneasy. Christopher Lake finds 'something a little unpalatable in the repeated exhortations to the unemployed to make a conscientious effort to find work, as though the frustrations of unemployment would be ameliorated through being conscientiously pursued'. To the contrary, in this respect liberal luck egalitarians may 'need perhaps to be mindful of the company they are keeping' (Lake 2001: 147).

I would second the need for caution here, for there is much about this vision that is troubling. Neoliberalism and New Labourism are both characterised by a strange double incitement to take risks for the 'common good' in the market economy whilst simultaneously being cautious, prudent and self-supporting. Ambition and entrepreneurship are held to be for the common good, and are laudable virtues of the new citizens. Indeed Hartley Dean's account of the New Labour vision of the active citizen has eerie resonances with the work of liberal egalitarians such as Dworkin and Arneson. For New Labour the new 'heroic citizens' are 'responsible risk takers: they embrace the risks implied in a world where one must provide so far as possible for one's own welfare ... seeking out the information they require and demanding the best deal on offer. However, not all citizens are heroic. Some ... are unreconstructed [and] must be cajoled into risk-taking' (Dean 2003: 700–1). As Tony Blair and Gerhard Schroeder have argued, 'For the new politics [of the Third Way] to succeed, it must promote a go-ahead mentality and a new entrepreneurial spirit at all levels of society' (Blair and Schroeder 1999: 5). In Blairite Britain we apparently need an economy with strong growth, and so there is a general incitement to take risks and to develop a more risk-taking culture. Nevertheless, it seems that we are to be left individually to pick up the tab for failure. This is the strange predicament of the neoliberal 'active' citizen then: whereas your success enriches all, failure should affect only yourself. Such a predicament is not resisted sufficiently clearly by luck egalitarians, whose arguments run parallel in all too many ways. As Elizabeth Anderson argues, 'for the outcomes for which individuals are held responsible, luck egalitarians prescribe rugged individualism: let the distribution of goods be governed by capitalist markets' (Anderson 1999a: 292).

Conclusions

It would be easy – all too easy – to claim that luck egalitarian theory represents a neat theoretical justification of the kinds of policies suggested within the Third Way discourse of social inclusion. There would be some truth to such a charge, but such a contention is not central to the aims of this chapter. Instead, the intention has been to demonstrate that the quite specific moves that New Labour discourse has made in response to the neoliberal 'challenge' have clear parallels in liberal luck egalitarian theory. As with Christopher Lake's cautionary note about the company luck egalitarians have been keeping, this serves not as a blanket rejection of the political and economic goals of luck egalitarians as political theorists, but as a means of highlighting the very real dangers of such an accommodationist strategy. If New Labour has thrown out the baby, the bathwater and the whole bathroom suite of equality in its attempts to develop an 'egalitarian' strategy that is immune to criticism from the right, then perhaps luck egalitarians should heed such a warning.

It has been assumed in this chapter that any theory of equality can best be understood by unearthing the 'problem' of inequality it attempts to solve (see Bacchi 1996, 1999). As with New Labour, much recent liberal egalitarian thought seems guided by the intuition that equality could be achieved if individual citizens could be persuaded to make the most of the choices available to them, assuming some more or less substantial notion of a level playing field. Although attention is sometimes focused on structural obstacles, it frequently falls on the will, desire and dedication of those who fail to become egalitarian citizens. Such a conclusion is possible because what we might expect to be the dynamic of the literature has been reversed. Rather than surveying a world of inequalities and recommending the eradication of at least some of them, the literature now starts from a presumption of equality and then goes on to ascertain which inequalities might be justified. The dynamic of the search within the literature has become the search for the one inviolable principle which will produce legitimate inequalities; thus equality, far from being a right which people are in some sense born with, or a condition of citizenship, can become something one must earn – but which, by implication, one might just as easily fail to earn, depending on one's 'choices'. Equality becomes a discretionary privilege to take a share of the goods produced by society, which will only be granted conditionally, if the individual measures up. There is a norm which needs to be aspired to, and there is a reward to the successful. Equality thus becomes a 'gate-keeping' concept, whereby the (spontaneous) common wealth is deserved only by those individuals who put their lives on the line. Although there are important differences, it is the claim of this chapter that there are also fundamental similarities with regard to the way in which the problem of inequality is framed in liberal equality and in discourse on social inclusion. If the discourse of social inclusion is to be chastised for its failings, it is difficult to hold liberal egalitarianism up as an alternative because by and large it has made a very similar set of moves. On balance, the view of liberal equality as posing a serious challenge to modern societies or to the economic system in Western societies seems highly problematic. To the contrary, if 'inclusion means accepting the fundamental inequalities of a capitalist system' (Levitas 1998: 69), so, it all too often seems, does liberal equality.

So where do we go from here? The chapters in Part II of this book seek to contribute in their own small ways to reframing the problem of inequality. What happens if the 'problem' of inequality is framed as an interactive or relational one? What are the consequences of beginning not with the characteristics of individuals that should be drawn out and then rewarded, but with the needs of citizens or, as Fraser puts it, the prerequisites for participation as peers in social life? Does the focus on chance and choice obscure the systematic and relational nature of inequalities, and if so, what are the implications of foregrounding oppression and hierarchy as the 'problem' of inequality? How might we begin to open up political possibilities that are foreclosed on the liberal account? The next chapter begins to address these questions by examining the role of the ideal of responsibility in egalitarian thought.

Notes

1 Callinicos initially seemed to place hope in the versions of luck egalitarianism set out by Marxist egalitarians such as Roemer and Cohen. But in a later piece he seems to be much more pessimistic about the potential of luck egalitarianism. Callinicos (2001b: 188) claims that the implications of the accounts these Marxist theorists have produced so far are more or less equivalent in theory, and indistinguishable in practice from those of liberal theorists such as Dworkin. He also charges that the central distinction of luck egalitarianism, between chance and choice, is as methodologically impoverished, abstracted and individualised in the analytical Marxist literature as it is in liberal writings. The evidence seems to be on Callinicos's side here, but surely all of this only serves to defer the purported radicalism of luck equality still further, for whilst Callinicos still seems to believe that the chance/choice distinction might be

transplanted onto a much more adequate social theory, it is not at all obvious how this is going to happen. This makes the initial hope expressed in Callinicos's book appear much more distant.

2 Sen's account will not be discussed further in this chapter because, despite fitting into the luck egalitarian mould to some extent, it differs in two crucial (and generally positive) ways. Firstly, Sen's account of valuable opportunities is considerably broader than the versions we can associate with theorists such as Dworkin and Arneson. His account of important human capabilities is examined in a little more detail towards the end of Chapter 5. Secondly, Sen brackets questions of responsibility, arguing that such considerations should not be at the forefront when deriving correct distributive principles, but rather come into view somewhere further down the line towards policy implementation.

3 This may or may not be the case (see note 1, above), but one issue that divides Roemer and Cohen from Dworkin, Rakowski and Arneson is that both Cohen and Roemer are much more sceptical about the role the market should play in delivering on luck egalitarian principles. We might, therefore, divide luck egalitarians into pro-market and market-sceptical varieties. I will not adopt such a distinction, but at a number of points in this and the next chapter I will make arguments about or criticisms against *liberal luck egalitarians* (see, for instance, the next note). When I do so, the implication is that my arguments relate to Dworkin, Rakowksi and Arneson and not, unless otherwise specified, to Cohen and Roemer, both of whom intend to enlist luck egalitarian principles to more radical effects.

4 This passage is cited by way of a rare example. The Marxist luck egalitarians Cohen and Roemer, to their credit, tend to steer well clear of the punitive rhetoric of the liberal luck egalitarians discussed here. Although they, too, ultimately struggle to establish a viable egalitarian politics on the back of the chance/choice dichotomy, they are to be exempted from many of the criticisms levelled at liberal luck egalitarians on that score.

5 Parallel arguments are sometimes made within the theoretical literature on disability. Disabled critics of the notion of dependency have long pointed to the way in which the dichotomy between dependence and independence is shaped by political and economic forces (as well as the professionalisation of 'disability'). Who is labelled dependent, how and by whom is strongly influenced by economic and political imperatives, as well as by cultural assumptions about 'normality' (Oliver 1990: 83–94). Nevertheless this does not mean that independence and free choice are not a value at all. Freedom to make decisions about the form and nature of care, for instance, is often a key aspiration even for many people who will find it hard to achieve physical independence, and the claim for direct input into policy-making on health and welfare has been a burning issue for many disabled citizens (and this is just the tip of the iceberg).

6 For much more detailed and sophisticated analyses of the uneasy relationship between equality and workfare, see the various contributors to Moss and McKinnon (2004).

II

ALTERNATIVES:

Equality and citizenship

4

Equality and responsibility:

Towards a more critical union?

Introduction

A S DEMONSTRATED in the last two chapters, contemporary liberal egalitarian theory has been profoundly marked by its encounter with neoliberal
discourses. For many liberal egalitarians – and luck egalitarians in particular –
there are good strategic reasons for this: Dworkin (2000), Arneson (1997a),
Cohen (1989) and Roemer (1996) all claim that the foremost 'discovery' of egalitarian theory over the last couple of decades is that equality and responsibility
need not, as neoliberals assert, remain enemies. Indeed Blake and Risse (2004)
suggest with some justification that 'responsibility-catering egalitarianism' is a
more appropriate term for this school of thought, for it is within this doctrine
that questions of responsibility and choice are most clearly foregrounded. Given
the prominence of neoliberalism, it is admirable that liberal egalitarians have
often attempted to meet the neoliberal critique – and the assertion of the importance of responsibility – head on, and thereby attempted to defuse its attacks on
equality. However, this engagement could take a number of forms. This chapter
seeks to examine the role(s) the idea of responsibility might play in egalitarian
argument. Its aims are in some sense modest. I will not attack the luck egalitarian co-option of the concept of responsibility, though I do not believe it can do
all of the work in an egalitarian account. Instead, it will be argued that the
concept of responsibility *could* play a useful role within egalitarian theory,
provided it is interpreted critically, and read 'against the grain' of the neoliberal
account. This chapter, then, has two aims – to show how neoliberal concerns
resonate throughout luck egalitarian theory and thereby diminish any radical
potential it might have had; and to suggest how the concept of responsibility
might be mobilised differently within a critical theory of egalitarian citizenship.

Section 1 raises some critical questions about the role of the ideal of responsibility within the luck egalitarian literature. Here it is argued that whilst the
neoliberal conception of responsibility is problematic in many ways, these problems have been transferred into, rather than resolved within, the luck egalitarian
account of responsibility. Like the neoliberal conception, the luck egalitarian

account of responsibility has often been narrowly economistic, focusing on the responsibility to refrain from making demands on the resources of the state (and indirectly one's fellow citizens), to be economically self-supporting, and to bear the consequences of one's prudent or imprudent economic decisions.[1] In luck equality, this concern is framed by the chance/choice dichotomy, and the goal of holding us responsible not for our circumstances, but for our conscious choices or gambles. But one way or another, the project of abstracting us from our circumstances in this way (even if we mean by this only *unequal* circumstances) is both impracticable and in many ways undesirable. This is not, however, the end of the road for the ideal of responsibility. Although there are serious problems with the luck egalitarian conception of responsibility, these do not mean that we should jettison the concept. Section 2 attempts to demonstrate that the idea of responsibility in both neoliberalism and luck equality is normative and moralised in specific senses. But this inherently normative character of the idea of responsibility raises other political possibilities. Section 3 endeavours to provide some leads towards a more genuinely critical account of responsibility, which might play a more progressive role within egalitarian theory and politics. Crucial to this endeavour is the notion of 'privileged irresponsibility' which is taken from Joan Tronto. Political discourses of responsibility construct images of responsible citizens as opposed to the actions and characteristics of irresponsible citizens, and it is well worth paying attention to the ways in which the latter are depicted. Whereas the 'irresponsible other' of liberal and neoliberal discourses on responsibility is the dependent, feckless, irrational or unproductive citizen, the idea of privileged irresponsibility shifts the focus onto those who are able to benefit from social activities and processes whilst insulating themselves from the effects of them (Tronto 1993: 121). Whilst Tronto is chiefly interested in analysing the way in which men are often able to benefit from caring work whilst opting out of its performance, it is argued below that this notion may be interpreted more broadly as a critical concept for egalitarian politics. Thus whilst the union between equality and responsibility does not need to be dissolved, it may need to begin again on quite different terms.

1   Interrogating responsibility

Duty or responsibility has been a key term of citizenship throughout its history; the identity of the citizen is substantially constituted in terms of her (or more usually his) citizenly duties. Such duties have been interpreted in a whole host of different ways: the duty to bear arms, to dig for victory, to participate politically, to engage in cultural life and democratic dialogue, to support the state financially, to preserve the language or traditions of one's community, to reproduce and educate the citizens of the future, to respect the duties of civility, reasonableness, or industry. Some conceptions of citizenship (such as republican or 'communitarian' visions) are on these dimensions much more expansive than others (such as classical liberal visions), which are fairly thin in terms of the range of responsibilities they assert. On any given account of citizenship, some of these possibilities may be emphasised, some underplayed, and all may be interpreted in very different ways: there is no core conception of responsibility which underpins all competing visions of citizenship. As different conceptions of responsibility are mobilised, the political effects will be different.

The neoliberal vision of 'active citizenship', whilst potentially very demanding in practice, is extremely narrow in the range of citizenly virtues it invokes. The responsibilities of active citizens are overwhelmingly defined in terms of the individual responsibility to be economically self-supporting, entrepreneurial and prudential in outlook, and to reduce one's dependency on the state (see Faulks 1998: 123–43). This neoliberal conception involves quite specific moves, then; it is overwhelmingly an *economic* category, rather than a political, social, cultural or ecological one. It is also an overwhelmingly *personal*, as opposed to *interpersonal* category: it primarily specifies *vertical* responsibilities vis-à-vis the state, not *horizontal* responsibilities towards fellow citizens. Within neoliberal discourse, social solidarity is expressed through an emphasis on the common threats posed by insecurity, lawlessness, immigration and the competitive global economy, rather than through an ethic of co-responsibility or interdependence. But even as a personal conception, it is significant that the 'person' here is conceived in his or her public (and largely economic) mode, not in his or her capacity as a private carer for dependants or as a giver of love. Such relations are crucial to any society, but are not foregrounded as expressions of citizenly responsibility. It is important to bring all of this to light, for there are many other ways in which the concept of responsibility could be mobilised within debates on welfare, economic justice and the role of the state, for instance, thereby producing different political conclusions. Unfortunately liberal egalitarians – and luck egalitarians in particular – have not brought this to light, and significant political consequences flow from this failure. Luck egalitarians have not asked enough questions of the conception of responsibility employed within New Right or neoliberal thought, the peculiarities of which they have therefore imported wholesale.

This incorporation is not completely surprising, since as with parties such as New Labour, luck egalitarians have been motivated by a desire to fend off the New Right challenge precisely by incorporating the ideal of responsibility (Cohen 1989: 933; Roemer 1996: 309; Arneson 1997a: 329). It is important to be clear that luck egalitarian theorists do not *oppose* the pull-up-your-socks meritocracy which New Right politicians such as Thatcher and Reagan counterposed to the bloated, responsibility-sapping excesses of liberal welfarism, but attempt to outdo the New Right by taking that idea to its hyper-meritocratic conclusion. In a sense, luck egalitarians call the bluff of neoliberalism: if you believe in connecting rewards to choice and responsibility, so do we, and let's see where it really takes us. What this incorporation also serves to demonstrate, at least for liberal luck egalitarians if not for all of its socialist adherents, is 'that egalitarians need not, in general, be hostile to markets' (Scheffler 2003: 14). By redefining equality of opportunity in terms of effort (and hence entrepreneurship), and by linking rewards to personal responsibility, barriers to equal opportunity can now be depicted as irrationalities and inconsistencies of the market. For a central tenet of the credo of the luck egalitarianism of Dworkin, Arneson, Rakowski *et al.* is the belief that in a suitably pure form, market mechanisms can be relied upon to reward the effort exerted by individuals. As Dworkin (2000: 178) affirms, 'the idea of an economic market, as a device for setting prices for a vast variety of goods and services, must be at the center of any attractive theoretical development of equality of resources'. By a simple manoeuvre of co-option, the luck egalitarian project seems to take on wholesale the mantle of academic respectability and pragmatism enjoyed by liberal economics.

The interesting thing that often gets missed here is that neoliberals have retreated in fully fledged panic from claims that the market actually does or can reward effort or talent. Hayek (1976) argues that the market simply cannot and should not be expected to respond to merit, and that this forms no part of its justification. The free market is only useful in that economic freedom safeguards political and social freedom (a highly dubious assertion, it is important to add), as well as efficiency. Any expectation that it will reward merit (in the form of either effort or talent) is frankly dangerous and can only be achieved, Hayek asserts, by way of totalitarianism. At the level of political theory Robert Nozick (1974) makes a similar argument. Markets are to be defended (only) because they protect freedom and individual rights, and any attempt to ensure that outcomes respond to merit will demand increasingly extensive interference in the operation of the market (and again, the main weakness of this argument lies in the role and theorisation of freedom, and not necessarily in the claim that markets are brutal and more or less arbitrary from a meritocratic point of view). In terms of party-political rhetoric, neoliberal politicians have made sweeping claims about the inherent meritocracy of markets. In the calmer confines of economic theory, neoliberals have been altogether more reticent. The neoliberal invocation of individual choice, personal responsibility and just rewards are scarcely delivered upon in practice; instead, we find an odd mixture of freedom *from* social responsibility for the rich, and a blend of coercion and incentivisation for the poor. Taken as a whole, the invocation of personal responsibility justifies a readjustment of the state, involving a hollowing out of social citizenship rights, and a redistribution of income and opportunity upwards to the already wealthy.

Luck egalitarians seem not to have noticed this, and appear intent on delivering on their bluff, by genuinely linking rewards to (rational) individual choices. For the most part, luck egalitarians have sought to render two different meanings of the word responsibility compatible. Specifically, they conflate its *moral* meaning with its *causal* meaning: individuals are to be held morally responsible for the (foreseeable) results of their conscious choices.[2] In an ideal system of distribution, if no individuals possessed advantages of power, ability or initial resources and if all were apprised of the possible outcomes of their choices, what we are entitled to is simply what we *get*. In such circumstances, if we end up with nothing because of sloth, nothing is what we deserve. If we end up with a spectacularly large amount of wealth simply because of our ambition and industry then that too is what we deserve. Indeed luck egalitarian visions are often structured around the economist's ideal of perfect competition, a world in which economic actors freely enter and exit the market, but are curiously unaffected by the accumulations of power and wealth that characterise real markets. Arneson, thus, asks us to 'Think of an individual facing a world that is fixed except for her choices' (1999: 488). On this vision we seem to play a metaphysical game of solitaire, where we make decisions and reap the consequences, isolated from the undue influence of other individuals. Dworkin's account is perhaps more sophisticated on this point, insofar as he recognises that the influence of risk and chance can never be expunged. Instead, in Dworkin's CasinoWorld, we speculate on risks, attempt to capitalise on them, and thereby subordinate brute luck (our physical natures, the world out there, other people) to option luck (our inner world of rational calculation).

One concern here is that such a vision is morally troubling. Luck equality attempts to obliterate the influence of (unequal) structure, circumstance or contingency, and to throw individuals onto their own judgement and ambitions. But the logic of this position is that if we could only achieve this self-determination, our moral claims on other individuals would surely disappear. As a variety of critics (Wolff 1998; Anderson 1999a; Phillips 1999; Scheffler 2003) and some liberal egalitarians (Barry 1991) have pointed out, luck egalitarian doctrine seems destined in practice to become harsh and degrading to the self-respect of individuals. Should we really leave people in the gutter because of their putative responsibility for decisions they made years ago? Is this what it means to treat people with equal respect, or is it merely callous and vindictive? Scheffler (2003) and Daniels (2003) ask whether it can be legitimate to refuse medical treatment to people who have fallen ill as a result of their own choices, as luck equality seems to demand.[3] They conclude that it cannot, and that here (as in many other cases) equal citizenship should 'trump' the single-minded obsession with personal responsibility, a judgement that is highly plausible. Whilst some luck egalitarians (such as Cohen 2000) have also appealed to other values, such as community and mutual support, it is not clear how these various commitments can be woven together within an account that is still identifiably luck egalitarian.

A second problem is that luck egalitarians have never shown how this goal of obliterating the influence of unequal structure, circumstance or contingency could be achieved, at least not without invoking the all-knowing, all-calculating administrative leviathan conjured up by neoliberals such as Hayek and Nozick. There are serious reasons for doubt about whether the luck egalitarian vision – a world in which the individual throws off the shackles of contingency and exerts control over his own destiny – can get off the ground in practice. In Dworkin's case, Chapter 2 showed that his theory's much-vaunted choice-sensitivity turns out to be a mirage: in the end, we are morally responsible for what Dworkin says we should be responsible for, and not necessarily for the choices we actually make (MacLeod 1998). Dworkin has certainly been reticent about specifying exactly what it means to integrate responsibility into the theory of equality, and to defend the version of the chance/choice dichotomy his theory seems to rely upon. Subsequent liberal theorists, however, have at least acknowledged the significance of the question of how individual causal responsibility can be reliably identified and hence rewarded. But they have had little success in advancing their cause.

The liberal inability to specify the line between chance and choice has been well detailed elsewhere (see e.g. Matravers 2002; Ramsay 2004), and the claim that the egalitarian impulse can be framed by the attempt to eradicate the influence of brute luck has been ably rejected by Susan Hurley (2001, 2003). It seems that luck egalitarians have begun to beat a tactical retreat too, and the work of Richard Arneson is particularly instructive on this point. Arneson originally defended a version of luck equality which he called 'equal opportunity for welfare'. This demands that each person, at the outset of their adult lives, faces a set of options that is equivalent to every other person's, in terms of the opportunities for preference satisfaction it presents. As such, our welfare becomes conditional purely on the rationality or irrationality of our choices (Arneson 1999: 488). What is particularly interesting about Arneson's work is that he so soon began to express doubts about its coherence, its desirability, and the possibility of its implementation.[4] Instead, Arneson came to argue that 'providing all individuals in society effectively equivalent options is surely utopian in a bad sense: in most circumstances there would be no conceivable way this goal could be reached' (Arneson 1999: 495). As such, attempts to integrate personal responsibility into distributive justice may appear to have driven into a dead end (Arneson 2001: 87). In the wider scheme of things, it looks as though Arneson sees luck equality as a failed experiment, a diagnosis which begins to look more and more plausible. One way or another, 'the idea that we might adjust our distributive-justice system based on our estimation of persons' overall deservingness or responsibility seems entirely chimerical. Individuals do not display responsibility scores on their foreheads, and the attempt by institutions or individuals to guess at the scores of people they are dealing with would surely dissolve in practice into giving vent to one's prejudices and piques' (Arneson 2000: 97). This is a possibility that is taken seriously in the next section.

2 Responsibility and moral discourse

There is a danger when refuting the practicability of the attempt to tailor distribution to responsibility that we move to the other extreme. Thus Ramsay (2004) appears to justify equality of condition on the basis that, at the end of the day, none of us can be judged responsible for anything. Some version of such an argument is in fact fairly common amongst some of the more radically minded liberal egalitarians, and can serve a useful role in casting scorn on the extent to which existing inequalities can be justified by reference to genuine choice (see e.g. Barry 2005 for a powerful attack on the range of inequalities that can be justified by reference to choice). It is hard, though, to extrapolate this into a positive claim for *equality*. Indeed there is something oddly paradoxical about claiming that equality means tailoring distributions to genuine choice, then denying that such choices exist and hence deriving an argument for something like strict equality. The point is that whilst such an approach works well as a counter-argument to right-wing rhetoric on choice, it tells us little about why equality itself is necessary or desirable.[5]

This is one reason, then, for scepticism about such a position. A second reason reflects a concern about the moral and political conclusions of denying the existence of genuine choice and hence responsibility. It is not, then, the argument here that all attributions of causal responsibility must fail entirely. In the absence of a resolution to the never-ending free will/determinism debate we still have to live together, and it seems both likely and appropriate that ascriptions of individual causal responsibility will continue to inform our moral judgements in many areas. Law and order is the most obvious example: if I were ever to be arrested for murder, I would sincerely hope that judgements about whether I was causally and intentionally responsible for someone's death would come very much to the fore (I might pin my hopes on the judges deciding that no one is ever truly responsible for anything, and releasing all criminals, but then again perhaps not). This brings us, in effect, closer back to the Rawlsian position that despite the intractability of debates over causal responsibility, a just and worthwhile society must require its citizens (sometimes individually, sometimes collectively) to bear responsibility both for the institutional structure of that society and for many of their individual actions (indeed such an approach may be undergoing a revival in the guise, for instance, of Young's 'political' or structural account of responsibility – see below). Like Rawls, I am sceptical that these working judgements about causal responsibility either could or should be extrapolated to the extent that luck egalitarians believe, to form the monolithic bedrock of a theory of equality though (see also Hurley 2001, 2003).

It is far from clear that suitably fine-tuned judgements can be made about causal responsibility in the fields of work, welfare and economics[6] – at least not if the staunch methodological individualism of luck egalitarians is preserved – and luck egalitarians increasingly seem to recognise this these days.

To invert the Rawlsian point somewhat, in the absence of serious progress in advancing our knowledge about human agency, the ideal of responsibility acts instead as a form of moral regulation.[7] In practice, when neoliberal politicians deploy the .concept of personal responsibility, these deployments are both informed by, and advance, a wide variety of political projects. When unemployment is redescribed as a moral failing, not a problem that is endemic within any free market, this cannot be understood as a simply factual statement. Similarly, when crime and teenage pregnancy are explained by moral failing, not socioeconomic circumstance, these are never – or at least never *only* – factual arguments. Arguments to the effect that individuals and their families, rather than the state, bear primary responsibility for their welfare are implicated in processes of economic and social change. At a higher level of generality, Charles Taylor has asserted that the autonomous, self-responsible individual is mythical – or perhaps better, that it is part of the project of modernity that the inherently dialogical nature of selfhood be obscured, and that whilst we come to believe that the self-responsible self is in some sense 'natural', it is in fact a social, political and economic artefact (Taylor 1989). Feminists and Marxists have rendered this same idea in different ways, linking the construction of the autonomous responsible self to structures of capitalism and sexism. Certainly, a highly moralised notion of personal responsibility has formed a major part of the attempt by neoliberal politicians to build a hegemony around free-market principles within Western states such as Britain (see e.g. Dean 2003: 704). It does not take much theoretical sophistication to see a connection between the reassertion of the responsible and prudent individual, and the neoliberal transformation of the state, with its accompanying reining back of social provision and naturalisation of inequality (for an excellent recent account of moral regulation in terms of welfare reform, poverty and the state, see Chunn and Gavigan 2004).

The fundamentally normative basis of the idea of responsibility is similarly evident in luck egalitarian theory. Dworkin makes no discernible attempt to ground a satisfactory causal notion of responsibility and ends up simply asserting that 'the fact of the matter is, people hold other people responsible' (see Matravers 2002: 569). His claims about individual responsibility and choice are not grounded on any factual account of determinism or free will, but represent his own (and apparently our) views about prudence and moral autonomy, and the apparently self-evident (but in fact highly controversial) boundaries of the self. Richard Arneson attempts to.justify his workfare schemes on the basis of choice, but our actual choices are substituted by the choices we should make, and what we *are* responsible for is thereby substituted for what we would be responsible for if we made the kind of decisions we *should* make (see Chapter 3). Arneson's final justification for this position is highly revealing. He argues that 'since many people in our society hold Charles Murrayish beliefs about the moral obligation to be self-supporting', (Charles Murray is an American neoconservative who has written on the moral decline of the underclass) then 'working to earn one's livelihood is in practice needed for now in order to earn the respect of one's fellow citizens' (Arneson 1997a: 349). The argument now becomes both circular and conventionalist; it implies that the assertion of responsibility is ultimately grounded in popular prejudices about the importance of responsibility. We are responsible for holding down jobs, it turns out, because (neoconservative) people believe we should be responsible.

John Roemer also comes to the same pass. Roemer has been far from sanguine about the prospects for solving the conundrum of causal responsibility, and instead has suggested an 'equal opportunity metric', which represents not so much a device for resolving the quandary, but, rather, a means of side-stepping it (Roemer 1996: 309). To achieve this goal, Roemer suggests what has been called a 'statistical' theory of responsibility (Fleurbaey 2002). When making a distributive decision, on Roemer's scheme, we first divide the population into a series of 'types', based on sex, race, income and so on. By putting someone into a type, and judging them against other members of that type alone, we thereby roughly speaking, abstract them from their circumstances. Thus the proper aim of egalitarian justice is to equalise achievement *between* groups, but not *within* groups. If we can equalise group attainment, where a given individual ends up within his group is, by hypothesis, 'due to his choice or effort' (Roemer 1998: 7). Only then can we say with any certainty that differences in the final condition of given individuals are down to individual choices, and not socio-economic circumstances – and that individuals should bear responsibility for them.

But on Roemer's own admission his scheme does nothing to advance the theoretical claims of luck equality. In fact, the theory is conventionalist on what counts as causal responsibility. As Roemer states, 'I do not have a theory which would enable me to discover exactly what aspects of a person's environment are beyond his control … In actual practice, the society in question shall decide, through some political process, what it wishes to deem "circumstances"' (1998: 8). The account is thus full of very Rawlsian assurances, such as 'we believe', 'our society considers', and 'we do not think' (1998: 5–6). If differences are simply divided into two categories (individual and social), without *actual* analysis, this does very little to support the claim that equality is compatible with responsibility or choice. This creates an interesting philosophical question, though; for two identical individuals might fare differently in different polities, simply because of differing conventions about the nature of choice and chance. Maureen Ramsay is correct to argue that if a society adopts a conservative position, holding individuals responsible for outcomes in a ruggedly individualist manner, Roemer has no grounds to argue (and therefore ends up in the same boat as Arneson). But if so, 'Making egalitarianism depend on social decisions lends support to the status quo and endorses existing inequalities which are undeserved on Roemer's own terms' (Ramsay 2004: 283). As such, we are not insulated from brute luck, but exposed to a different *kind* of brute luck, that of whatever conventional views on causal responsibility happen to be. What Roemer gives us, then, is a policy-maker's device for moral regulation, for inserting popular views about responsibility into practical effect. We are responsible for our fates, on his scheme, when and only when our peers consider us responsible; our political fates will therefore vary across time and across societies, regardless of whether we are actually causally responsible or not. As such Dworkin, Arneson and Roemer in their individual ways illustrate a shift in luck egalitarian theory from a conception of responsibility based directly on individual causation or control, and towards a more overtly moral account. As Mason (2006) observes, it is now much more commonly claimed that individuals should be held responsible when, and only when, their actions can intelligibly be the subject of *moral appraisal*. Although this shift enables luck egalitarians to avoid difficult questions about the nature of genuine choice, it does produce its own complex set of moral quandaries.

In fact this shift seems to me to be inevitable: in the absence of any usable scientific method for isolating genuine choice, and putting to bed once and for all the age-old debate between free will and determinism, our ideas about responsibility will be unavoidably normative. They will reflect back to us dominant views on the boundaries of personhood, on the nature of citizenship, and dominant conceptions of rationality. Susan Mendus has argued that one of the problems of pinning too many of our hopes on the chance/choice distinction is precisely that we disagree so frequently about where the boundary lies, not least because 'what we are disposed to attribute to the accidents of nature of contingency or circumstances depends partly on the role we ourselves occupy and partly on the scheme of justice within which we situate ourselves'. Many people, after all, 'are inclined to construe famine, poverty and unemployment as accidents of nature' (Mendus: 2000: 123), while others, who may be on the receiving end, are not. The point, as Mendus (2002) suggests, is that rather than being a neutral scientific artefact which political philosophers then deal with the consequences of, the distinction itself is the subject of moral contestation, and as such is highly political. To put our faith in an essentially a- or pre-political 'solution' to the problem is merely to defer some of the more pressing moral issues of our or any time. Although science for instance may inform our views (perhaps by casting rather ambiguous aspersions on the idea of free choice), it cannot provide answers independent of moral and political debate. As has been suggested in this section, the distinction is at the heart of our moral conception of what it means to be a person, and what the relation between individuals, and between individuals and the state, should be. And this has indeed been borne out in the recent work of luck egalitarians. Rather than criticising luck egalitarians for failing to 'solve' the problem of responsibility, this normative turn should be welcomed. If we accept this, the possibility of other moralised, counter-hegemonic conceptions of responsibility opens up.

3 Towards a critical ideal of responsibility

Critical attitudes towards responsibility tend to be double-edged. On the one hand, within leftist and feminist circles, there has been a degree of caution towards invocations of citizenly virtue and personal responsibility (as Kymlicka and Norman 1994: 361, put it, 'the left has not yet found a language of responsibility that it is comfortable with, or a set of concrete policies to promote those responsibilities'). This caution is often justified, for in the absence of serious attention to the kind of structural inequalities that characterise economic life, and/or the domestic division of labour, for instance, assertions of personal responsibility will usually be conservative in effect. Any genuinely critical invocation of responsibility must go hand in hand with a serious scrutiny of the structural inequalities that characterize contemporary societies, and must be accompanied by serious attention to who is expected to bear which responsibilities, when and why. On the other hand, the idea of duties towards others does seem to suggest one means of defying the resolutely contractual, individualistic and right-based character of much contemporary political and philosophical discourse on citizenship (see e.g. Dietz 1987). Rejecting the view that duties are derived purely from abstract principles as corollaries of rights, Selma Sevenhuijsen asserts that 'obligations and responsibilities are always made, experienced and lived in specific social practices', and that our discourse on responsibilities should be 'situated' within a concrete analysis of relationships, interdependencies and needs. There is certainly a striking difference between the liberal and neoliberal bearer of responsibilities and 'the moral subject in the discourse of care', for example, who 'always already lives in a network of relationships, in which s/he has to find balances between different forms of responsibility (for the self, for others and for the relationships between them)' (Sevenhuijsen 2000: 10). Similarly, there is little or no discussion in the literature on luck equality of issues of collective responsibility, of interpersonal responsibilities to care for vulnerable others, and very little attention to relational responsibilities towards those on whom our acts of production or consumption have an impact.[8] But other currents in contemporary political theory suggest alternative approaches.

It is not the intention here to provide the language of responsibility that Kymlicka and Norman argue the left has been lacking, or to provide an account of who must be responsible for what, when and how. This would be a far larger and more difficult project than could be dealt with here. Rather, the intention is to begin more speculatively to open up some alternative political options. Responsibility as a register of citizenship does not look like being easily dispensable, and neither should it be – but what needs to be remembered is that the luck egalitarian resort to responsibility is but one among many possibilities. There is potential for invoking a relationship between equality, responsibility and citizenship in many different ways. The rest of this section will investigate three specific ways of broadening out the idea of responsibility, thereby to discover how it might function differently within an account of egalitarian citizenship. In particular, it foregrounds the notion of 'privileged irresponsibility', a term taken from Joan Tronto's feminist work on caring responsibilities (Tronto 1993). Whereas the 'constitutive other' of the responsible citizen within luck equality is the feckless, greedy and dependent idler, the more pressing issues for egalitarian citizenship, it will be argued, involve the ability of the powerful to abdicate from caring responsibilities and to make economic decisions that impact on the security of others and the environment that sustains us all.

First of all, even within the narrow terms of formal economics, the literature on luck equality seems devoid of any serious consideration of corporate responsibility, or the responsibility of powerful economic actors. Where do we look to find condemnations of the irresponsibility of executives who take decisions based on the interests of their shareholders and not their employees or the communities they are rooted in? And who invoke responsibility to shareholders to justify despoiling the environment, or skimping on training or safety at work?[9] If we want to deploy the ideal of responsibility in the interests of equality, this would surely be one of the first places to start. In contemporary political practice, all too often the responsibility of the individual to enter the labour-market and be responsive to the needs of employers is asserted without a corresponding state responsibility to ensure that jobs are available (see Rosanvallon 2000). Luck egalitarians such as Arneson, Dworkin and Rakowski have not escaped from this vicious circle either. Why, on liberal luck egalitarian theory just as much as New Labour practice, is the only responsibility that counts my responsibility to make the best of the economic choices available to me? Why is it my job to adapt and retrain when businesses relocate, as New Labour will assert? What are the needs which are accepted behind the scenes here, my need for a secure income, or employers' need for cheap and 'flexible' labour?

In this context it is worth pointing out that the increased emphasis on personal responsibility which characterises neoliberalism is often intimately tied to an erosion of any idea of social responsibility (Chunn and Gavigan 2004: 232). This is not to claim that choice and responsibility are zero-sum issues, but it is true that choice for one person is often expanded by someone else's lack of choice, and that one person's responsibilities often underwrite other actors' *lack* of responsibilities. On a similar theme, Sevenhuijsen (2000: 24) persuasively argues that the 'revolt of the elites' described by Giddens – the tendency for the rich to opt out of common institutions, to resent or reject the responsibility to contribute to their upkeep, to concentrate on private consumption and indeed to encourage the privatisation of public space and public goods – can be legitimately described as a kind of 'privileged irresponsibility'. An attack on this irresponsibility should be at the top of the agenda when responding to the neoliberal focus on personal responsibility. Although she does not foreground the notion of privileged irresponsibility, Iris Young has suggested a 'political' or structural account of responsibility that shares some of these concerns. For Young (2004), individuals who benefit from global inequalities of wealth and power – including those of us who buy products produced in oppressive or exploitative conditions in poorer countries – have a responsibility to act in order to combat such exploitative relations. Whether we can each individually be considered causally responsible for such exploitation is a difficult issue, but is not the only issue for Young. Rather, her argument is that we benefit from such relations, and that we may therefore incur political responsibility merely by virtue of the fact that we stand in unjust relations to exploited peoples. In effect, this approach echoes the Rawlsian assertion that citizens must accept responsibility for the institutional structure of contemporary societies, but allies that assertion with a broader conception of the basic structure (as noted in Chapter 5) which includes, for instance, the 'institution' of global capitalism. Although Young's account has only been set out briefly as yet, such an approach looks likely to be extremely useful.

Secondly, it is regrettable that the luck egalitarian literature tends to say little about ('private') issues of the interpersonal responsibilities for care (especially with regard to children, the elderly and disabled) that are disproportionately shouldered by women, and in many places by ethnic minority women. Any society is sustained on a day-to-day level by the unpaid work of carers and volunteers, but the (formal) economistic focus of much contemporary political theory obscures this, at the same time as contemporary political practice devalues such work (see Levitas 2001, Young 1997b). Care, 'insofar as it is undertaken in the private sphere of the home, tends to be discounted as an expression of active citizenship responsibility' (Lister 2003: 23). But failing to integrate issues of care within egalitarian arguments allows the 'privileged irresponsibility' of men to continue. The feminist concern to see care as an activity accorded a proper place within theories of equality and justice reflects a much broader and long-running concern to see the system of reproduction accorded normative and analytical priority alongside the system of material production. Feminists have long struggled to achieve recognition of this within Marxist theory (see e.g.

Beneria 1979; O'Brien 1981; Butler 1998; Bryson 2004), and the same struggle apparently continues within liberalism.

The idea that, when theorising equality and responsibility, we might have to foreground obligations to care for others is entirely occluded in theories like Dworkin's. For Dworkin (2003b: 136–7), it is crystal clear that 'it is government and not we that must have equal respect for all ... equal concern and respect is not required of us as individuals'. Where individual responsibilities to care have been theorised at all, it has been a staple assumption of luck equality that these are generated by individual choices – as, for instance, in the assertion that parents must bear the costs of their choice to have children. Thus Rakowski (2002) argues that the parents of 'genetically disadvantaged' children, rather than the state, should bear the sole financial responsibility for their care, if they could have prevented them being born disabled or impaired (Rakowski 2002; see Casal and Williams 2004; Mason 2000: 231). But in a whole host of cases (such as care for siblings, for parents, for extended family members, for the elderly, indeed for children who are wards of state, fostered, orphaned or not conceived through choice), this seems much less appropriate. And in a world scarred by war, famine and ecological catastrophes, to acknowledge our caring responsibilities only when these are triggered by our own choices seems highly dubious, to say the least. As Baker *et al.* (2004: 221) point out, 'The millions who become refugees throughout the world each year because of war and political repression are also deprived in a most serious way of relations of love, care and solidarity', and yet their needs will surely be ill served by a purely contractualist account of responsibility.

In its broadest sense, the labour of care includes 'everything that we do to maintain, continue and repair our "world" so that we can continue to live in it as well as possible. That world includes our bodies, ourselves and our environment, all of which we seek to interweave in a complex, life-sustaining web' (Fisher and Tronto 1990: 40; see also Sevenhuijsen 2000: 12; cf. Adrienne Rich's description of the work of 'world-protection, world-preservation, and world-repair', quoted in Longo 2001: 278). Again we could fruitfully adopt a 'structural' or 'basic structure' perspective here, insofar as recognising the omnipresence and the necessity of care provides a good reason to explore the possibilities for a broader, more critical and importantly more interpersonal notion of responsibility. Ruth Lister (2003) for one fruitfully investigates the possibilities of a conception of the 'citizen carer'. Care should be stripped of its outmoded and romanticised association with docile femininity, and celebrated as a political virtue of all citizens.[10] This is a particularly pressing theoretical imperative given the fact that care, love and intimacy increasingly take place outside of the conventional family (see Roseneil 2004). Pnina Werbner (1999) also argues that a feminist account of citizenship will have to foreground the values of caring, compassion and responsibility for the vulnerable, whilst

Sevenhuijsen (2000: 6) argues that we cannot begin to theorise the rights and responsibilities of citizens 'without taking care into account in the fullest possible manner'. But for this renewed focus on care to become fully egalitarian in its implications, it must resonate far beyond the feminist movement (Baker *et al.* 2004: 225), and achieve integration within all discussions of equality and/or citizenship.

Even if we are unconvinced by the salience of care as a political *ethic*, then, care as an essential social *activity* immediately triggers questions of issue of equality and justice. The need for a serious philosophical engagement with responsibilities for care – and the relationship between citizenship and caring work – is especially pressing in a time when care is being increasingly commodified, with serious and inegalitarian implications for the frail and vulnerable among us (see Player and Pollock 2001; Henderson and Forbat 2002). We thus find a growing feminist concern with the justice of time – with issues concerning the work–life–care balance, and possible egalitarian arguments about the enjoyment of free time, caring time and working time (see also Fraser 1997a on universal caregiving). Within the liberal egalitarian literature individuals are simply presumed to make autonomous choices about their work–life balance, and to accrue economic rewards accordingly (see e.g. Rawls 1993: 181–2, on which see Van Parijs 1995: 97–8; Dworkin 2000, on which see Iorns 1993); but this ignores the interpersonal nature of our choices about time, which are bound up in (sometimes hierarchical) relationships with significant others, and are in turn conditioned by economic 'realities' privileging full-time, permanent and regular work.

Thirdly, and finally, where do we look in the literature on luck equality to find a genuine discussion of ecological responsibility?[11] The prominent ecological political theorist Andrew Dobson (2003) has argued for a conception of ecological citizenship as a useful corrective to liberal and republican accounts. In doing so, he convincingly establishes that any adequate notion of responsibility will inevitably disrupt all sorts of cherished boundaries – most notably those between public and private, active versus passive citizenship, and national versus global relationships of responsibility. A notion of ecological responsibility will also put pressure on the ethical individualism of the luck egalitarian account: i.e. its concentration on personal as opposed to collective moral responsibility. In some cases ecological responsibilities might well be levelled at the door of individuals because of choices they have made (the 'polluters pays' principle in miniature). In most other cases such reckonings cannot be made, and any notion of responsibility must be collective.[12] The idea of an ecological footprint may prove to be particularly useful here. This idea involves a version of the categorical imperative: that we should not consume resources (or produce pollution) at a level that would be unsustainable if enjoyed by all. If a community such as the USA makes up 4 per cent of the global population but consumes 25 per cent of its energy, then its ecological 'footprint' has been exceeded and such behaviour can be viewed as ecologically irresponsible. The details of an ecological footprint are subject to dispute and are in many ways ambiguous (Dobson 2003), but the core idea seems highly plausible. Significantly, the idea of an ecological footprint could be applied at both individual and collective levels, and even at the level of entire global generations vis-à-vis our successors on this planet. Interestingly, Dobson argues that many of the non-reciprocal, non-contractual and highly generalised responsibilities demanded by ecological justice are best framed in the language of care. As such he takes a lead from Lister's emphasis on the citizen carer, arguing that although caring is at present a gendered activity, one task of ecological citizenship would be 'to reclaim it as a citizenly, rather than a gendered, virtue' (Dobson 2003: 65).

This section has discussed, then, just three ways in which we might theorise the relationship between equality and responsibility in a more critical way, *in opposition* to the narrow and ultimately inegalitarian conception we find in neoliberal thought. The general argument has been that in integrating 'the ideal of responsibility' into egalitarian thought, luck egalitarians have been uncritical about precisely *which* ideal they are talking about. I do not want to deny that there is space for a suitably critical egalitarian account of responsibility. But liberal theorists have not made the interconnections between equality and responsibility on the one hand, and care and global and/or ecological justice on the other, and the political consequences are regrettable (for a brief and very rare exception, see Sen 2004). For theorists such as Cohen (2000) and Wolff (1998) who argue for the importance of an 'egalitarian ethos' in sustaining a just society, there is surely a great deal of scope for connecting with the notion of responsibility in a more circumspect way. For such a putative egalitarian ethos, the concepts of interpersonal, non-contractual responsibility and care could well be key concepts (for an account of the role that love, care and solidarity could play as mobilising narratives in an egalitarian movement, see Baker, Lynch *et al.* 2004: 220–6). By the same token, a critical exploration of the interplay between the ideals of equality, responsibility, care and global economic/ecological justice would be highly fruitful. It has been suggested that the notion of 'privileged irresponsibility' may well be useful as a broad category for a critical egalitarian politics. The notion of privileged irresponsibility (Tronto 1993) directs our attention not so much to individual acts of causality, but to the ways in which some people are able to benefit from relations that oppress and exploit others. As such, the 'other' of the responsible citizen is defined not so much in terms of the undeserving poor, but in terms of those who neglect caring responsibilities which sustain us all, who with impunity make economic decisions that disrupt the lives of others (see also Young 2004), and who participate in processes of ecological degradation that affect us all, but which impact particularly strongly on the poor and disempowered. All of this serves to suggest that, although the issue of responsibility can do some (but not all) of the work in grounding an egalitarian conception of citizenship, there are other and more productive routes we could take in attempting to integrate considerations of responsibility into egalitarian theory.

Conclusions

This chapter has considered the role that the concept of responsibility might play in egalitarian argument. Specifically, the first two sections dealt with some of the downsides of the luck egalitarian attempt to head off neoliberalism by incorporating key elements of its rhetoric, specifically on the issue of responsibility. But this is not to reject the ideal of immanent critique, or of serious engagement with the ideological opponents of equality – far from it. There is no reason why the idea of responsibility cannot be turned to egalitarian ends, and mobilised *against* neoliberalism, by revealing the particular and contingent ways in which it has been constructed within right-wing discourse, thereby opening up different political possibilities. No concept can be monopolised by any one ideological project, and each offers a potential site for contestation or subversion. It may be politically valuable to attempt to seek out other, 'counter-hegemonic' ways of theorising the ideal of responsibility, and such a project was at least begun in Section 3.

It might well be said, of course, that for all of their assertions about the discovery of 'the ideal' of responsibility luck egalitarians are simply interested in one specific form of responsibility, and that much of the above argument is extraneous to their concerns. Maybe so, but I hope to have shown why it might be fruitful to look beyond the narrow terms of the luck egalitarian discussion of responsibility not just because of what we can *add* to this discussion, but also because a genuine recognition of the terms of human interdependence could *transform* that debate. With regard to the luck egalitarian co-option of responsibility, then, I want to express two reservations. The first concerns the *uncritical* way in which the ideal of responsibility has been taken over from neoliberalism. The luck egalitarian gamble – to accept the focus on choice and responsibility, to raise the stakes and see where we end up politically – fails because liberals have not asked any searching questions about the ways in which the ideals of choice and responsibility have been constructed and mobilised within neoliberal discourse. Whilst some luck egalitarians might be appalled by the political consequences of neoliberalism, they have largely reproduced the core elements of the neoliberal ideal of responsibility, and as a result possess inadequate resources for challenging the substance of many neoliberal policies. The second reservation is that, although we can choose to integrate ideals of choice (as discussed in Chapter 3) and responsibility (as discussed in here) into egalitarian theory, these concepts cannot do *all* of the work. For both practical reasons (i.e.

the difficulty of implementing luck equality) and moral reasons (i.e. the punitive and degrading judgements luck equality requires us to make), the attempt to ground equality *purely* on considerations of responsibility and choice fails. More positively, there is growing recognition of this amongst luck egalitarians themselves, as well as a growing awareness that other egalitarian aspirations (for an egalitarian ethos, for community or solidarity or the enjoyment of public goods, against hierarchy and oppression) may be ill-served by the monological nature of the luck egalitarian project. A satisfactory egalitarian project will need to be more pluralist in its theoretical approach (cf. Cohen 2004: 24). Though notions of responsibility and choice may perform some role within a satisfactory egalitarian project, their role looks likely to be both *different* and more *limited* than luck egalitarians have suggested.

Notes

1 This chapter will omit one half of the story when it comes to injunctions on rational economic behaviour. Neoliberal discourses on the imperatives of the modern capitalist subject have a register of production (involving normative assumptions about work, training, speculation and enterprise), and a register of consumption (involving normative assumptions about desire, accumulation, the satisfaction and multiplication of wants). This chapter focuses on the register of production, tracing the commonalities here between neoliberal and luck egalitarian rhetoric. It would be an interesting project to trace the lines of neoliberal rhetoric on consumption throughout the luck egalitarian literature on expensive tastes, adaptive preferences and so on, but such a task cannot be pursued here.

2 Andrew Mason (2006) usefully distinguishes between two different ways in which luck egalitarians have argued that responsibility can be attributed to individuals. The *control* conception assigns responsibility for outcomes (only) when they were under the control of a given individual, and he or she could plausibly have acted otherwise. The *responsiveness to reason* conception, on the other hand, assigns responsibility for outcomes (only) when an outcome can plausibly be regarded as a product of the *judgement* of an individual, in the sense that it makes sense to appraise them morally. The arguments of this paragraph chiefly relate to the control conception which, as Mason notes, has proven very difficult to defend adequately. As a result, the responsiveness to reason conception has begun to look more attractive to a number of luck egalitarians. This approach does raise a number of difficult issues itself, though, some of which are highlighted in Section 2 of this chapter.

3 Alexander Kaufman (2004) provides an interesting corrective to this view, arguing that luck equality could and should incorporate a defence of an unconditional minimum of welfare (and presumably health) provision. As such, the luck egalitarian emphasis on responsibility would be scaled back, at least in such desperate cases. Insofar as this would render luck equality more pluralist in the bunch of distributive principles it advocates, such a move could represent a useful beginning.

4 Arneson also expressed some very suggestive doubts about the 'starting-gate' aspect of his theory. A starting-gate, snapshot view of equal opportunities, according to which we are required to have equal opportunities at one particular moment – however fleeting – is not unusual, and such a 'cardinal moment' is usually pitched at

adulthood (see e.g. Rawls 1971). This has some appeal, but Arneson declares that in the wider scheme of things this seems 'capricious'. This is because however equal our opportunities might be at the starting-gate of adulthood, any decisions we make thereafter will immediately shape and constrict the remaining opportunities left open to us. In this sense, the way our life goes in later life is very definitely not a matter of our individual control in the relevant sense (1997b: 239). As he pointedly asks 'why does sheer bad luck that befalls an individual after this initial moment [of] redistribution demand no redress, while similar sheer bad luck that befalls an individual prior to the canonical moment demand full redress?' (1999: 490). The only non-capricious (though impractical) alternative is to re-equalise our opportunities after every choice, because this is the only way in which chance (in Cohen's (1989) sense of everything that is not choice) can be conquered. This would surely require continual equality of condition. Paradoxically, providing everyone with equal opportunities at all moments effectively means that we will *always* possess equal resources or opportunities for welfare, or whatever, *regardless* of our actual choices, and hence the choice or responsibility that luck egalitarians claim to tailor distribution towards actually disappear from view. The choice for luck equality is therefore between capriciousness or contradiction.

5 Samuel Scheffler (2005: 7–8) has recently made this point at greater length, arguing that whilst there are good reasons for egalitarians to employ 'limited and defensive' arguments on responsibility – in effect, by denying that current inequalities can be justified by reference to choice, in the way that right-wing politicians sometimes argue – luck egalitarians commit a mistake when they claim that equality per se can be justified solely on the basis of an egalitarian theory of responsibility.

6 It is not the aim here to reject the idea that political policy should integrate some notion of individual responsibility even in the fields of welfare policy, but it is to register several provisos. For one thing, as is claimed below, such an integration is likely to be conservative in impact unless it is preceded by a serious attack on the structural inequalities of the economic market, and a serious attack on the sexual division of caring labour – neither of which are consistently on offer from any of the liberal luck egalitarians discussed here. Secondly, it may be that such considerations will generally be better integrated at the ground level, according to the judgment of the relevant professionals and affected citizens (see Shapiro 1999), and are often poorly served at the generalised level of political theorising or political rhetoric. On this issue Elizabeth Anderson's (1999b) views are broadly sensible. Thirdly, it seems inappropriate – and again this makes more sense in context of the discussion below – to theorise individual responsibilities in abstraction from the already-existing social web of relationships of care and dependency that characterises any society. A number of feminists and ecologists have endeavoured to theorise responsibility 'from the ground up' – i.e. beginning with an account of interdependency and human needs rather than an abstract account of deontological obligations (see below) – and this represents at the very least a valuable corrective to liberal and neoliberal accounts of responsibility.

7 Moral regulation refers to 'a project of normalizing, rendering natural, taken for granted, in a word "obvious", what are in fact ontological and epistemological premises of a particular and historical form of social order'. As such, various forms of moral regulation are implicated in processes of state formation and reformation: 'state forms are always animated and legitimated by a particular moral ethos' (Corrigan and Sayer 1985: 4).

8 To give a striking example, Christopher Lake's book *Equality* and *Responsibility* (Lake 2001) sets out to examine the ways in which liberal egalitarians have tried to connect

the two concepts. The book does indeed present a thorough and tightly argued account of those ideas; but in a short footnote to the very first sentence of the book, Lake notes that that he will only be discussing *personal* or *individual* responsibility. No explanation or justification is given for this remarkable foreclosing of possibilities, or for the altogether unremarked fact that Lake concentrates on economic responsibilities (to work, possess or produce) alone. In terms of reflecting the nature of the debate that has occurred within liberal theory, though, Lake is surely justified in pursuing such an approach. Luck egalitarian theorists have failed to open up any real distance between themselves and what Hartley Dean (2003: 696) calls the 'post-emotional' vision of neoliberalism, which 'entails a hollowed-out form of compassion for others and a distinctively apolitical preoccupation with one's own interests and well-being, or those of one's immediate family'.

9 Brian Barry (2005) has offered precisely these things in characteristically indignant style but would not, I presume, describe himself as a luck egalitarian.

10 It is important to recognise that members of the disabled people's movement have often found the ideal of care invoked within feminist debates on the 'ethics of care' deeply troubling. But for two interesting attempts to navigate these complex issues and produce an account of care that can satisfy both feminists and the disabled people's movement, see Hughes *et al.* (2005) and O'Brien (2005).

11 This is not to claim that the egalitarian theorists discussed in this chapter are unconcerned about environmental issues. G.A. Cohen (2000), for one, certainly is. The point, rather, is that this concern appears thus far disconnected from their erstwhile invocation of the importance of responsibility.

12 Andrew Mason (2000) observes that the luck egalitarian position fails to give us any leads in such cases, so grounded is it in the assumption of individual, autonomous causality. As he rightly argues, 'In some cases, responsibility may be irreducibly collective … there are cases where a group of individuals engaged in a cooperative venture bring about an outcome which none of them individually [cause] but where there is no way, even in principle, of determining the relative contribution that each individual has made' (Mason 2000: 233). Though Mason makes his point in a different context, it seems to apply directly to situations in which ecological degradation is visited on some communities because of the 'lifestyle choices' of others. Though the burden of these responsibilities will ultimately be felt by individuals, such obligations are generated by diffuse and collective action. Young (2004) also makes this point very clearly.

5

Opportunities, outcomes and democratic citizenship:

Young and Phillips on equality

Introduction: the hegemony of opportunity

IT WAS noted in Chapter 3 that liberal debates on equality increasingly concentrate on the ideal of equal opportunities for all individuals. There are, to be sure, different interpretations of equal opportunities: thus the luck egalitarian literature kick-started by Dworkin, in particular, attempts to replace the old meritocracy – the talent-based equality of opportunity which Rawls rejected – with a 'new' meritocracy where the effort and ambition of all individuals can be rewarded. But the hegemony of equality of opportunity as an ideal remains profound. I expressed serious reservations about this project in Chapter 3, which drew a comparison between the new meritocratic ideal and the project of social inclusion pursued by centrist political parties in Europe and North America. The rhetoric of these 'modernising' parties, on my analysis, has seen equality 'repackaged' as the right to engage in productive work, and the opportunity to develop the skills and 'flexibility' necessary to insert oneself into the increasingly competitive global labour market. Considerations of economic opportunity strongly inform political rhetoric on the equality of women, ethnic minorities and the disabled. Robin Cook (2003), for instance, lauded the fact that Britain's multiculturalism gives it 'a competitive advantage in the global economy', which may be true, but feels like a very odd justification for cultural equality. By the same token the gender equality agenda of recent decades has been overwhelmingly framed by the need to ensure entry of women into the formal labour market (Bacchi 1999), and we can make similar points in terms of the disabled. All of this reflects some quite profound processes of ideological realignment: notably, this repackaging is informed by a broader shift in the discursive role of the state. Whilst up to the era of social citizenship the state was largely portrayed as a localist guarantor of social rights and privileges against the vicissitudes of the global market, the state now increasingly acts as a relay between global market and individual citizen, 'encouraging' the latter to engage productively with the former; the imperatives of this global market are assumed as given (see Cerny 1995).

It has been my contention that insofar as liberal theorists such as Dworkin have replicated neoliberal rhetoric within their theories, they seem peculiarly incapable of challenging such developments. But this is not the end of the matter, for there are further questions to be asked about how a satisfactory egalitarian politics can move forward in light of these problems. This chapter examines the role of the notion of equal opportunities within egalitarian theory, a question which allows us to address the place of social groups within egalitarian theorising. There are two possible responses to the hegemony of ideals of economic opportunity. One is to reject equal opportunities in favour of another conception of equality, or at least to argue that the ideal can only play a *limited* role within an egalitarian project. Another would be to seek to *radicalise* the idea of equal opportunities: to argue that equality of opportunity can be a transformative ideal if it is interpreted sufficiently broadly, or to claim that if we engaged in a sufficiently rigorous analysis of the nature of contemporary inequalities we would be much less willing to accept them as rooted in personal choice. This chapter examines how two prominent political theorists, Anne Phillips and Iris Young, respond to this dilemma. Their positions have much in common, and both are concerned to challenge the way in which inequality is narrowly framed within the liberal egalitarian literature, as an issue of relative disadvantage within a more or less unproblematised institutional order. But there are also crucial differences between them, which suggest that Young – in her recent work at least – has a greater investment in the discourse of opportunities than does Phillips. As such, whereas Young concentrates on the second strategy, Phillips leans towards the first.

In terms of general strategy, Iris Young's concern is to *broaden* and *deepen*, rather than abandon, the emphasis on equal opportunities that we find in the liberal literature. Young argues that Rawls is right, for instance, to focus on the ways in which the basic structure of society conditions the opportunities or life-chances of individuals, but that we need to broaden our understandings of both the basic structure of society and the nature of the life-chances in question. First of all, the definition of social structure that Young works with consciously echoes that of Rawls: 'structures refer to the relation of basic social positions that fundamentally conditions the opportunities and life prospects of the persons located in those positions' (Young 2001: 14). But in analysing the operation of the basic structure, Young argues that Rawls unduly focuses on its distributive aspects: that is, the way in which the basic structure affects the distribution of various social goods. If we are concerned with how social institutions constrain our life-chances, this simply misses too much. Secondly, whilst opportunities are indeed what matters from a moral point of view, Young believes that these opportunities should be construed much more widely than they have in the liberal literature. The chief aim of Young's account is therefore to examine the 'institutional conditions necessary for the development and exercise of individual capacities and collective communication and cooperation' (1990: 39), and in this respect her approach shares some features with the ideal of equality of capabilities, as advanced by Amartya Sen.

Anne Phillips, by contrast, appears much more circumspect about the merits of arguments for equality of opportunity. Her specific concern is to show how a commitment to equality of opportunity, correctly interpreted and implemented, must drive us towards the conclusion of substantial equality of outcomes. But we need to be clear here that for Phillips this is an exercise in external critique: it is an attempt to enlist the support of defenders of equality of opportunity for conclusions which she thinks can be defended on other grounds. In fact Phillips maintains that equality of outcomes might be *better* defended in other ways: and especially by resorting to the overarching value of the political equality of citizens.

In what follows I will examine the arguments of Young and Phillips side by side, for they are complementary at many levels. This is certainly the case at the level of critique, where they both develop broadly parallel critiques of liberal equality, and at the practical level, where they develop broadly similar accounts of equality within the fields of work and political representation (though this chapter will concentrate on the first case). But ultimately the two accounts pull in different directions. On the crucial question of whether equality of opportunity can provide an overarching framework for egalitarian politics, it seems that Young's response is in the positive, whereas Phillips's is in the negative. Whilst many of Young's interventions are salutary, this chapter concludes by siding with Phillips on this question, by arguing that equality of opportunity is not capable of standing in as an overarching normative principle for egalitarian politics.

Section 1 of this chapter considers Young's arguments for the centrality of social groups to the analysis of inequality. Whilst liberal theorists usually argue that differences in occupational or income profile between groups are not in themselves troubling, Young suggests that such disparities are likely to provide evidence of injustice. Both Young and Phillips argue that equality of condition between social groups based on class, sex or ethnicity should be the critical standard for assessing just social relations. This critical principle suggests that a just society will be free from substantial inequalities in political power, economic wealth and social position between major social groups. Section 2 moves on to discuss Phillips's critique of liberal defences of equality of opportunity, and her argument that if properly understood and operationalised, a commitment to equality of opportunity should produce equal outcomes.

The concern for groups is not purely analytical, however. Section 3 examines suggestions advanced by Phillips and Young for how to *remedy* group inequalities. For both theorists, equality must involve a commitment to closing the gap between social groups across various dimensions, including occupational role, income, and political representation. Specifically, this Section discusses issues relating to work as an example. Both Young and Phillips are concerned to disaggregate work-related inequalities from race and sex, and their arguments represent valuable correctives against accounts such as Rawls's, which discusses the distribution of benefits between various broad social positions without adequately problematising how those positions, and the relations between them, are constituted. Finally, Sections 4 and 5 return to examine the ways in which equality has been theorised by the two writers under discussion, before this chapter concludes with some reflections about the appropriate role of the ideal of equal opportunities within egalitarian argument. It is argued that Young and Phillips are right to defend what I call a critical group-oriented principle of equality, but that this principle is not best defended solely through the logic of choice and opportunity. Instead we must turn towards the logic of equal and democratic citizenship.

1 Young on equality and institutional structure

This section has three goals. Firstly, it examines Young's arguments that if we are concerned about the way in which the institutional structure of society conditions the opportunities of individuals, then we should be concerned about the relations between social groups. Secondly, it moves on to the critique of liberal – and chiefly luck egalitarian – thought advanced by Young, which implies that a focus on the relative positioning of groups is central to the identification of inequality and injustice. Thirdly, it examines Young's defence of what I shall call a critical group-oriented principle of equality.

As part of her critique of the 'distributive paradigm', Young (1990) charges that liberal theories of justice are superficial, in the sense that they concentrate on the surface redistribution of concrete goods such as income and wealth, at the expense of a proper critical examination of institutional structures. Even Rawls is vulnerable to this criticism, especially since he equivocates between the claim that the goal of a theory of justice is to assess the basic structure of society, and the more narrow claim that its proper focus is 'the distributive aspects of the basic structure' (Rawls 1971: 9). Indeed within this focus on distribution, for heuristic purposes Rawls focuses on the 'proxy' of earned income when setting out his proposals, and the wider implications even for institutional reform of the economy remain significantly underdeveloped. This distributive focus is replicated in the work of Dworkin who, far from problematising the basic institutional forms of contemporary capitalist economics, assumes that they must be at the centre of any scheme of distributive justice.[1] Even Kymlicka, an erstwhile defender of Dworkin's theory, therefore concedes that his suggestions are 'primarily focused on *ex post* corrections to the inequalities generated by the market' (Kymlicka 2002: 82), and fairly tentative ones at that.

[*120*]

Young's arguments on the need for a proper focus on institutional structure are complex, and we can only deal with one aspect of her case here. Young contends that, if we are concerned about the way in which social structure and social institutions condition the life chances of individuals, as Rawls says we should be, then we should be concerned about group relations *as institutions*. Our social position in relation to groups organised around sex, race, and ability or impairment, for instance, affect our lives, as Rawls would have it, 'right from the start'. As Shane O'Neill (2004: 89) suggests, what should concern us is 'the fact that the basic structure of all modern societies creates and produces inequalities that result in the historical formation of relatively stable hierarchical group relations'. These structural social groups, as Young puts it, 'are constituted through the social organisation of labor and production, the organisation of desire and sexuality, the institutionalised rules of authority and subordination and the constitution of prestige' (Young 2001: 12). These hierarchical group relations constrain and condition our opportunities in just the same way as the institutional forms of the economy, the family, and so on. As Young argues, 'a person's social location in structures differentiated by class, gender, age, ability, race or caste often implies predictable status in law, educational possibility, occupation, access to resources, political power and prestige ... each of these factors enable or constrain self-determination and self-development' (Young 2000: 95).

It is important to note that for *analytical* purposes Young does not want to make any claims about the essential 'identity' or interests of these groups, or what group membership means to a group's 'members'. To the contrary, it is important to recognise the relational nature of these groups. The 'disabled' are only understandable as such insofar as there is another group which we can call 'able-bodied'. 'Femaleness' has historically been understood in opposition to 'maleness', 'whiteness' in opposition to 'blackness' and so on. Crucially these major dualisms are always hierarchical: in most cultures one is constructed as superior by the contrast to the inferiority of its 'constitutive other'. In that sense group difference itself is a function of the relations between groups (1990: 171). From the point of view of the analysis of inequality, the important issue is simply that we *are* positioned in social life through these groups: if 'a person complains of being the victim of arbitrary search because he is Black, we do not need to know very much about how this person defines his Black identity, or whether he does so at all' (2002a: 6–7). The fact is, 'Individual people come into a world where social groups are a given, and people treat one another partly on the basis of imputed group membership' (2002b: 285).

Groups, though, are noticeable only by their absence in many liberal accounts. Our second concern, then, is with how Young's assertion of the analytical importance of groups motivates a specific critique of the liberal egalitarian literature. Young has been fiercely critical of the methodological individualism of liberal egalitarianism, which fails to get to grips with the relational nature of inequality. As noted in Chapter 2, since Dworkin the emergent luck egalitarian literature has driven forwards a categorical distinction between the choices we make, and the circumstances we face. The concern of egalitarians, on this account, is to protect us from, or more often compensate us for, the influence of the latter. But as Young points out, 'A large set of the causes of an unequal distribution ... is attributable neither to individual preferences or choices nor to luck or accident. Instead, the causes of many inequalities ... among individuals lie in social institutions, their rules and relations, and the decisions others make within them' (Young 2001: 8). The luck egalitarian approach fails to do justice to the causes of injustice, and the disproportionate regularity with which it impacts on particular groups of people. Once issues get conceived in this way, oppression, domination, sexism, racism, are all crowded out, or reconfigured as part of the social 'circumstances' which must somehow be compensated for. Within the luck egalitarian literature, as Elizabeth Anderson has rightly noted, the world seems populated by the industrious, prudent and rational, in addition to 'beach bums, the lazy and irresponsible, people who can't entertain themselves' (1999a: 288). We are given no clue, though, to what has happened to the oppressed, to those marginalised by inequalities of class, gender, race and caste.

As an indicator of this, the second chapter concurred with Robeyns, who suggests that Dworkin's theory is 'structurally unable to account for the cultural aspects of gender, race, and other dimensions of human diversity that create unjust inequalities between people' (Robeyns 2003: 541). Although it may not be the case that contemporary liberal theorists do not want to explain inequality, their arguments seem to be framed in such a way that individual choice becomes our first port of call in accounting for concrete inequalities. Indeed in the case of Dworkin, individual choice threatens to become the final port of call. This issue comes into clear focus when we consider recent work by Young and Brian Barry side by side. Barry has resorted to arguments about what he calls 'achievement oriented dispositions' in accounting for different levels of economic 'achievement' shown by members of different social groups (Barry 2001: 94). If such groups possess different amounts of material resources, or populate different occupations to different degrees, why should we assume there is some form of injustice or oppression at work? If members of different groups really *value* different things, for instance, what is wrong with them following different courses in life? When conceived in this way the question becomes one of how much *presumptive legitimacy* we can give to such differential profiles, based on the supposition of different ambitions. The answer given by Young is: very little. As Paul Kelly usefully notes, 'Where Barry is inclined to see [unequal] outcomes as benign unless there is evidence to the contrary, Young is persuaded that the existence of group difference is precisely what needs justification. For

Young, equal outcomes form the baseline against which departures are to be judged' (Kelly 2002: 68). This sets a high critical standard for equality.

So Young is concerned, then, about the major, *systematic* forms of privilege and marginalisation that characterise modern societies. This leads her to suggest a group-oriented definition of equality. In her work on status equality, Young gives the clearest indication of this concern. She claims that the kind of inequality that should concern us in terms of status consists in

> differential honor or deference afforded to some people by others on account of their social and institutional position. Our society contains many small status inequalities, not all of which are matters of justice ... the sort of status inequality that ought to worry us ... is that experienced systematically by certain groups of people ... It is the systematic nature of this status inequality that raises issues of justice. (Young 2002a: 2)

This status inequality exists when a group of people are relatively disadvantaged on dimensions of job status and pay, residence, autonomy or respect from others (2002a: 3).

It is important to note, however, that it is not wholly clear whether Young defines any inequalities between social groups based on sex or race as unjust *per se*, or merely *likely* to be unjust. Young initially seemed to argue the former, as when she argued that 'basic equality in life situations for all persons is a moral value' (Young 1990: 14). But she now seems to reach towards the latter position, affirming that inequalities on some measure between groups are not unjust unless we can specify how social structures are unfairly constricting the opportunities of some (2001: 15, 16).[2] Whilst identifying aggregate differences in social location between groups is a beginning, then, it is not the end. It directs us towards injustice, but we still need to tell a 'plausible structural story' about how these inequalities arise, and how they constrict individual opportunities, if we are to establish that they are in fact unjust (cf. Roemer 1998). I will deal with some of the practical implications of this shortly, but I will turn first to Anne Phillips's immanent critique of equality of opportunity.

2 Phillips on the immanent critique of equal opportunities

Phillips shares with Young a concern that the liberal literature on equality 'obscures ... structural inequalities that cannot be understood in such individualist terms' (Phillips 1999: 59). Again, the chief object of criticism here is the 'luck egalitarian' literature inspired by Dworkin, which recasts the problem of inequality as one of choice and personal preferences, versus brute circumstances. As such, this literature 'has redefined what is predominantly a problem of inter-group relations – the inequalities between rich and poor, male and female, black and white – as a conundrum about luck and choice' (Phillips 2004:

17). Along with Young, Phillips argues that 'current thinking misrepresents the effects of social relations and institutions as if these were generated by individual choice ... This draws us into a discourse of individual variation that has less and less purchase on the larger issues of inequality' (2004: 15). In this literature, 'Instead of discrimination, we see only individual differences in qualification or talent; instead of inequality, we notice only the effects of luck and choice' (Phillips 2001b: 125). In political terms this has two downsides. For one thing these theories 'tend to anaesthetize people against what they know to be major differences in opportunities and power. In abstracting from social relations, they also abstract from dominance: the fact that one person's choice is so often enabled by another's lack of choices, or that one person's success may depend on exploiting other people' (1999: 57). For another, as noted in Chapter 3, such accounts all too easily coincide with a 'rather punitive frame of mind' (2000: 242) when it comes to political policy. Just as Bacchi (1996) observes, this framing of the problem means that the focus shifts so that the characteristics of the 'claimant' (women, ethnic minorities, the disabled) becomes 'the issue', rather than the privilege of the advantaged, or the hierarchical relations between social groups.

Phillips's critique of liberal ideas of equal opportunities tackles this tendency head on. In particular, she wants to argue that – unless we accept some rather distasteful assumptions about the character of different groups of people – any serious commitment to equal opportunities will lead us inexorably towards acceptance of equal outcomes. For Phillips, any defence of equality of opportunity must lead to a defence of equality of outcomes between social groups, unless we presume that the members of such groups differ in their average genetic makeup, or 'natural talents', or 'native endowments'. And this, Phillips asserts, is wholly implausible. In this way any *serious* defence of equal opportunities must lead, crucially, to a defence of equal *outcomes* between groups. As she puts it, 'there is no significant space to be inserted between equality of opportunity and equality of outcome when it comes to sexual or racial equality. If the outcomes turn out to be statistically related to sex, the opportunities were almost certainly unequal' (Phillips 1999: 50). This does not mean that we must be committed to the eradication of all inequalities between *individuals*, because individuals do of course vary in their abilities and dispositions. But it does mean that we should be concerned with those 'historical accidents' by which inequalities become clustered around sex and race (1999: 63) or other social categories.

Phillips suggests that we should be committed to substantial equality in the way in which resources, roles, responsibilities and time map across social groups based on race and sex (2004: 10). There is a question, though, about how we should take Phillips's critique. Is she herself committed to equal opportunities – and *therefore* to equal outcomes? Or is she in fact much more reticent about the idea, and therefore seeking to pull defenders of equal opportunities back onto the right course, whilst distancing themselves from their obsession with opportunities? The evidence points to the latter, and as such suggests some real critical distance between the accounts of Young and Phillips, as I will argue in the last section of this chapter. For now, I will contextualise some of these issues by moving on to arguments advanced by Young and Phillips about equality and work.

3 Equality, work and hierarchy

A key argument of radical critics of liberal egalitarianism has long been that on closer inspection, the apparently abstract and deontological reflections of theorists such as Rawls and Dworkin do in fact assume the existence of specific social institutions. As Young puts it, 'In his theory Rawls implicitly assumes many institutions as given ... such as competitive markets, political bureaucracies, and monogamous heterosexual families, without ever raising questions about whether the positions and relations these institutions entail are just' (Young 1981a: 286). This argument is important: although such liberal theories are often condemned for being detached and abstract, that charge misses the point. The real problem is that the appearance of abstraction allows quite concrete (albeit generalised) assumptions about social institutions such as the exchange economy, the family and the bureaucratic state to be assumed without adequate defence, even though these institutions are often hierarchical in nature. If this is the case, the 'problem' equality tries to solve is to ensure fair competition to fill the relevant positions within such hierarchical institutions.

Radical critics, though often accepting the principle of competition in some way, tend to want to expand the agenda to include issues surrounding the constitution of such positions, and the relations between them. In the case of work, there is considerable evidence that many liberal egalitarian accounts inadequately problematise the 'basic positions' of economic life. Rawls, for instance, explicitly argues that he is concerned with the distribution of benefits between people in 'representative social positions'. In economic terms, we are left to presume that this maps onto distinctions between mental and manual, white collar and blue collar, or as Rawls puts it entrepreneurial versus unskilled classes (see e.g. Rawls 1971: 78); but the nature and validity of this basic division of positions is not problematised. In Dworkin's case we could make similar observations: as a consequence, a valid interpretation of equality of resources would seem to be for people to sign up for a scheme whereby they regularly switched positions within profoundly hierarchical structures. Furthermore neither theorist adequately addresses the relations between the advantaged and disadvantaged at the global level, or the fact that in the rich North we stand in specific social relations with individuals in the South, defining positions which have an effect on the way our lives go right from the start (consumer/producer, lender/borrower, donor/recipient, coloniser/colonised).

Ensuring equal access to an unequal and hierarchical system of rewards and valuations may or may not be valuable, but it certainly does not tackle all of the fundamental issues. Instead, Young argues, 'a major issue of justice should be who decides what are the appropriate qualifications for a given position, how they will be expressed, and whether particular individuals have them' (Young 1990: 193). Debates over qualifications are deeply political, and a counter in power struggles between various social groups. In practice, the ability to define talent tends to be monopolised by professional elites, and reflected back as a technical, apolitical issue. This enables such elites to be self-serving in several ways. For one thing they can be self-selecting, setting the terms of admission to their privileged roles. For another thing elites have a greater say in determining both their own pay and conditions and those of workers 'lower down' the professional hierarchy.[3]

Young's real problem, then, is with the way in which 'the ideology of merit seeks to depoliticize the establishment of criteria and standards for allocating positions and awarding benefits' (1990: 211). By comparison, attempts to question dominant conceptions of talent – or the nature of the institutional hierarchies individuals will fill – appear highly political. Most worryingly, such attempts can easily be depicted as attempts not to reassess the rules of the game in an inclusive way, but to seek special treatment for particular minority groups. This is clearly what has happened in the debate on affirmative action, which is widely represented as an act of unfair discrimination. Whilst affirmative action strategies as commonly understood tend to redistribute desirable positions among groups, however, they are of minor significance in the broader picture, and are often forwarded merely as a relatively 'safe' policy option (1990: 200). 'Changes in the overall social patterns of racial and gender stratification in our society', Young argues, 'would require major changes in the structure of the economy, the process of job allocation, the character of the social division of labour, and access to schooling or training' (1990: 199), which take us far beyond the distributive focus of affirmative action.

Job allocation is the case Young devotes most attention to. She believes the idea that we can unproblematically ascribe appropriate qualifications for any given task within modern organisations is dubious for a number of reasons, chiefly to do with the complexity and interdependence of roles within such organisations. In fact 'the idea of merit criteria that are objective and unbiased is ... impossible' (1990: 202). In particular the conventions that value mental over manual, white collar over blue collar work are just that: conventions, which often reflect nothing more than the fact that the relevant decisions are made by white collar workers. So, Young argues, are many workplace conventions based on the idea of a full-time male breadwinner (1990: 205), and presumably what counts as 'work' in the first place. On these questions, there is no impartial standpoint from which such decisions can be made: all judgements are implicated within group struggles.

Once we admit that what counts as merit is both thoroughly political and an object of struggle, the legitimacy of a hierarchical division of labour is seriously questioned. Nevertheless, Young's position here is highly controversial: is she seriously claiming that anyone could be a nuclear physicist, or a midwife? (see Fletcher 1998: 203). On reflection, her position is less categorical than it at first appears. Though she is sceptical about our current ideas of merit, she does not want to reject the idea of merit itself. Given that these ideas are deeply political, though, she advocates a strategy of democratisation. Young argues that 'decisions that establish and apply criteria of qualification', pay scales, and all other major workplace decisions, 'should be made democratically' (Young 1990: 212). In particular, she argues for the representation of oppressed groups such as women and ethnic minorities on workplace committees, for it is only in this way that the uninterrupted and uninterrogated privilege of dominant groups can be overcome. The results of this fair discussion will significantly challenge, but will not obliterate, hierarchies of authority and of differential pay, which are often legitimate (1990: 216). As such, Young intends not to abolish hierarchies, but to democratise them, to make their constitution a genuinely common project. Although Young rejects an ideal of impartiality based on the transcendence of group membership, she does seem to prefigure here a version of impartiality based on the inclusion of social groups in fair discussion.

Phillips's concerns are broadly parallel. She claims that there should be no difference between social groups in terms of roles, unless we are very sure they are the product of genuine choice (Phillips 1999: 68) – and for reasons outlined above, she is very sceptical that we will be able to justify disparities in social roles in this way. Moreover Phillips is concerned about the rewards and responsibilities that accompany roles such as jobs (and Phillips would attach to this category other social roles such as sexual roles in reproduction and 'domestic' work). Like Young, Phillips is concerned that the influence of prejudice and hierarchy should be stripped out of our ideas about ability. But she is particularly concerned to unsettle the manner in which some forms of work are valued over others, and by how these valuations and devaluations map onto groups. Phillips is troubled by the ways in which valuations of work map onto race, and as a feminist, she also sees a key part of this struggle as breaking down the hierarchy between women's and men's work. As she points out, 'it does not take a great deal of theoretical sophistication to perceive the connection between the sexual division of labour and norms of masculine behaviour' (1997: 112). As a result, 'even if we allow the legitimacy of differential rewards for differential work, the valuation currently attached to particular jobs is often highly questionable' (1999: 69). The only feasible strategy to combat this is to equalise care work between men and women (1997: 111; cf. Fraser 1997a on universal caregiving).[4] Any *sound* argument for fair access

[*127*]

requires, as Phillips suggests, broad equality between social groups organised around sex, class or ethnicity. Nevertheless, it is important to note that the fair access argument could be met by a society with huge gulfs of income and privilege between those who occupied particular roles. The subsequent argument about rewards is therefore essential, for it promises to close the hierarchies of position which individuals can compete for places in. Satisfying this principle, as Phillips observes, would entail some pretty radical reforms (Phillips 1999: 68). It would demand that we become far more sceptical about the fairness of market outcomes, the merits of current incentive structures and, presumably, the widespread horizontal and vertical segregation along the lines of sex and ethnicity that characterise many contemporary labour markets.[5]

Overall, Young and Phillips actually follow a fairly well-trodden line, which poses a radical conception of equality of opportunity against a liberal one. Such a radical conception of equal opportunities has three chief characteristics. Firstly, we find the idea that 'since it is manifestly the case ... that women and black people are the equals of men and whites, the actual distribution of occupational rewards should reflect this fact ... The absence of an equal distribution is, ipso facto, evidence of unfair discrimination' (Jewson and Mason 1986: 315). Secondly, it is therefore claimed that equal opportunities can only be measured by examining the relative positionings of social groups (see e.g. Schmid 1984). Thirdly, it is charged that 'the terms "ability" or "talent" are not the politically or morally neutral ones that they purport to be' (Jewson and Mason 1986: 315); as a result, a radical approach therefore recommends the politicisation of work life, on the understanding that 'decisions within an enterprise or institution are not made according to technical or bureaucratic criteria or rationality', but are instruments of struggles between social groups (1986: 320). By introducing these concerns into the literature on equality, Young and Phillips promise to broaden the frame of the debate. These arguments are salutary, and restore a concern with institutional hierarchy that has been lacking in mainstream accounts of economic justice (for exceptions to this rule, though, see Walzer 1983 and Shapiro 1999). In Young's case, at least, they represent a transition to what I would call a third generation conception of equal opportunities. Whilst the earliest view prescribes that those with equal qualifications should compete on equal terms (the French Revolutionary ideal of the career open to talents), the now-dominant view (in post-Rawlsian philosophy, at least) prescribes that if such competition is to be fair, all should have equal opportunities to *develop* marketable talents. The third incarnation of this principle, which we can associate with Young and other defenders of radical equality of opportunity, accepts the first two stages but argues that all must have an equal opportunity to *define* talent and to determine its fair rewards. Only in this way can we ensure that competition is genuinely fair, in the sense that our chances are not influenced by our background social position.[6]

These developments are promising. Nevertheless, it is interesting that although their conclusions are quite different, the premises of these arguments are not wholly opposed to those of many of the liberal theorists Young and Phillips criticise. Some of the concerns of Young and Phillips therefore hit the target when directed against political practice, but threaten to talk past their target of academic liberal egalitarianism. After all, Rawls had serious doubts about the role ideas of meritocracy could play in a plausible version of distributive justice, and, as I noted in Chapter 1, shared many concerns with critics of meritocracy such as Michael Young (1961) and R.H. Tawney (1921). Dworkin (2000) even more firmly declares that no one should have more income simply because they possessed more 'natural' talent, and instead advocates what I call a 'new' meritocracy, where effort or ambition alone are rewarded.

It is not entirely clear how Young and Phillips stand on these issues. Both apparently share with luck egalitarian theorists the view that differences in effort and hard work should be rewarded (Young 1990: 214, 216; Phillips: 2004). More broadly Phillips and Young in fact show sympathy for the central plank of the luck egalitarian argument, namely the idea that whilst talent is morally arbitrary, inequalities arising from genuine choices should, within certain constraints, be tolerated (see e.g. Young 2001: 8). Interestingly, this threatens to make the argument vulnerable to the same problems that plague luck equality, such as whether we could ever reliably reward effort in isolation, as opposed to talent. Indeed many of Young's concerns about how difficult it is to appropriately specify relevant talents in a modern, diverse organisation apply quite straightforwardly to effort too. It is curious that Young considers talent to be riddled with cultural stereotypes, immersed in power struggles and subject to definition 'from above', whereas effort and ideas of 'hard-workingness' are not problematised in the same way. In fact, there have historically been many social stereotypes – aggregating around ethnicity for instance – about predispositions to work hard, and not just about talent itself.

More interestingly still, it is not in the end clear that Young or Phillips do object to the rewarding of talent either. Phillips agrees that rewarding talent is arbitrary, and therefore appears unjust. Nevertheless she argues that much in life is arbitrary, and we should not be concerned too much with the rewarding of individual talent, so long as we strip out of rewards the results of any prejudices based on 'historical accidents' such as racism and sexism (Phillips 1999: 63). Young, too, seems to be content that merit finds its own reward, so long as that merit is democratically defined and hence insulated from the influence of group privilege and oppression. We could say as a result that Young and Phillips do not in fact reject all versions of the choice/chance distinction, but that they are content to situate both effort and talent on the side of choice, which may be rewarded, so long as we situate the influence of social structure – arising from judgements about groups – on the other side. In this way the approach of Young and Phillips is more ambitious than liberal egalitarians – because both want to ally it to a profound scepticism about existing hierarchies and the legitimacy of systematic inequalities. But it is also less ambitious than their luck egalitarian rivals – because they are more tolerant of inequalities arising from differential 'talent', so long as they are not *systematic* – in the sense that such inequalities map onto social group membership.

4   Young on equality and capacities

> Equality refers not primarily to the distribution of social goods, though distributions are certainly entailed by social equality. It refers primarily to the full participation and inclusion of everyone in a society's major institutions, and the socially supported capacities to realise their choices. (Young 1990: 173)

In her recent work Young defends a strong version of equality of opportunity, pitched at the level of the self-development of important capacities. Moreover, this equality of opportunity matters at the level of the individual, although group analysis may provide a useful way of identifying structural injustice – that is, the way in which social structures unfairly constrict the opportunities for self-development of individual citizens. 'Measuring inequalities between groups', Young asserts, is merely 'a means of arguing that structures of privilege and disadvantage give individuals unequal opportunities' (2001: 17).

Although Young is fiercely critical of the positions taken within the liberal 'equality of what' debate, her criticisms are therefore more relevant to some of those positions than to others. Her criticisms are especially relevant to theories of equality of resources, but they are less obviously relevant to theories of equality of welfare, or of capabilities. In fact Young seems to share much in common with theorists who define equality in terms of specific skills, abilities or 'capabilities'. Whereas some liberal egalitarians have unduly focused on equal chances to earn income, Young's view is that opportunities should be construed much more broadly, in terms of the ability to participate on an equal footing in all social institutions. Specifically, we should be interested in defending two sets of opportunities. The first set is associated with 'developing and exercising one's capacities and expressing one's experience'. This would include fulfilling one's material needs, living in a decent environment, playing and communicating with others, learning and deploying skills, and experiencing pleasures (1990: 37). The second set is associated with 'participating in determining one's actions'. This would involve 'participating in the life of institutions and receiving recognition for doing so, and expressing our experiences and feelings in supportive settings' (1990: 37).

Young (2001: 98; 2000: 31) has explicitly developed the connection between this broader ideal of equality of opportunity to develop important capacities, and the theory of equality of capabilities, which is most closely associated with the economist Amartya Sen. Sen (1992) defines a capability as an opportunity to develop a 'functioning' – that is, the ability to perform a valuable task such as eating, sleeping, educating oneself, enjoying good health, or participating in political institutions. Equal opportunity means, then, the opportunity to achieve sets of functionings that are valued by the individuals concerned. This account clearly has virtues.[7] Despite its huge influence, though, the theory remains ambiguous in many ways. Indeed the theory's 'unique adaptability' (Olson 2001: 21) may be both a strength and a weakness. Young's resort to such an argument brings to bear some difficult questions.[8]

The most pressing question is whether we can specify in advance what the most valuable human capacities are. Whether we do or not, we face two horns of a dilemma. Sen (1992) argues (at least sometimes) for *equivalent sets* of functionings rather than actually specifying those functionings which must be guaranteed for all: in fact he shows a reluctance to set out an objective account of human flourishing (Sen 1993: 47). Rather, he asserts that the capability approach is compatible with a variety of 'theories of value'. As a result, though, Sen must therefore presume some notion of 'commensurability' – the idea that the *value* of one capability can be judged against the value of another. This is the first horn of the dilemma, because such an approach presumes that we can make statements of some accuracy and intelligibility to the effect that being able to play a musical instrument, for example, is broadly comparable in value to being able to speak a foreign language. But this is objectionable for two reasons. Practically it seems that we simply do not have any reliable metric for comparing such functionings, or indeed for measuring opportunities more broadly – although to be fair most of us blithely continue to use the idea of equal opportunity. Morally or politically, the notion of commensurability may be offensive. It is surely a working assumption of democratic life that no number of gold watches can compensate us for the absence of a vote. By the same token, it would surely not be sufficient merely to award financial compensation to the socially or culturally oppressed.

Some theorists have attempted to bypass this problem of commensurability precisely by setting out an objective set of core human capabilities. For instance Martha Nussbaum (2000) defines core capabilities in terms of life, physical health and integrity, play, mental faculties, emotions, practical reason, affiliation, relationships with other species and control over one's environment. Young too seems to be specifying a set of *core* capacities which should be available to all. But here we face the second horn of the dilemma, for the issue of paternalism rears its head. Most accounts of the core functionings necessary for citizens in a democracy are in fact Aristotelian and/or republican in orientation, and often avowedly 'essentialist' in their claims about human nature (see e.g. Nussbaum 1992; see also Anderson 1999a). Given her rejection of essentialism, and her caution about universalism, we would expect Young to be highly suspicious of such an account, but she does appear to depend on such an account herself. These problems are serious, and as yet unresolved.

This is not to reject the capacities approach, however; for these theoretical problems need to be put in context. Specifically, they need to be put in the context of a world marred by desperate inequalities across and within nations. Assembling a list of core human capacities is a tricky and to some extent arbitrary process, which throws into relief questions about the good life, pluralism, particularism and universalism. But this does not mean that the danger of essentialism is worse than the dangers of starvation, malnourishment or social and political exclusion. There seems to be no reason why a list of basic human capacities or capabilities should not form a key part of the struggle against global injustice, and such an approach may unite theorists from quite different theoretical positions (see also Phillips 2001a: 259; Barry, 2001: 285). Though safeguarding these capabilities across the globe would require substantial material redistribution, as well as social and cultural change, this basic list is philosophically fairly 'thin'. What is less clear is whether we can take the notion of capability or capacity equality 'all the way', and thereby produce an overarching theory of justice that will govern modern societies, and here I am highly sceptical. At least at some points, the position taken by Nussbaum is that the notion of capabilities works best in its capacity as a baseline, as an element of a wider conception of justice. For Nussbaum (2000: 75), a concern for 'central capabilities is not a complete theory of justice [but specifies] a decent social minimum'. It concerns the 'threshold' of justice but may not take us further than that. Whilst Young might disagree, it remains to be seen how she can navigate these difficult theoretical questions. This throws us directly back onto the question of how much work opportunities can do in a theory of equality, to which I shall return in the conclusion.

5   Phillips on opportunities, outcomes and democracy

My primary focus is on what democracy suggests about the relations between citizens, and the promise it holds out (but on which it so rarely delivers) about our status as political equals ... I see the furthering of that equality as requiring ... a new settlement between women and men ... I also see it as intimately bound up with reducing income differentials and reforming the division of labour. (Phillips 1999: 18)

Phillips's argument from equal opportunities is much more strategic than Young's. Her criticisms of existing defences of equality of opportunity are, I would argue, well taken. In the absence of, firstly, a proper critical scrutiny of the way in which structural injustices are produced, and, secondly, an adequate interrogation of the institutional hierarchies of work and politics, for example, such defences can only legitimise substantial inequalities. She sets a high standard for any theory of equality of opportunity, arguing that the only situation in which we can be sure that equality of opportunity actually holds is one on which substantial equality of outcome obtains too (2004: 13).

Phillips also states, however, that she has serious concerns about arguments from equal opportunities, and implies that she merely wants to show defenders of opportunities why they should be committed to a critical principle of equality between groups. The more profound justification for such a principle is located by Phillips in the political equality of citizens. Phillips is keenly aware that the political equality of citizens is at best an incomplete project: 'there is a great deal of unfinished business', she declares, 'in working out what it means to treat citizens as equals' (1999: 126). On this account, political equality means something more than equal opportunity for influence during elections or public debates, for instance: Phillips argues that the ideal of political equality is potentially much broader and deeper than this. It refers us back to the very ideal of the equal respect for human worth which is in turn inherent in the ideal of democratic citizenship. In that sense, like Young (2002a), Phillips accords a central place to the idea of equality of *status*. Such an ideal of equal worth or status simply cannot be sustained in the presence of great extremes of wealth and poverty, of occupational segregation by sex and race (1999: 94–95) and the kind of upper- and middle-class flight that mean that we no longer genuinely share common institutions. Phillips is particularly exercised, then, by 'the emptiness of proclaiming people political equals when the disparity of their incomes and lifestyles means they inhabit almost separate worlds' (2001a: 259).

So precisely what kind of economic equality is required to underpin the value of egalitarian, democratic citizenship? Here there are two strands to Phillips's arguments, relating to groups and individuals respectively. In terms of groups, Phillips defends what I have called a critical group principle of equality: no inequalities of outcome that aggregate around race or sex should be accepted. But what about inequalities between individuals? This strand of Phillips's argument is somewhat less demanding, insofar as Phillips is arguing for *less* inequality of outcome between individuals, rather than strict equality. But Phillips wants to insist on two provisos. Firstly, inequalities arising from free choice can only be tolerated *so long* as they do not jeopardise political equality. We therefore have a parallel of Rawls's point about the fair value of the political liberties, but which for Phillips imposes a cap on *relative* inequalities and not just absolute ones (1999: 71), and hence implies an attack on the wealth and power of the rich. Secondly, Phillips asserts that 'a humane society would ensure that everyone has enough resources to maintain a decent standard of life' (1999: 68). Phillips advocates, that is, an unconditional minimum beyond which we cannot fall. She devotes little time to making clear what form such a guaranteed minimum should take, however. Is it based on a standard welfare scheme, albeit a substantial and democratised one? If so, how does it relate to work (either of the so-called formal or informal varieties?) Or would Phillips advocate an unconditional basic or citizens' income? Carole Pateman (2004) has argued forcefully for the utility of a basic income for the achievement of a feminist, democratic and radical form of citizenship, and there would appear to be good grounds for giving such a strategy serious consideration.

More work on this would be welcome, but either way, what becomes clear is that although Phillips engages in an instrumental critique of liberal ideals of equal opportunity in order to elicit support for her critical group principle of equality, the ideal that she has the most genuine investment in, and which seems to hold the most immanent power, is the ideal of equal citizenship within a democratic polity.

Conclusions

The arguments of both Phillips and Young represent persuasive critiques of the economism and superficiality of many liberal approaches to equality, and the failure to deliver on the radical promise of the ideal of equality of opportunity. Both argue that any serious defence of equal opportunities, if followed through, will entail a commitment to what I have called a critical group-oriented principle of equality. It is significant here that both theorists invoke democracy at crucial points in their arguments, albeit in somewhat different ways. Young's defence of core capacities is an attempt to broaden the meaning of opportunities to include all sorts of meaningful democratic, social and communicative activities, in addition to the primarily economic opportunities upon which liberal theories have often concentrated. It is not, then, a rejection of equality of opportunity, but an attempt to extend its terms (cf. Kelly 2002), to include values of democratic communication. I regard this endeavour as worthwhile and persuasive. The conflation of 'opportunity' with 'opportunity to earn income in a market economy' should not go uninterrogated, for there are many other opportunities that have meaning to us, and which any theory of equality should therefore register a legitimate interest in (on this point, see also Van Parijs 1990). Nevertheless, there are profound questions to be answered about how such a broad account of opportunities could be operationalised, and here Young's theory seems to face the same dilemmas as the theory of equality of capability (see e.g. Sen 1992). The evidence here suggests that the notion of capabilities can play a much less ambitious (or rather, more basic) role within an adequate theory of justice than Young would seem to imply.

Phillips, by contrast, places much less faith in the ability of the ideal of equality of opportunity to give force and shape to the egalitarian project. She invokes democracy, in the end, precisely to show how we need to go *beyond* the ideal of equal opportunities. For Phillips, whilst opportunities may be important for various reasons, they do not exhaust the concerns of the egalitarian. A concern for equality of condition may be justifiable on other grounds, such as a concern for community, solidarity, equal status or, most fundamentally, the political equality of citizens. Indeed the view of 'life as a race' may undermine these very things. Such concerns might suggest that we circumscribe the areas within which inequalities can be justified *even* by reference to uncoerced choice.

There are great merits to both theorists' accounts, but on the crucial question of how much work the ideal of equal opportunities can do in an egalitarian theory, Phillips seems to occupy the more secure position. Equality of opportunity will be a part of any adequate theory of justice: opportunities are clearly valuable, not least insofar as it is important that we should have some control over the way our lives go. But as a broader idea about rewards – and specifically in invoking the idea that society can be arranged so that effort and choice alone are consistently rewarded – the idea seems to overstretch itself, and this is evident in the problems encountered in the capability approach as well as within contemporary luck egalitarianism. A more likely hope is suggested by Paul Kelly (2002: 76), who argues that 'We can combine the opportunity and outcome perspectives in a substantive egalitarianism that conceives of equality as the core value underpinning social and moral relationships in a civilized and inclusive society. In this way, equality is a good of political structures and institutions and not merely a principle that applies to the distribution of individual goods'.

This chapter has endorsed the critical group-oriented principle of equality suggested by Phillips and Young, then. The ultimate standard for a critical egalitarian politics should be to end substantial equalities in incomes *and* social roles such as caring aggregating around hierarchical constructions of race or ethnicity, or binary constructions of sex and sexuality. In addition a critical egalitarian politics should involve at least a continual scrutiny of established hierarchies of respect and reward within the major institutions of society. But there must be a *double* justification for such standards. Part of such justification will undoubtedly refer to the likely outcomes if opportunities were genuinely equal. But such counterfactuals can only take us so far. A substantial part of the justification must also refer to the equal status of citizens within a democratic polity. And, as Phillips suggests, this latter idea will often override our acceptance of inequalities arising even from uncoerced choice. It is worth noting that this moves us closer to many pre-Rawlsian egalitarian arguments. John O'Neill, for one, tries to recover some of the critical force of an earlier socialist egalitarianism – running from Marx through to Tawney – when he notes of such 'traditional' egalitarianism that

> While the elimination of the social lottery was central to the egalitarian project – life chances ought not to depend on accidents of the social position into which a person is born – the elimination of cosmic misfortune in the distri-

bution of natural capacities was not ... The ideal of equality is tied to the creation of a particular form of community in which certain forms of power, exploitation and humiliation were eliminated, relations of solidarity, fellowship and mutual aid were fostered, and basic needs universally satisfied. (O'Neill 2000: 307)

In view of the theoretical problems experienced by the contemporary liberal doctrines of capability equality and luck equality, a reengagement with such arguments would appear invaluable.

Notes

1 Despite their very real weaknesses, it may nevertheless be inaccurate to claim, as Young (1990) appears to, that liberal theorists have pursued an entirely 'distributivist' approach to social justice. Dworkin, for instance, has always made it clear that his view of equality has never been about distribution alone. Certainly he argues that equality of resources is the single, purely distributive expression of the equal moral worth of persons, and certainly that account has to be seen as highly problematic. But he also argues that there are other, *non-distributive* implications of that moral ideal. In fact Dworkin (2003a: 190) claims that he sees social, political and economic equality as equally important, and argues that 'a genuine society of equals must aim at equal stake as well as equal voice and equal status for its citizens'. Equality then has more than one terrain. It may well be the case that Dworkin tells us less about political equality than economic equality – and almost nothing at all about social equality – and that he tells us next to nothing about the relationship between the three. But it is not the case that his approach to equality or justice in the broadest sense is distributivist.

2 This leaves it open whether equality of outcomes between individuals should be the ultimate goal and standard for egalitarians. The view of both Young and Phillips would seem to be that it should be (and the various strategies examined in this chapter would move us significantly closer to that goal), but that the practical energies of egalitarians should be focused on group-related inequalities, at least as a point of leverage for more radical change. This brings to bear many complex issues, but generally I would want to concur with such a view.

3 For evidence on the ability and willingness of executives to ensure exceptional benefits for themselves, see Bebchuk *et al.* (2002).

4 For a parallel argument which makes use of Walzer's notion of the stigma which adheres to groups undertaking what is defined as 'hard work', see Armstrong (2002).

5 The phrase 'horizontal segregation' refers to the way in which various subgroups of the labour force are consigned to particular jobs or sectors of employment, as illustrated by the over-representation of women in professionalised child-care work, but their under-representation in the field of information technology. The phrase 'vertical segregation' refers to the ways in which various subgroups are consigned to the higher or lower echelons of a particular industry, as illustrated by the over-representation of black males as professional footballers, but their severe under-representation as professional football managers.

6 This typology has some overlap with Adam Swift's (2001: 99) delineation of minimal, conventional and radical interpretations of equality of opportunity, though for Swift

the radical view is a broadly luck egalitarian one, as opposed to the democratic view I describe here.

7 Young's interest in the capability approach is not isolated. Elizabeth Anderson has also defended an ideal of democratic equality that draws on the work of Sen. 'Following Sen', Anderson argues for 'equality for all in the space of capabilities'. Specifically, she calls for a set of capabilities 'necessary for functioning as an equal citizen in a democratic state' (Anderson 1999a: 316).

8 Her resort to an idea of capacities or capabilities may also throw some doubt on Young's claims about her own brand of political theorising. Young (1981a, 1990, 2001, 2002b) asserts that she is not providing a new theory of justice, but is instead arguing for an approach to justice that takes on board the concerns of specific emancipatory social movements. This suggests a contextual approach to justice, located in the struggle against specific injustices at specific times. On the other hand, her opposition to oppression and domination is grounded in a conception of human functioning that is openly universalist and non-contextual: rooted, in fact, in the idea of the equal moral worth of persons (1990: 37). At this point, we can ask questions about which argument is bearing the real weight in Young's approach to justice. Roger Paden (1998) argues with some justification that the universalist account of capacities is doing the theoretical work, and that Young is therefore prepared to ignore claims from oppositional movements when they do not forward her underlying goals of capability and participation. Either way, whilst Young (2000: 31) asserts that her ideals of self-development and self-determination are 'fairly uncontroversial' they clearly are not.

6

Equalities:

recognition, redistribution and citizenship

Introduction

THIS CHAPTER examines Nancy Fraser's work on recognition and redistribution, and her account of justice as participatory parity. Fraser's work provides invaluable insights into how a concern with inequalities connected to culture and 'identity' might be integrated with more traditional concerns with economic inequality. At the same time, the guiding concern of her account mirrors one of the central questions discussed in this book: namely that of what the prerequisites are for genuine membership in a democratic community, and for interaction as peers within social life. It has to be said that Fraser does not explicitly foreground the concepts of equality *or* citizenship in her account of justice. Far from it, her much-noted work on the recognition/redistribution debate seemed to pose a significant challenge for defenders of equality, insofar as it consigned the politics of equality to a subcategory of political struggle, key to economic justice but out of place in the fight against cultural or symbolic injustice. But on closer inspection this apparent opposition fades from view, as the egalitarian content of her work is rendered increasingly explicit. By the same token, although Fraser rarely resorts to the language of citizenship per se, she aims to kickstart a radical politics bridging both economy and culture, and united on the basis of an account of egalitarian, democratic membership. In so doing she both provides resources, and raises crucial questions, for those concerned to formulate a genuinely radical and democratic account of equal citizenship.

The chapter proceeds as follows: Section 1 examines Fraser's celebrated discussion of what she calls the recognition/redistribution dilemma, as well as her suggestion for how we might navigate that dilemma by pursuing a strategy of socialist economic reform, and cultural deconstruction. It also explores her notion of parity of participation, which is intended to provide an overarching normative framework for a variety of struggles for justice. Section 2 examines the role of the concepts of equality and citizenship in Fraser's work. In her earlier work on the recognition/redistribution dilemma, Fraser appeared to downplay the significance of equality as a critical tool, by describing it as the key concept for a politics of redistribution, but not of recognition. In her more recent work, the egalitarian character of Fraser's work has been revealed to be much more significant. For one thing, equality has been rediscovered as a core component of struggles for recognition. But more importantly, the notion of parity of participation has been redescribed as an egalitarian ideal. This section, in fact, interprets it as an ideal of equal citizenship, and goes on to draw a parallel here between Fraser's work and that of radical democrats who suggest that only the ideal of citizenship is capable of providing the grammar with which to articulate the diverse demands of oppositional groups in a pluralist society.

Though much in Fraser's account is persuasive and helpful, I do want to raise some critical questions about it. In Section 3, the major concern is with Fraser's social-theoretic arguments. The key problematic of Fraser's work is how the apparent bifurcation of radical struggle might be remedied, by investigating how economic and cultural struggles sometimes complement each other. Fraser's work attempts to steer a course between an 'ontological' dualism which presumes a substantive separation between economy and culture, and ('anti-dualist') approaches which assume that economics and culture wholly interlock, but which may as a result be unable to theorise the complexity of different forms of group-based injustice. Fraser instead favours an approach that distinguishes analytically between economy and culture, but rejects an empirical separation. It is argued that her position here is highly ambiguous, as is the notion of a 'partial uncoupling' of economy and culture that it is based on. In fact, the trajectory of her recent work tends to undercut her resistance to anti-dualist positions. In Section 4, I argue that this suggests we should employ critical categories that cut across such putative boundaries. This final section therefore returns to briefly address the political utility of the concepts of recognition and redistribution, arguing that, ultimately, these do not close the gap of critical cultural-economic politics, whereas opposing citizenship to oppression and hierarchy might do the job better. Thus whilst Fraser's suggestion that (something like) parity of participation can function as an overarching norm for egalitarian politics is to be welcomed, it is much less certain that the twin ideals of recognition and redistribution represent the surest routes to achieve it.

1   The 'recognition/redistribution' dilemma

> A critical theory of contemporary society ... must clarify the prospects for emancipatory change for a time in which struggles for recognition are increasingly decoupled from struggles for egalitarian redistribution – even as justice requires that the two be joined. (Fraser 2003a: 5)

An increasingly prominent theme in political theory is the question of how economic and social/cultural struggles for equality might relate to one another.

Though it has received increasing attention recently, this question has had a long life within both political practice and political theory. Similar questions have often arisen at the nexus of socialist and feminist struggles in particular. In the old Soviet Union, in socialist parties across the world, and within the trade union movement, the priority of apparently 'cultural' emancipation for women or economic emancipation for the workers has been hotly debated. Would emancipation for women come 'after the revolution', as many socialists argued, or did it need to be fought for now, not only in the wider world but also within the often sexist confines of the socialist movement? At a theoretical level, this concern led to the 'Dual Systems debate' within socialist feminism (see Sargent 1981), which contested the relationship between the systems of patriarchy and capitalism. Is the materiality of economics analytically (or even historically) prior, thereby determining the 'cultural' injustice faced by women? Or vice versa? What are the implications either way for radical egalitarian struggle?

In the end, this debate remained fundamentally unresolved, not least since the deeper questions it posed were so difficult: are social or cultural ideas ultimately shaped by economic forces, or vice versa? Are 'economy' and 'culture' two systems – which might be more or less independent over time – or two faces of a single interlocking system? Though substantial agreement over these questions was never achieved, the concerns they expressed have not disappeared. Far from it: the very same concerns were reinvented in the new language of the equality/difference debate, and have latterly re-emerged relatively unchanged in what has come to be known as the recognition/redistribution debate.

The precise language of this latter debate owes much to the tradition of critical theory. Specifically, the so-called recognition/redistribution debate arises in response to the way in which critical theorists had addressed the emergence of the 'new social movements' of the post-war period. Whilst the black civil rights movement, the second wave of feminism, the growth in environmental consciousness, and struggles for equality for disabled people and against hetero-sexism were widely welcomed, the emergence of these movements often suggested a difficult question. Was a new 'identity politics' in the process of displacing struggles for economic equality? This question was answered in the affirmative by Jürgen Habermas, for whom 'the new conflicts' characterising the contemporary political scene were 'not ignited by distribution problems but by questions having to do with the grammar of forms of life' (Habermas 1987: 392).

Whilst Habermas's became an influential position, the younger generation of critical theorists, and especially Nancy Fraser and Axel Honneth, have been critical of the way in which it seemed to suggest an unsustainable substantive (or 'ontological') dualism between economy and culture (or, as Habermas puts it, system and lifeworld). Could we really say of a movements such as feminism or the civil rights movement, for instance, that they concerned 'forms of life' (or cultural politics) and not issues of distribution? That they were, in Judith Butler's loaded words, 'merely cultural' (Butler 1998)? Axel Honneth's response has been to assert the fundamentally cultural nature of economic relations, and hence to reject Habermas's distinction between the two types of struggle. Instead, all of these movements, *and* movements such as socialism, can be seen as struggles for some form of cultural 'recognition' (see Honneth 2003). He presents, according to Fraser, a form of ontological monism: what feminists once would have called a culturalist unified systems approach.

Nancy Fraser (2003a) rejects Honneth's approach too, which she argues renders economics as a mere effect of culture. Nevertheless Fraser has grappled with exactly the same issues. She asserts that within radical politics we have witnessed the eclipse of a 'socialist imaginary', centred on terms such as interest, exploitation, and redistribution, by a new 'postsocialist' political imaginary, centred on notions of identity, difference, cultural domination, and recognition (1997a: 2). Such developments may not be limited to radical movements either, but have parallel registers throughout contemporary political practice. As Anne Phillips (1999) has observed, parties such as New Labour seem to have abandoned meaningful redistribution, focussing instead on an agenda of (partial) cultural equality and (limited) constitutional reform. Indeed many mainstream parties in Europe and the North America increasingly engage in a much less progressive politics of identity, continually ratcheting up the intensity of their rhetoric on law and order, and engaging in moral panics centred around underclasses, 'deviant' minorities, asylum seekers and terrorism (see e.g. Feldman 2002: 419).

Assuming for now that this bifurcation of radical politics has occurred, there has predictably been intense interest in how we might we draw the strands together again. In fact, there seem to be two questions involved here. The first is: can we provide analytical tools to theorise the potential conflicts, and potential harmonies, between the two types of struggle? And secondly, can we provide a broad normative language to unite (and assess) demands for (apparently) cultural and (apparently) economic forms of justice? In recent years, the critical theorist Nancy Fraser has made much the most influential contribution to answering both of these questions. This is not surprising, since Fraser has long been one of the most thought-provoking contributors to debates at the nexus of issues concerning feminism, socialism, the welfare state and the politics of 'identity'. In this chapter I raise a number of critical questions about her account, but also argue that Fraser's linking of the different claims of justice to what is in effect an egalitarian, dialogical model of citizenship is particularly suggestive.

Two paradigms of justice

Fraser's response to Habermas's insupportable opposition of economic and cultural spheres is complex. As she has explained it most recently (Fraser

2003a), her approach to critical theory pitches itself at three levels: that of moral philosophy, of social theorising, and of political praxis. Moreover, it attempts to show how the three levels can be navigated, producing a new synthesis of 'pragmatic' critical theorising. As such, her account is hugely ambitious, for not only does it provide us with the tools for engaging in social criticism, but it also tells us how that endeavour is to be conceived, and the broad standard it is to be judged against.

Central to Fraser's argument is the claim that whilst economy and culture are theoretically separable, they cannot, contra Habermas, be seen as *actually discrete* systems. Any such substantive dualism needs to be rejected (2003a: 61). However Fraser argues that in specific social relations, culture and economy may have relatively different levels of importance. What we see in modern complex societies is a 'partial uncoupling' of economy and culture, such that we can talk of differentiated 'arenas' or 'zones' of market and status (2003a: 53). This can only be seen as a statement about relative autonomy: any 'uncoupling' is only partial, and the two systems interlock considerably. Nevertheless this partial uncoupling means that the injustices suffered by diverse groups may be different in character, and fighting them will require careful and contextual political action. For this reason, we do not find, in Fraser, a hard and fast ontological distinction between two separate forms of injustice. What we do find is the claim that it can be profitable to separate the two forms of injustice *analytically*, so that we might better theorise the relative importance of each in particular struggles for justice; Fraser calls this approach 'perspectival dualism'. The approach seeks to avoid the mistakes of ontological dualism, whilst still providing us with the tools for contextual, case-based social criticism.

Analytically, then, Fraser (1998: 432–3; 2003a: 13) differentiates between 'socio-economic injustice' (which includes exploitation, economic marginalisation, and deprivation), and 'cultural or symbolic injustice' (which includes cultural domination, non-recognition and disrespect). Moving on to moral philosophy, Fraser argues that remedial strategies for the two forms of injustice can be collected under two separate flags: namely, a paradigm of 'redistribution' and a paradigm of 'recognition'. For their part, matters of redistribution are clearly answered by some kind of 'politico-economic restructuring', which is likely to involve an ethic of equality. There is an extensive and sophisticated literature on this, Fraser notes, as conducted by theorists such as Rawls and Dworkin (Fraser 1997a: 13, 2003a: 10). Failures of recognition, however, are best remedied by 'cultural or symbolic change', aimed at 'valorizing diversity' (1997a: 14). The politics of recognition seeks to break down hierarchies of status which aggregate around cultural membership, binary sexuality, or race/ethnicity, for example, either by revaluing devalued identities or by attacking the hierarchical construction of identity directly.

So how does all of this map onto concrete struggles? Rather than adopting a broad-brush approach to these issues, Fraser's most distinctive contribution rests with her assertion that different approaches will be suitable for different types of social group, given that they are frequently differently situated in terms of the two forms of injustice. For some groups, the remedy is presumably straightforward: for instance, the poor seek not recognition, but redistribution alone. As Fraser argued, 'The task of the proletariat ... is not simply to cut itself a better deal, but "to abolish itself as a class". The last thing it needs is recognition of its difference' (1998: 437, but see below). At the other end of the spectrum, Fraser argued that homosexuals are disadvantaged in the cultural or symbolic arena, and not in the arena of economic life, since 'homosexuals are distributed throughout the entire class structure of capitalist society, occupy no distinctive position in the division of labour, and do not constitute an exploited class' (1998: 437). In the first type of case, the appropriate remedy is apparently redistribution alone. In the second case, on the other hand, the remedy is not redistribution but recognition: specifically an end to the cultural or symbolic valuing of heterosexuality over homosexuality.

So we have two kinds of justice claim, for recognition and for redistribution. Fraser also layers a second distinction onto this one. She suggests that we can pursue either *affirmative* or *transformative* remedies for either kind of injustice, and that each may be appropriate for different cases. By affirmative remedies for injustice Fraser means 'remedies aimed at correcting inequitable outcomes of social arrangements without disturbing the underlying framework that generates them.' Transformative measures by comparison imply 'remedies aimed at correcting inequitable outcomes precisely by restructuring the underlying generative framework' (1998: 443). In terms of economic injustice, this largely maps onto Young's (1990) distinction between the transformation of institutional structure versus surface distribution. An affirmative approach might use welfare payments to ameliorate the worst effects of the economic cycles of capitalism, whilst ignoring or even supporting the inequalities in wealth that characterise such a system. A transformative approach, by contrast, would directly target such inequalities, calling for a revolt against the entrenched hierarchies of economic life. In terms of cultural injustice, we can point to the way in which 'Whereas affirmative recognition remedies tend to promote existing group differentiations, transformative recognition remedies tend, in the long run, to destabilize them so as to make room for future regroupments' (Fraser 1998: 444). Affirmative remedies for injustices of recognition seek to value the previously undervalued, be it femininity, blackness or disability. Transformative remedies would disrupt the very terms of femininity/masculinity, whiteness/blackness, ability/disability, to reveal their arbitrary and oppressive nature. Such opposed approaches are clearly displayed within feminism, for instance, with proposed solutions to sexism ranging from the celebration of essential sexual difference to universal androgyny or the multiplication of gender identities.

For Fraser, justice theorists have not been sufficiently clear about when and why the two different forms of remedy are appropriate, and what the relations are between them. For example, Fraser (1995) takes particular issue with Iris Young's approach to group difference (see Chapter 5), which she argues is insufficiently sensitive to the nature of the various forms of difference. Young (1990) famously suggested a politics of the affirmation of difference for all oppressed groups, but Fraser implies that whilst this is appropriate for groups in need of cultural or symbolic recognition, it is much less appropriate for groups like 'the poor', which are constituted only by their inferior position in respect to economic structures. Indeed, whilst Young does recommend the kind of economic restructuring that would tackle poverty directly, her simultaneous recommendation of group representation for the poor *could* be taken to imply the kind of assumption that Rawls has been roundly criticised for – namely, that classes in some form are likely to be a permanent feature of society.[1] In short, Fraser claims that Young pays too little attention to the ways in which the specific situations of different groups suggest different approaches to the affirmation or transformation of group difference.

If Fraser is recommending different political strategies for different groups, her position could be interpreted as deepening the bifurcation of political struggle, rather than effecting some kind of reconciliation. But for Fraser, this would be mistaken: rather, her point is that whilst both forms of struggle are important, we cannot simplistically assume a harmonious relation between them. The two could well pull in different directions, and the job of the political theorist is to suggest areas of potential common ground. As a result, Fraser argues that we need to carefully *seek out* the areas of complementarity, rather than simply assuming them. The task for theorists of justice is therefore 'Figuring out how to conceptualize cultural recognition and social equality [redistribution] in forms that support rather than undermine each other ... it also means theorizing the ways in which economic disadvantage and cultural disrespect are currently intertwined with and support one another' (Fraser 1998: 431).

The best lead for how we might do this arises when we consider groups which suffer injustice along both economic and cultural dimensions. The paradigmatic cases here are gender and race. These 'bivalent collectivities' may endure 'both socioeconomic maldistribution and cultural misrecognition in forms where neither of these injustices is an indirect effect of the other, but where both are primary and co-original. In that case, neither distributive remedies alone nor recognition remedies alone will suffice. Bivalent collectivities need both' (1998: 438). The oppression of women, for instance cannot – contra reductionist Marxists – be reduced to purely economic causes. But neither can it – contra some radical feminists – be simply reduced to cultural or symbolic origins. The category of gender is bivalent because it is always and everywhere a category of both economy and culture. So, too, is the category of 'race'. Indeed, we might well place disability in this 'bivalent' category too: though Fraser herself maintains a puzzling silence on the disabled, we could presumably make exactly the same points about the intermeshing of cultural and economic injustice with reference to disability or impairment.[2]

As Fraser argues, 'All this suggests a way of reformulating the redistribution/recognition dilemma. We might ask: for groups who are subject to injustices of both types, what combinations of remedies work best to minimize, if not altogether to eliminate, the mutual interferences?' (1998: 446). Some combinations are clearly unsuitable. For instance, the redistributive strategy of liberal welfarism often produces stigmatisation for those who are 'dependent' (see Fraser and Gordon 1994 for an earlier and very persuasive analysis of gender and dependency), and hence this strategy is incompatible with genuine recognition for single mothers, welfare families, racialised 'underclasses', and so on. But some combinations are more harmonious. In particular 'The long-term goal of deconstructive feminism is a culture in which hierarchical gender dichotomies are replaced by networks of multiple intersecting differences that are demassified and shifting. This goal is consistent with transformative socialist-feminist redistribution' (Fraser 1998: 449). Transformative economic policies will tend to disrupt the fixity of group memberships, and so by definition will a deconstructive cultural politics. Both are in a sense aiming at the same thing: a world where individuals can seek to autonomously define their own positions in social life, in the absence of structural injustices. This provides a promising route forwards for gender politics, and similar conclusions are suggested for injustices organised around 'race' (1998: 450). This represents Fraser's most celebrated contribution, at least in terms of political praxis. In both of these categories at least, we have a promising area of positive interference: cultural deconstruction appears compatible with economic transformation. Whilst she was reluctant to draw over-sweeping conclusions from this, she suggested that it might betoken a way of finessing the recognition/redistribution dichotomy more broadly. Thus Fraser – at least in her early work – suggested that as a general formula, we might embrace 'socialism in the economy plus deconstruction in the culture' (1998: 451).

Parity of participation

Fraser's initial contribution was warmly welcomed, for it seemed to promise a way of reuniting the disparate elements of radical theorising. One question remained outstanding, however: united in precisely *what*? It was not clear what really united the two struggles beyond the fact that they could be pursued simultaneously. Although compatibility may be a necessary condition for a critical coalition politics, it is clearly not a sufficient one. What were advocates of socialist transformation and cultural deconstruction really united in fighting *for*? Fraser was adamant that socialism, multiculturalism, political liberalism and communitarianism would not fill the vacuum (1997a: 2), but what could? To begin with, Fraser simply asserted that both struggles were required by 'justice', but what might this idea of justice look like? This apparent lack of a centre also became apparent in another way, which is that her account did not seem to offer a standard for *discriminating between* rival claims for either recognition or for redistribution – or, we might say, for deciding which claims were genuinely critical, and which were not. As Fraser puts it, 'Clearly, not every claim for recognition is warranted, just as not every claim for redistribution is. In both cases, one needs an account of criteria and/or procedures for distinguishing warranted from unwarranted claims' (2003a: 37).

Both of these issues suggested that if the dichotomy was to be bridged at all, it would have to be shown that the two forms of struggle in fact worked towards a single, and well-defined ideal. As her work on recognition and redistribution has progressed, Fraser has increasingly fleshed out this integrative, overarching ideal, which she calls 'parity of participation'. This notion refers to the ability of individuals to participate meaningfully in common institutions in the absence of structural disadvantages. This is clearly an interactive ideal: parity of participation 'requires social arrangements that permit all (adult) members of society to interact with one another as peers' (2001: 29). These social arrangements are both cultural and economic. Participatory parity requires adequate cultural recognition, but 'equal participation is also impeded when some actors lack the necessary resources to interact with others as peers' (2000: 116). Without these resources, a person cannot be 'a full member of society, capable of participating on a par with the rest' (2000: 113).

It seems then that justice claims are to be mediated by and decided with reference to an idea of effective, autonomy-promoting membership within a democratic community. This idea of fully autonomous interaction in social, political and economic life provides the grammar that must be used by legitimate justice claims, and defines their regulatory ideal. This conception certainly seems to offer a way to finally repair the bifurcation of political struggles in what Fraser calls a 'post-socialist' age. We will examine this idea further in the next section.

2   Equality and democratic citizenship

At this point it is useful to turn to a slightly contentious issue, which is how equality comes into the picture in Fraser's scheme, how and where the ideal of equality figures in the theory of justice as participatory parity. On this issue Fraser's position has shifted over time. In her original contribution, Fraser argued that egalitarianism provided the proper and logical language for debates about socio-economic injustices. But not for cultural injustices: these were ill-served by the language of equality, which was out of place in discussions of the hugely important issues of social or cultural recognition. This position has been moderated, though, and two shifts are particularly significant here (see also Armstrong 2003c).

Firstly, Fraser now makes much less of the contention that the language of equality can play no useful part in demands for recognition. In this respect, her work may have been influenced by her engagement with Axel Honneth's notion of recognition, which indicates that norms of equality are a key tool for those who would claim recognition. In Honneth's highly influential account, it seems that for both political and social forms of misrecognition, equality is, directly or indirectly, the appropriate remedy (Honneth 1992).[3] Either way, Fraser now uses the notion of *status equality* to describe a situation of mutual recognition, so that claims for recognition can now be understood as claims for a kind of equality. From the point of view of egalitarian theory, this is a significant shift. Indeed, it is possible to argue that any progressive rendering of recognition is *inevitably* egalitarian in nature. The idea of recognition surely depends upon an egalitarian specification to gain force: what, otherwise, do marginalised or oppressed groups demand recognition *as*? No doubt in the first instance many groups demand recognition of their existence, and their – sometimes radical – difference. But ultimately in political life the claim for recognition moves beyond this, and becomes a demand for the acceptance of the equal validity of one's 'identity', choices, experiences, and needs, and one's right to possess and express legitimate knowledge about these things. Without this egalitarian specification, the 'recognition of difference' can even be a mechanism of exclusion.[4]

The crucial move in this context is Fraser's gradual elaboration of what she now calls a 'status model' of recognition (Fraser 2003a). What should concern us, she asserts, is not misrecognition of our distinct identities per se: recognition does not seek to reinforce an 'authentic' understanding of 'essential' difference, after all. Rather, what we should be concerned about in terms of misrecognition is the extent to which negative cultural evaluations impede the ability of some to live as fully participating members of a democratic community. Fraser's status model of recognition has elicited much discussion, but her basic intuition appears sound. What matters is not misrecognition in some cognitive or objective sense, but the fact of hierarchy, and the ways in which this hierarchy impedes equal standing and interaction on a par with others in social life. As such, equality (in the sense of equal participation and even equal citizenship – see below) comes very much to the fore in the pursuit of recognition. It has to be said, though, that Fraser continues to use misleading language on this issue. In an earlier piece (1996: 223) she rightly argued that the claim that equality suppresses difference is only based on particular, and unduly narrow theories of equality. Nevertheless Fraser continues to counterpose 'social equality' and 'the recognition of difference' (2003a: 26–7), 'the politics of difference' and 'the politics of equality' (2003a: 8; 2004: 126), even where the more pertinent distinction now seems to be between 'social equality' and 'status equality' (2003a: 26, 29). This ambiguity aside, Fraser's relegation of equality to a sub-category of justice has been substantially undercut.

Secondly, and just as importantly, the notion of parity of participation is a clearly egalitarian ideal. To begin with, Fraser seemed reluctant to position equality as an overarching concept in her work, claiming instead that she was uniting the language of recognition and redistribution under 'an expanded understanding of justice' (2001: 23) that did not resort to explicitly egalitarian language.[5] Nevertheless, in response to questioning by Honneth (2003), Fraser asserts that her idea of parity of participation is, in fact, 'a radicalization of widely held norms of folk equality' (2003c: 210). The meaning of this declaration remains somewhat obscure, since these norms of folk equality are not elaborated. In fact, what Fraser seems to be doing is making an argument about the immanent logic of 'liberal equality' (2003c: 222), and attempting to radicalise that ideal. Her argument is one about 'the emergent historical "truth" of the liberal norm' of equality (2003c: 232), and its political potential. Specifically, it is based on 'the central moral idea of modern liberalism: the equal autonomy and moral worth of human beings' (2003c: 228). This idea of autonomy is a foundational value – as Fraser argues, 'The basic idea is that equal autonomy, properly understood, entails the real freedom to participate on a par with others in social life ... Thus, participatory parity simply *is* the meaning of equal respect for the equal autonomy of human beings qua social actors' (2003c: 231). However this principle gets worked out in practice, what is certain is that 'denial of access to parity's social prerequisites makes a mockery of a society's professed commitment to equal autonomy' (2003c: 229).

Citizenship, need interpretation and political struggle

It is interesting to note that whilst Fraser has elsewhere tried to rehabilitate the idea of citizenship (Fraser and Gordon 1992), she does not resort to the language of citizenship to frame her broader position here.[6] But her account seems to turn around something very much like it. On the best available definition, the notion of citizenship refers to two things. The first relates citizenship to that set of practices and institutions which define individuals as equal members of a polity, which apprehend a person as a competent member of society, 'and which as a consequence shape the flow of resources to persons and social groups' (Turner 1994: 2). And, secondly, citizenship is the result(s) of those practices. Namely, it is a status, or, more precisely, a complex and sometimes shifting set of statuses (see Lister 2001: 102), which determines both a set of rights and responsibilities, and the relation of individuals to governing powers and each other. The reason why equality and citizenship are so often co-implicated concepts (or so it was claimed in the Introduction to this book) is that, in the modern West, debates about the meaning of citizenship as a status of equal membership have been a key place where demands for equality have been collected and inter-related. It appears that in Fraser's work this link is bubbling below the surface. Parity of participation asserts the moral equality and autonomy of all members of a democratic community, and sets about the task of interpreting the prerequisites for that common status to become meaningful.

In some ways Fraser's work on parity of participation has echoes with the Rawlsian position outlined in the first chapter, albeit with some crucial differences.[7] One obvious similarity is that the notion of parity of participation – which I have likened to the ideal of equal citizenship – is supposed to function as a thin but nonetheless overarching justificatory resource which will reflect and give force and shape to the actual normative language commonly used by citizens. Indeed the echoes with Rawls are occasionally quite strong on this point: as Fraser puts it, participatory parity 'represents the *principal idiom of public reason*, the preferred language for conducting democratic political argumentation' (Fraser 2003a: 43, italics in original; 2004: 132). But a key difference is that whereas Rawls (at least on first view) interprets this as a more or less static idea that can simply be worked up philosophically, Fraser's account is more dynamic, in the sense that every consensus, as Fraser asserts, is fallible, 'each provisional determination open to later challenges' (2003a: 44). Although parity of participation or equal citizenship will continually function as the reference point of political struggle, it is an ideal that is flexible and open-ended, not one that points towards a predetermined destination. In Fraser's account this is also a less metaphysically ambitious ideal than in Rawls, and as such is largely 'negative', in the sense that this process of endless revision and contestation of the terms of citizenship works 'upwards' from specific, situated claims about *injustice*, rather than 'downwards' from an overarching (e.g. Kantian) ideal of autonomous individuality (see Zurn 2003b).

We might draw an interesting parallel here between Fraser's current position on parity of participation, and her earlier work on 'the politics of need interpretation', although she does not make this link herself. In her work on the concept of need, Fraser (1989: 156, italics in original) called for the replacement of '*monological, administrative processes of need definition* [by] *dialogical, participatory processes of need interpretation*'. Whereas in welfare politics for example the needs of individuals have tended to be defined 'from above' in a (pseudo)objective manner, our needs are at least partly socially constructed, since they involve substantive questions about personhood and about how we are to live together in the absence of oppression. The job of political theorists is to make this explicit, and encourage open-ended discussion of these socially interpreted needs. This idea of the dialogical politics of need interpretation seems to me to be a good contender for a motto for egalitarian, democratic citizenship. Once we acknowledge needs to be at least partly non-objective in the sense that they inevitably relate to how we want to live together and the kind of world we want to inhabit, the idea of citizenship comes to represent one of the most promising locations for such need interpretation. At a somewhat higher level of generality, this is exactly what her account of parity of participation appears to be doing: it advocates a continual and dialogical discussion of the pre-requisites of effective and meaningful membership, always open to reinterpretation, but still grounded in an ideal of equal and autonomous interaction.

As such, Fraser's approach has some parallels within recent political theory, and particularly with the project of radical democracy pursued by Butler, Laclau and Mouffe, amongst others (see e.g. Butler *et al.* 2000). Though there are important differences between the two positions, Fraser's work here at least runs close to Chantal Mouffe's claim that the diverse struggles for egalitarian and democratic change expressed by a myriad of antagonistic political groups can only be articulated through the language of citizenship. In this context citizenship represents not just a status, but a positive commitment to principles of freedom and equality for all (Mouffe 1993). Although the claims for justice of cultural, ethnic or sexual minorities, for example, may appear to be self-serving, each potentially pushes us in the direction of universalism and equality for all, by challenging the way in which equality is presently defined in such a way as to serve the interests of dominant groups. As Smith (1998: 135) puts it, citizenship becomes the 'articulating principle' by which our diverse commitments and radical impulses are mediated, the 'nodal point' for a future counter-hegemonic bloc which might deliver on the promise of freedom and equality for all citizens. Whilst oppositional groups will disagree about their claims and their grievances, these disagreements should pass through a normative filter guaranteeing a commitment to democracy, equality and human rights for all. And this normative filter is citizenship. What the principled commitment to equal citizenship represents is an aspiration towards 'a non-teleological universalism, which is to say a universalism that leaves open the possibility of new articulations within the given, new identities and thus the need for new reformulations of those very values. As such it is a non-essentialist and non-"totalitarian" universalism leaving spaces open to reformulation, negotiation and contestation' (Tormey 2001: 6–7). Equal citizenship is the ground on which these reiterated and expanding universalisms are built, but it shapes and informs that building rather than determining its details.

To return to Fraser, I think this is what we are witnessing in her recent work, albeit below the surface. Fraser foregrounds the idea that all parties to social interaction must be able to interact as peers, and that the genuine fulfilment of this liberal ideal has economic and cultural prerequisites. Some form of continuous, democratic process of need interpretation is the best way to fulfil this interactive norm, for Fraser. Her notion of parity of participation is a promising development, and this chapter has interpreted this ideal as a version of equal citizenship, which might form the idiom of an open and dialogical politics of (citizenly) need interpretation. As argued in the Introduction to this book, equal citizenship has long provided a critical resource for collecting, organising and framing a variety of egalitarian commitments, and it may continue to do so in an age of global diversity (see Chapter 7). What is much less secure, though, is the claim that the twin principles of recognition and redistribution – each operating within its own distinctive arena – provide the best way to defend such an ideal. This suspicion in turn raises questions about the social-theoretic assumptions on which Fraser's position rests, and which will be examined further in the next section.

3   Equalities: economy, culture and anti-dualism

Although Fraser's ideal of parity of participation has much to say for it, we will turn now to some questions arising from Fraser's *social* theory of contemporary society. Fraser's political project is informed by, and provoked by, an important social-theoretic concern. Does the increasing opposition between advocates of cultural and economic change reflect a genuine opposition between economics and culture, so that we really do need to make either/or choices? Or is there no such opposition, implying that an integrated cultural-economic politics can proceed instead? Here, Fraser has tried to navigate between two poles – the substantive dualism of Habermas on the one hand, and the unified systems approaches of Honneth or economic reductionists on the other. Although Fraser's answer to this question has been highly influential, it will be demonstrated that her answer is more unstable than at first appears to be the case, and that in her more recent work she concedes enough ground to the anti-dualist position to call her own resolution into serious question. This, in itself, has implications for critical politics, which are addressed in Section 4.

Perspectival dualism in question

So Fraser's intervention into debates on justice is motivated by an attempt to heal the rift between radical cultural and politico-economic struggles, but in doing so to avoid both the monism of Honneth, and the substantive dualism of Habermas. Fraser's solution to this dilemma lies in her 'perspectival dualism', which is supposed to provide a useful way of thinking about the issues involved, without assuming an untenable 'ontological' or 'substantive' separability between two 'spheres' of social life. Nevertheless, it is clear that her own account is based on some notion of the autonomy of the systems in question: there has to be some ontological basis to the analytic distinction, we might say, otherwise the analytical distinction is not helpful in practice. But Fraser is ambiguous about the empirical nature of the distinction between the economic and the symbolic or cultural. She is clear that we must reject the idea of two separate

[*151*]

'spheres', but instead talks of 'zones' and 'arenas', two spatial metaphors which remain underspecified. Furthermore her project seems to hinge on the notion of a 'partial uncoupling' of economy and culture that looks, sounds and acts like an ontological distinction.

On Fraser's view, there is substantial overlap between economy and culture – and gender and race clearly fall into that overlap. But there is a partial uncoupling between economy and culture, and as a result there are areas that remain substantially monological. One fringe area, we might imagine, corresponds to symbolic discourse on sexuality, which is *relatively* unconnected to economic rationalities. A second fringe area pertains to economic processes with little or no cultural or symbolic significance – to the brute realities of economic competition or class politics, perhaps. But the putative existence of either of these 'monological' areas is less clear than this implies. It is notable that in her more recent work Fraser acknowledges that 'virtually all real-world axes of subordination can be treated as two-dimensional', and that overcoming injustice 'in virtually every case' requires both recognition and redistribution (Fraser 2003a: 28). It is questionable what the 'virtually' is doing in either case, though. For one thing it threatens to downplay the intersecting nature of injustices, albeit only for analytical purposes. But one of the lessons of black or lesbian feminisms, for instance, has been that injustices are never experienced in isolation from each other (that is, no one ever experiences sexism *as a woman*, but always as a gay white poor woman or a straight black wealthy woman). Thus a heterosexism divorced from economic over-determination, which Fraser seems to suggest, is not a heterosexism that is easy to recognise. More broadly, it was surely *always* remiss to downplay the economic role in the construction of identities around binary conceptions of sexuality (see e.g. Evans 1993). Judith Butler (1998) has argued forcefully that if we expand a Marxist frame to include issues of reproduction as well as production, then we can see that sexuality is, amongst other things, a category of political economy. Fraser seems to take this on board to the extent of acknowledging that sexuality is a category of economic life, but still claims that the 'ultimate cause' of heterosexism is the status order (Fraser 2003a: 24). But if we are not to fall into an ill-advised substantive dualism, what are we to make of this depiction of 'ultimate causes'? By the same token, it was surely always implausible to identify class as an economic and not a simultaneously cultural category, as Honneth (2003) shows. More recently, Fraser accordingly declares that she now sees class as a two-dimensional (i.e. economic and cultural) category (Fraser 2003a: 23).

The concessions above are welcome and necessary, but leave us in a strange predicament. This is because despite her erstwhile claims, Fraser now provides no real-world instances of one-dimensional injustices at all. The intriguing issue here is that the perspectival approach now begins to look rootless: is this a rather elegant theory desperately in search of a reality to describe? Iris Young summarises the central paradox this produces pithily: 'Fraser denies that this dichotomy describes reality. What, then, justifies its use in theory?' (Young 1997a: 150). Indeed Young's question has even more bite now than it did at the time, for in Fraser's current position the 'partial uncoupling' of economy and culture seems to recede to vanishing point, as all the group-based forms of injustice Fraser discusses can be seen to be simultaneously cultural and economic. For this reason it is worth questioning whether Fraser's model marks out its superiority to anti-dualist positions which see economy and culture as *inextricably* and *necessarily* co-implicated. Certainly Fraser's rejection of what she calls the 'postmodern anti-dualism' of Butler is not wholly persuasive (Fraser 2003a: 60–1). By the same token, during the original Dual Systems debate within socialist feminism Iris Young (1981b) argued with some force for a single-systems theory acknowledging the inherently social nature (and specifically gendering) of capitalism, and the inherent materiality of women's oppression.[8] Interestingly Young's early assault on Dual Systems theory represent a dry-run for criticisms that she later levels at Fraser. From a feminist perspective the biggest problem is that this kind of Dual Systems theory, in portraying capitalism as a system at least theoretically separable from sexism, threatens to accept the idea of economics as gender blind and strategic. But there are good reasons to doubt this. For one thing, as Majid Yar (2001: 292) observes 'The organization of economic life is "always already" bound up with moral claims about rights and entitlements that cannot be analytically distinguished from claims for recognition', and the business of economic life is surely always 'infested' with cultural presuppositions, prejudices and desires (a good lead here is provided by Bob Jessop's analysis of what he calls 'cultural political economy').[9] Even as an ideal type, the depiction of economics as rational, calculative, strategic and in short as a form of action divorced from the complexities of desire, emotion, identity or subjectivity is a constitutive myth of modern society. It is a myth which Fraser sometimes seems to accept, but it is a myth nonetheless.

This forces us to confront a very serious question. Whilst the original point of Fraser's intervention was to address the disarticulation of economic and symbolic or cultural struggles, her more recent position throws serious doubt on whether that disarticulation truly existed other than at the level of political rhetoric. As such, the provocative – but perhaps fruitful – question to ask is whether the problem she set out to resolve was ever a concrete as opposed to 'merely conceptual' one. Is the economy/culture division, to use an old-fashioned term, 'ideological'? There is much to be said for the position of Lisa Duggan, who argues that although liberal ideologies do organise social life in terms of such oppositions, 'the categories through which liberalism ... classifies human activity and relationships actively obscure the connections among these organizing terms' (Duggan 2003: 3). Duggan herself points to the ways in which political reality in liberal states places advocates of cultural politics in a double bind. The modern capitalist state simultaneously operates through 'cultural' categories such as gender and race (see e.g. Stevens 1999) itself, and yet locates culture as essentially private and non-political, thereby serving to keep 'cultural' issues off the political agenda. This double movement is reproduced by contemporary liberal theorists such as Brian Barry (2001), whose opposition to cultural politics recycles one of the cardinal myths of liberal ideology – that we can separate culture from state or economy, that these categories are not inextricably linked already.[10] Radical critics have to some extent bought into this dichotomy too. But one of the points of Judith Butler's intervention is that we must not accept this ruse in the first place (Butler 1998). The process by which 'identity and cultural politics [are] presented as the irresponsible, trivial, divisive "other" of serious left analysis and organizing' (Duggan 2003: 71; cf. Žižek 1997) should be resisted. Although culture and economics may be 'rhetorically disarticulated', they are never genuinely separated. Metaphors are powerful, and pervade all political theories. But in this context, it might be suggested that the different processes Fraser discusses are so bound up in each other that any search for origins is irrelevant, and that the drive to categorise zones or to discern origins is in fact a drive to *create* such distinctions.

We should insist, therefore, that although such concepts may represent a useful shorthand, 'economics' is always already cultural, and vice versa. Many of Fraser's quite illuminating suggestions for how we might heal the rifts of radical politics paradoxically establish precisely this. In terms of her most recent work, her resort to the notion of 'cross-redressing' is particularly instructive here. Cross-redressing, for Fraser, 'means using measures associated with one dimension of justice to remedy inequities associated with the other – hence, using distributive measures to redress misrecognition and recognition measures to redress maldistribution' (Fraser 2003a: 83). To give an example, we might try to improve the material condition of a subgroup of women, hence improving their 'exit options' from marriage and *thereby* reducing their vulnerability to domestic violence (2003a: 83–4). In this case redistribution indirectly serves the goal of recognition. To give another example, legalising gay marriage (which Fraser seems to consider a 'cultural' move) would improve the economic position of homosexuals, by safeguarding their entitlements to welfare and inheritance, whilst preventing workplace discrimination against homosexuals (again, apparently cultural) will improve their economic position (2003a: 84). In this latter case, a strategy of recognition achieves an advance in terms of redistribution. I would endorse these proposals. Fraser's suggestions here are laudable, and represent significant contributions to the relevant debates on political praxis. But what the examples above imply is precisely that marriage is an irreducibly economic institution, and that the modern workplace is profoundly gendered, rather than that these systems happen to coalesce at given points in time. Postmodern anti-dualism may well have the last laugh.

4 Conflicting categories and overarching principles

The recognition/redistribution framework has been enormously influential within a variety of academic disciplines, but its political utility remains open to question. Are the twin goals of recognition and redistribution as useful as they might seem? To take redistribution first, it is far from certain – as Young (1990) has long maintained – that the language of distribution serves to direct our attention towards the more profound injustices that characterise contemporary societies. Indeed Young's words of caution seem especially applicable to the even narrower language of *re*distribution. Although redistribution looks like a very good word for 'affirmative' economic policies such as liberal welfarism, it may be much less salient as a descriptor for more radical and fundamental struggles to redetermine the categories and relations of economic life. If we really do want to challenge hierarchies in the division of labour and conventional definitions of roles and abilities, for instance (see Chapter 5), then it may be that redistribution simply fails to provide a very good descriptive or organising term for that kind of struggle, or that it is just too amorphous to capture such an objective (see Phillips 2003: 270). The language of recognition, too, is ill-placed to capture the complexity of the struggles Fraser analyses. As with redistribution, the language of recognition seems well suited to describing and organising affirmative cultural practices, but less useful as a category of deconstruction (which, after all, seeks precisely the opposite of the 'recognition of difference').[11] To be sure, Fraser (2003a) is at pains to reject the idea that recognition aims at the acknowledgement of some authentic and pre-existing identity, which the state or other political actors have a duty to endorse. Recognition, instead, means the rectification of status subordination, rather than a failure to uphold some duty to cherish diverse identities. But if this is so, 'recognition' comes to look less and less useful in descriptive terms, in capturing the multifaceted tasks of a critical cultural politics. For recognition seems to conjure up precisely this kind of public endorsement of identity (as Phillips 2003: 271 puts it, 'describing mobilizations as struggles for recognition can encourage precisely that validation of identities Fraser warns against').[12]

None of the above is to be taken to imply criticism of Fraser's own substantive positions, but it is to express serious doubt about whether the normative concepts of recognition and redistribution are reliable and useful vehicles for the full range of egalitarian commitments. A related issue concerns the expansiveness of the two ideas. Perhaps because of their remarkable success, the notions of recognition and redistribution seem capable of describing a huge variety of struggles. These struggles pursue all kinds of goals, not all of which may have been envisaged originally by Fraser. This is both a symbol of success and a potential problem, for it may be that the taxonomy of recognition/redistribution has actually been *too* compelling. This raises the question of 'whether the recognition/redistribution dichotomy has outlived its usefulness, either as an analytic distinction or heuristic device' (Phillips 2003: 268). Such problems could perhaps be avoided if Fraser set out in clear terms exactly what recognition and redistribution imply for political practice. Unfortunately, any such precise specification of recognition and redistribution has been attenuated in her recent work. What was particularly attractive about Fraser's earlier position on recognition and redistribution, for many, was precisely the political pay-off: her advocacy of a specific route out of the apparent bifurcation of cultural and economic struggles. To begin with, Fraser expressed a strong preference for deconstructive (i.e. transformative) approaches to cultural difference, and socialist (transformative) approaches to economic issues. This was her celebrated solution, that is, of deconstruction in the culture, and transformation in the economy. But more recently Fraser has distanced herself from this solution in several ways. On the one hand Fraser's position on economic change is now surprisingly unclear (Fraser 2003a: 69), but apparently less opposed to affirmative strategies. Whilst she had originally opted squarely for socialist transformation, Fraser now simply declares it to be an 'open question how much economic inequality is consistent with parity of participation' (2003a: 101). Beyond a gesture towards the work of Rawls and Dworkin, Fraser's position on economic justice remains open. More recently however Fraser has gestured towards the idea of a Basic Income as a tool for embedding an affirmative approach to economic justice that might over time facilitate a more radical transformation (2004: 137–8). This is an idea that might put more flesh on the bones of the idea of 'non-reformist reform' (2003a: 80). Although this is a promising development, its avowedly gradualist nature does mean that the distinction between affirmation and transformation looks less and less germane to her project.

Fraser's position on recognition has also changed. Initially, her opposition to affirmative strategies of recognition was so strong that she was able to make use of a metaphor that advocates of affirmative cultural politics would surely find highly patronising: she argued that for her preferred strategy to work, people would have to 'be weaned [*sic*] from their attachment to current cultural constructions of their interests and identities' (1997a: 31). This position has now been moderated to the extent that it is not at all clear that Fraser prefers any such sweeping strategy. For instance, whilst Fraser had initially seemed hostile to affirmative approaches to cultural 'identities' (such as maternalist accounts of gender), that hostility is definitely softening (Fraser 2003a: 81; see also Feldman 2002: 414). This may be partly because she now sees the affirmation of identities as a crucial part of struggle within economic life too: she thus asserts that participants in economic struggle (such as welfare recipients) may need symbolic affirmation in all sorts of ways. Fraser also makes a similar judgement in terms of multicultural politics, arguing that cultural minorities might benefit from affirmative strategies, at least as a short-term measure (Fraser 2004: 139). Here, too, the emphasis on non-reformist reform illustrates how the complexity of Fraser's current position renders her earlier distinction between affirmation and transformation increasingly marginal. In terms of recognition, her preference is no longer for affirmation or deconstruction, but a strategy which seeks to minimise the subordination experienced by some groups whilst leaving it 'to future generations to decide whether a given distinction is worth preserving' (2004: 139).

In a way, all of the above points to an interesting shift in Fraser's project. Her theoretical analysis of the impasse that she originally described – between the politics of recognition and the politics of redistribution – has been hugely successful. Her typology of justice claims and her more recent writings on parity of participation are having an increasing impact on critical work throughout the social sciences, and Fraser appears to be devoting more time to this project of providing a framework for critical theory. At the same time, however, her original intervention was interesting not for its theoretical elegance, but precisely because it promised a political route out of the impasse which she herself diagnosed. It suggested, that is, a way of finessing the dilemmas of radical praxis in an age of pluralism and diversity. But at the same time as her attempts to define the ground of critical theorising continue to gain adherents, the political distinctiveness and utility of Fraser's position has been weakened, as she has been increasingly circumspect about her original solution: that of socialism in the economy and deconstruction in the culture. Fraser now seems to advocate both affirmation *and* deconstruction in the culture, and some form of transformation *through* reformism in the economy, with only 'pragmatism' supplying the answers.

Alternatives

It must be reiterated that the concern of this section is not with Fraser's substantive positions, which are considered and thought-provoking. Instead, what all of the above suggests is that the categories of recognition and redistribution, affirmation and transformation, are less and less capable of capturing the complex political projects Fraser wants to advance. The thrust of her current work denotes an attempt to span these categories in pursuit of a politics which will genuinely marry cultural and economic concerns. It is worth asking, then, whether the two paradigms of justice genuinely serve the purpose Fraser intended. Although the ideal of parity of participation provides an overarching metric for justice, the twin goals of recognition and redistribution remain separate, each operating within its own arena, and according to its own logic. It is far from obvious, however, that groups really do express demands in terms of recognition or redistribution alone. On this theme Barbara Hobson (2003: 14), summarising the arguments of the various authors whose work is collected in

Hobson (ed 2003), all of them dedicated to Fraser's framework, observes that 'we could not find any pure ideal types of either structure of claims-making'. For instance neither the objectives of lesbian and gay movements nor workers' movements, Hobson notes, can be defined entirely in terms of either recognition or redistribution. Above it was indicated that Fraser's own position now confirms this.

So where does this leave us? The suspicion is that the project is incomplete unless we transcend these distinct categories too. Earlier, I indicated broad sympathy with the anti-dualist positions of Butler (1998) and Young (1997a), and claimed that 'cultural' processes and 'economic' processes are never truly separate, although they are often rhetorically opposed. If this is the case, the pertinent question shifts slightly. It is not 'how can we do cultural politics and economic politics simultaneously?', for each form of politics also entails the other. Economic policies have cultural effects, and cultural politics either challenges or endorses existing economic hierarchies. As Isin and Wood (1999: 154, italics in original) argue, the question that faces us is not *whether* to engage in cultural recognition, economic struggle, democratic activity, 'but *how* to do all and at the same time'. Whether we like it or not, 'this "strange multiplicity" is upon us, in all its forms at once'. The pertinent question becomes how we do these various forms of politics *radically.* And answering this question seems to push us in the direction of categories and principles that cut across such putative distinctions.

Analytical tools

Fraser is absolutely right that the real issue at stake 'is not the number of categories but their epistemic status and explanatory power' (Fraser 1997b: 128). But on this issue, there are good reasons for favouring approaches that cut across the putative culture/economy divide. The aim is not to provide an alternative account here, but rather to suggest with Davina Cooper that the language of social dynamics and organising principles may be more useful. Organising principles refer to social categories that name, but also help to enact, the major forms of inequality, and would include 'gender, class, sexuality, age, bodily capacity and race' (Cooper 2004: 51). Social dynamics, by contrast, refer to social processes that 'reach across and combine social life in ways that provide the motor for both social stability and change' (2004: 54). For Cooper (2004: 55), situating the analysis of inequality in relation to social dynamics such as production and reproduction, community boundary formation, desire and the intimate/impersonal can allow us to get a grip on such processes at the same time as 'avoid[ing] the dualism that Nancy Fraser has been criticised for constructing between economic and cultural processes, since social dynamics combine and cut across these divisions'.

The crucial point is that major organising principles such as class, race, sex and sexuality articulate simultaneously with all of the major social dynamics such as production, desire, and community boundary formation, albeit in different ways. None of them operates within its own sphere or arena; instead all cut across the various social dynamics. Whilst Fraser's original model has class operating along the dimension of economic life and status operating along a cultural/symbolic dimension, this makes for a more complex but ultimately more illuminating model. In a way, this brings us quite close to Young's position on the basic structure, which was examined in the preceding chapter. There, Young suggests a focus on social structures that involve the division of labour and production, desire and sexuality, hierarchies of authority and subordination, and the valuing or disvaluing of relationally defined 'identities' (Young 2001; cf. Cooper 2004: 54). It also draws us parallel with R.W. Connell's powerful analysis of gender in terms of production, power, emotion and discourse (see Connell 2002), and opens up possibilities for analysing other organising principles in similar ways. Conceived in such a way equality seeks to tackle 'organising principles' such as race, gender, class and sexuality: as Cooper puts it 'The pursuit of equality ... requires challenging – even eliminating as socially significant – such organising principles' (Cooper 2000: 271). The task of egalitarian theorists becomes that of unearthing the ways in which the major organising principles interact with the various social dynamics, and to work to undermine the ways in which they constrict the ability of individuals to interact as peers in social life.

Political principles

By the same token there are good reasons to favour broad normative principles that cut across putative divisions between culture and economy. The last chapter endorsed two related claims, which were extrapolated from the work of Phillips and Young. One was the critical group-oriented principle of equality. The other was the attack on hierarchies within the division of labour, and in economic structures and categories themselves. Neither is an economic or cultural strategy; instead each one is both 'cultural' and 'economic'. This suggests that 'one-dimensional' principles such as recognition and redistribution are of limited utility. But, if so, what general principles might serve the purpose better? There are plenty of good candidates, including oppression, dominance/domination, subjection/subjugation, hierarchy and exclusion. Again, rather than setting out an authoritative account I want to be open-minded about which of these might be useful. Any of these can succeed – and has succeeded – in organising resistance to various forms of injustice. But in the argument thus far my preference has been for two categories – oppression and hierarchy – to be applied contextually across the various social dynamics. In terms of oppression, Young's (1990) conception represents a very good start. Young's definition describes oppression in terms of exploitation, marginalisation, powerlessness, systematic violence and cultural imperialism, all of which are more likely to be experienced by people defined as members of some groups rather than others, and all of which are in that sense structural features of contemporary societies. The virtue of Young's account of oppression is that it consciously spans the putative boundaries of arenas or spheres.

The second idea suggests that equal citizenship is opposed to hierarchy – not that it aims to obliterate hierarchy or social structure, but that it involves a continual suspicion of institutional hierarchies, and a commitment to mitigating their inegalitarian effects. There are many ways in which this idea might be applied. One concerns the fact of political marginalisation, and the ways in which decision-making may be monopolised by some groups rather than others. Another concerns the division of labour, which has been discussed briefly in some of the previous chapters (and what is especially significant here, as Young 1997a has argued, is that the notion of the division of labour spans the economic and cultural, or recognition and redistribution). Another is identity: for what it's worth, Fraser's more recent position on hierarchies of 'identity' is generally convincing. Whilst Fraser had strongly criticised the apparently sweepingly affirmative strategy of Young's as unpersuasive, an unremittingly deconstructive approach to difference threatens to operate above the level of human suffering. As Fraser suggests, we might need instead to pursue both strategies simultaneously; with the overarching goal of mitigating the impact that the hierarchical construction of difference has on the lives of individuals. This requires effort, as Judith Butler (1995: 141) puts it, 'to expose and ameliorate those cruelties by which subjects are produced and differentiated'.

But at the broadest level, the resistance to hierarchy implies a resistance to the way in which membership or citizenship is based around the exclusion or marginalisation of others, whose energies are required to sustain the way of life of citizens but who are excluded from the possibility of becoming citizens themselves. In the context of citizenship the opposition to hierarchy implies a commitment to resisting the dependence of one person's full membership on someone else's exclusion or otherness. Walzer (1983: 277) suggests that 'Democratic citizenship is a status radically disconnected from every kind of hierarchy.' If this is so, it surely implies a critical interrogation of the ways in which rich and powerful communities' 'ways of life', and citizenship regimes, are dependent on their privileged place in the global system (an issue discussed further in the next chapter).

To sum up, the argument of this chapter has welcomed Fraser's suggestion of the ideal of parity of participation as a mobilising category for egalitarian politics. It has also endorsed many of Fraser's political suggestions. Compared to many of the approaches that characterise the egalitarian literature – such as Rawls's or Dworkin's – the framework of Fraser's model of egalitarian citizenship represents a significant advance. It takes seriously the claims of oppositional movements, rather than suppressing their concerns by insisting on a model of equal treatment that seems ill-placed to grasp the complex nature of contemporary injustices. It takes seriously, that is, the claim that 'differences differ' (Longo 2001: 282). The present argument has also welcomed Fraser's attempt to heal the apparent division of radical theorising into a camp concerned with economic change and a camp concerned with 'identity'. Such a division is politically debilitating, and moreover masks the systematic blurring of 'economic' and 'cultural' life. It is therefore to Fraser's credit that she has contributed so significantly to this goal, and also thereby to theorising the prerequisites for meaningful membership (or citizenship) in a democratic community. But whilst it has been argued that the ideal of parity of participation is a promising one, I have expressed reservations about the twin means Fraser suggests such parity will be served by: recognition and redistribution. If this argument is right, Fraser's advocacy of these two principles prevents her from finally closing the gap of radical politics, whereas categories such as oppression and hierarchy might be more promising.

Notes

1 On this point it would, however, be unfair to Young to identify her approach to the identity of 'the poor' as merely affirmative – as Fraser seems to do. To be sure Young's arguments that the poor need special representation might seem to suggest that the poor will indeed 'always be with us'. But her advocacy of industrial democracy, which was discussed briefly in the last chapter, seeks to break down the distinctions between white collar and blue collar, manual and mental work (and workers), and in that sense is a transformative and not merely affirmative approach.

2 Hugemark and Roman (2002) argue that Fraser's account is helpful in theorising the injustices faced by disabled people. Smith and O'Neill (1997: 124) also argue that any adequate approach to equality and disability needs to supplement a concern with the distribution of resources with a concern for 'individual autonomy and equal citizenship', an approach that seems close to Fraser's own position. Danermark and Gellerstedt (2004) note Fraser's neglect of disability but argue that, although her framework is useful, it is marred by an inability to theorise the 'personal', face-to-face or small-scale interactional nature of the injustices disabled people face.

3 I say 'directly or indirectly' because strictly speaking, Honneth recommends equality only as the remedy for 'social' misrecognition. For 'political' matters, his recommended remedy is universal rights, supported by the principle of the equal right of all citizens to participate as full members of the community. Although this disrupts Honneth's neatly triadic typology, the remedy for political misrecognition could therefore also be described as an equality claim. Only in the arena of 'personal' or bodily needs is equality out of place, because, rightly or wrongly, Honneth seems to identify equality as an essentially political (as opposed to private) concept (but see Baker *et al.* 2004 for an innovative account of the egalitarian politics of love and care). In any case equality serves at least two of the three desirable forms of recognition.

4 Chetan Bhatt argues that in practice the acknowledgement of difference can be right-wing and exclusive as well as left-wing and inclusive in intent (Bhatt 1994: 140).

Judith Squires similarly asserts that 'It is no use simply celebrating unassimilated otherness as though all differences are chosen with pride, are democratic in impulse, and glorious in manifestation. What might plausibly make a pluralism radical is an awareness of the existence of structural oppressions and the need to act positively to overcome them' (Squires 1994: 98). For Chantal Mouffe, even more strongly, 'There cannot be a pluralism which accepts *all* differences. We must be able to determine which differences should exist within a liberal democratic regime, because those differences are necessary for the realization of principles of liberty and equality' (Mouffe 1996: 136, italics in original).

5 This ambiguity is preserved in the idea of 'parity' (rather than equality) of participation. Clearly the idea of parity – our status as peers – captures something important, but Fraser sometimes (instructively) slips into discussing 'equal participation' instead (see e.g. Fraser 2000: 116).

6 Fraser's explicit concerns about the language of citizenship relate to its association with the statist Westphalian system, with all of its accompanying exclusions (2003a: 91). Nevertheless, her concerns about the exclusions of the Westphalian system closely parallel those of many contemporary citizenship theorists, who are examining the possibilities of post-Westphalian citizenship practices. These issues are discussed further in the final chapter.

7 It also, on one interpretation, has commonalities with the basic thrust behind Michael Walzer's account of complex equality (Walzer 1983). Of course there are significant differences which will not be explored here, but Robert Van der Veen's (1999) interpretation of complex equality as an account of equal citizenship is generally convincing. On this interpretation the principle of equal membership, or citizenship, provides the grammar for democratic debate around the socially interpreted needs of all individuals. Thus 'on Walzer's account, "membership" is the only natural locus for reflecting on the overall justice of institutions ... Its core principle defines the status of individuals as political equals, and defines the political community as a collectively self-governing community of citizens ... It is as politically equal citizens that [we] are best placed to articulate the social criticism of dominance and inequality' (Van der Veen 1999: 247–8).

8 Young (1981b: 47) claimed that 'it does not seem possible to separate patriarchy from a system of social relations of production even for analytical purposes'. Anticipating her arguments in *Justice and the Politics of Difference*, Young argued instead for the centrality of the concept of the division of labour in theorising the gendered nature of capitalism, and the material nature of sexism. As Young (1997a) rightly notes, it is not clear whether the division of labour (or decision-making power for that matter) can be adequately theorised as issues of either recognition or redistribution. In terms of the division of labour, it should be clear from feminist struggle, as Young asserts, that 'Changes in the division of labour ... do not amount merely to "redistributing" tasks ... but often in redefining the cultural meanings and value of different kinds of work' (1997a: 154).

9 The notion of an economic imaginary could be particularly interesting here. For Jessop, institutions such as political parties, think tanks, bodies such as the OECD and World Bank, business associations and trade unions, social movements, the mass media and so on are perpetually engaged in the construction of rival 'economic imaginaries'. These imaginaries concern 'the boundaries, geometries, temporalities, typical economic agents, tendencies and countertendencies, distinctive overall dynamic, and reproduction requirements of different imagined economies', and importantly 'successful economic imaginaries do have their own, performative, constitutive force

in the material world' (Jessop 2004: 5). Following Gramsci, Jessop argues that new economic regimes do not emerge for purely technological reasons, but are often at least in part the product of political moral or intellectual leadership. Jessop persuasively discusses the new (post-Fordist) economic imaginary of the Knowledge Based Economy as an example.

10 Seyla Benhabib argues instead that 'Culture is political; Barry wants to assume that there is a "baseline" of a non-political culture in a liberal society, whereas feminist critical theorists claim that much of the work of democracy proceeds through the political give-and-take within an already politically suffused culture' (Benhabib 2002: 120, italics in original). Benhabib is right about this, but the other half of the argument, I think, is that politics *is* cultural, and that political forms such as the state, nation and citizen are, to reverse Benhabib's argument, 'already culturally suffused'. As Aleksandra Ålund (1999: 149) puts it, 'social struggle is conducted through culture'.

11 On this issue, Simon Thompson (2006) has argued that 'deconstruction' cannot, on any meaningful interpretation, be seen as a variety of recognition. If this is so (and I believe Thompson is correct in this), the implication is that Fraser's goal of parity of participation cannot be served by recognition or redistribution alone, and that these two categories do not exhaust the claims of justice.

12 Indeed is there something in the language of recognition that threatens to deflect our attention from the role of political actors such as the state in *constituting* the identity of groups or individuals? This suspicion is registered by Patchen Markell: 'If identities are not pre-politically given but constituted in and through politics, then an act of recognition, by endorsing the terms of a certain articulation of identity and enshrining those terms in legal or political institutions, may do much more than simply acknowledge people as what they "already really are"'. To the contrary, such an act might 'strengthen the underlying relation of power and domination that have helped to *make* people who they are' (Markell 2000: 498). See also Cooper (2004: 77).

7

Equality and citizenship in global perspective

Introduction: the spreading of citizenship?

THE PRECEDING chapters of this book have enquired whether a commitment to an egalitarian, democratic form of citizenship is capable of organising and giving shape and force to a variety of egalitarian commitments. Whereas the arguments collected together in the first part of this book criticised the approach taken by prominent participants in the 'equality of what' debate, the second part of this book has investigated ways in which we might avoid some of same pitfalls by theorising equality in relation to citizenship. This approach does raise its own questions, of course, and this chapter deals with one which has until now mainly been kept to one side. This question is: if a commitment to equal citizenship is going to provide a useful vehicle for egalitarian arguments, should we conceive of citizenship in a national or global way? If equal citizenship is to be opposed to hierarchy and oppression, is a commitment purely to nation-state based visions of citizenship capable of challenging the sweeping inequalities that characterise the contemporary world?

For theorists such as Rawls and Marshall, it was taken for granted that citizenship as a practice and as an identity would be coterminous with the institution of the nation-state. As such the immanent value of the ideal of equal citizenship simply ceased to make any demands beyond the borders of the nation-state. Even if there were reasons for objecting to inequalities on a world scale (and by and large Rawls and Marshall maintained a deafening silence on this issue), these reasons would not relate to citizenship as a value or an aspiration. Although such a view has a number of contemporary adherents (see e.g. Walzer 1996; Miller 1999b; Brown 2001), it is increasingly challenged on two related grounds. Firstly, politicians, journalists and academics increasingly tell us we live in an 'interdependent', even 'cosmopolitan' age, the by-product of an inexorable process of 'globalisation'. This globalisation is, to be sure, usually presented as a mixed blessing. As Anheier *et al.* (2001: 7) put it, 'Globalisation is an uneven process which has brought benefits to many but which has also excluded many.' This is an understatement, of course, for what is called globalisation is associated not with an inevitable coming together of peoples and places, but (though often in highly complex ways) with drastic and widening inequalities in relation to poverty (Pieterse 2002), health (Evans 2002) and gender (Pettman 1999), and has made possible a world in which three men own assets greater than the GDP of the world's 48 poorest nation-states (Keane 2001: 34). But either way, we now share what Held and McGrew (2002) call a single 'community of fate', such that actions in one part of the planet inevitably impact on others, and we face common problems that can only be dealt with by means of common political action. Given the increasing economic and cultural inter-penetration of societies, the resolutely Westphalian approach to justice and equality of both communitarians and liberal nationalists is, it is said, both naïve and politically disabling.

Secondly, for many commentators the dominant nation-state based model of citizenship is in the process of disintegrating as a focus of political identity and power, and as a conduit for egalitarian politics. Although the political project of citizenship has been successfully 'fixed' at the level of the nation-state in recent centuries (Behnke 1997), this link is under threat on a number of fronts. The growth of transnational identities and mass migration, the vagaries of the global economy, or the collapse of the vision of the homogenous nation-state have led to a progressive unwrapping of the citizenship 'package' that characterised much of the twentieth century, based on state sovereignty, social protection and a common identity (Sassen 2003; see also Benhabib 2001, 2002). Political iden-tity has become increasingly detached from its 'monogamous' association with a single nation-state, and replaced (at least for some) with a system of fluid, multiple citizenships. Here we could usefully distinguish between horizontal and vertical dimensions of change. Horizontally, there is a gradual erosion of the hostility to dual or multiple citizenships characteristic of the Westphalian era (Rubenstein and Adler 2000), so that increasing numbers of people can move between national citizenship regimes at will (presuming they have pass-ports in the first place). Vertically, the rise in 'layers of governance' within the contemporary world (such as sub-state regions, the EU or UN) points, for Held (1995: 233), towards a world of 'multiple citizenships', where individuals would be 'citizens of their immediate political communities, and of the wider regional and global networks which impacted on their lives'. This latter trend is essential, because the various processes of globalisation have seen a flight of political power from the nation-state, and towards transnational bodies, multinational corporations and as-yet undemocratic global institutions. The state is simply no longer the only meaningful player on the world stage, and although this may not imply the death of the state, it does suggest a changing *role* for the state, and a change in the nature of citizenship. As Held and McGrew put it,

States no longer have the capacity and policy instruments they require to contest the imperatives of global economic change; instead, they must help individual citizens to go where they want to go via the provision of social, cultural and educational resources [...] Individuals must be empowered with the cultural and educational capital to meet the challenges of increased (local, national, regional, global) competition and the greater mobility of industrial and financial capital. (Held and McGrew 2002: 93; cf. Steger 2005)

Assuming that both of these trends are indeed evident, the question that is posed in response is how we might 'tame', 'domesticate' or 'civilise' these processes, or to recapture political control over a 'runaway' world. One increasingly common answer harks back to the very old ideal of 'world' or 'global citizenship'. The same forces that have led to an unbundling of the project of national citizenship have opened up possibilities for imagining forms of solidarity and belonging less marked by the exclusionist histories of the modern nation-state (Purcell 2003). On this version of events whilst globalisation is both a blessing and a curse, global citizenship offers an antidote to the inegalitarian and undemocratic tendencies of global integration. Such an approach has also been taken up by some of the theorists discussed in the second part of this book, albeit very fleetingly. Iris Young (2000: 273), for example, argues for 'a global citizenship status for all persons, so that they would not have to depend on a state for acknowledgement of their basic rights'. Nancy Fraser (2005: 14–15), similarly, argues that correcting the 'mismatch' between nation-state based citizenship and new transnational power-relations and solidarities requires 'institutionalizing elements of ... quasi-global citizenship'. Beyond these gestures no more has been said, yet, about what this might mean in practice, and this chapter aims to investigate some of the possibilities.

The major task of this chapter, then, is to examine the prospects for, and nature of, a putative regime of global citizenship. As such, it aims to examine whether the dichotomy between curse (globalisation) and cure (global citizenship) bears up under scrutiny. Andrew Linklater (2002), in an influential formulation, suggests that a nascent form of global citizenship is marked by three components: a cosmopolitan, universal system of individual rights; a set of duties additional to or even competing with duties to fellow nationals; and finally an emerging world-wide democratic public sphere, or 'global civil society'. Section 1 examines the 'universal' discourse on human rights and human responsibilities, to assess some of its political implications. The assessment here is in fact fairly sceptical, for two reasons. Firstly, if a regime of global citizenship based on human rights is emerging, it appears in practice to be taking a broadly neoliberal form. And, secondly, despite the universal language of human rights discourse, responsibilities for their 'achievement' are usually laid at the door of individual nation-states, leaving global inequalities broadly untouched. All of this is not to say that the vision of global citizenship rights and responsibilities has no critical appeal, but it does imply that we need to be very cautious about some of the eager declarations of cosmopolitan theorists. Section 2 turns to the 'politics' of a putative global citizenship regime, and specifically the character of the much-vaunted 'global civil society'. Again, it is argued that there are reasons for scepticism about the radical potential of global civil society, and this section sets out two competing narratives of its critical potential as the guarantor of a nascent form of democracy on a global scale. Section 3 assesses the claims for global citizenship presented in the first two sections. It is shown that, despite the claims made on behalf of the discourse of global citizenship, certain parts of the emerging citizenship order remain resolutely non-'global'. Rather than 'local' sovereignty and citizenship being displaced by 'global' forms, the current global order seems to be characterised by a complex inter-relation between the two, and the political and economic effects of this division of labour are broadly conservative. This does not confirm the view of Rawls, Marshall, Walzer *et al.* that the value of citizenship cannot organise egalitarian commitments at the transnational level, but it does imply that such a project is more complex and difficult than has often been imagined. Just as there are many possible *globalisations* (to echo the name of a recently launched journal), so there are many possible global citizenship forms, some of which will have more radical implications than others. This final section, then, suggests how the ideal of equal citizenship might be mobilised in more progressive ways.

1 Human rights and human responsibilities

For those who would claim that a global regime of citizenship is emerging, its most prominent manifestation is the universal framework of human rights. For Yeatman (2000: 1501) the idea of human rights forms the 'master discourse' of international politics, and sovereignty itself is increasingly rhetorically linked to a state's success in implementing basic human rights (Reus-Smith 2001). 'States are no longer able to treat their citizens as they see fit', but instead are obliged to conform to common standards of provision and protection (Held and McGrew 2002: 20); those which do not may be labelled 'failed states' and subjected to military, political or economic intervention. This view of human rights as global 'trumps' is a relatively recent phenomenon, and is associated with the United Nations Charter of 1945. The rights in question were set out in detail by the UN's *Universal Declaration of Human Rights* of 1948, and include – amongst other things – the right to life and liberty, to impartial justice, to free movement, free expression, to own property and to work (and to equal pay and holidays), and to participate in political and cultural life. These rights were elaborated still further in subsequent covenants – foremost amongst these are the *Covenant on Civil and Political Rights*, and the *Covenant on Social, Economic and*

Cultural Rights, both agreed by the UN General Assembly in 1966 and ratified by many – though not all – states since.

Despite its supposed role as the master discourse of international politics, there is significant debate on the content, implementation and universal applicability of these rights. Rawls (1999b) characteristically argued that the rights regime of the international arena is 'hardly controversial', and therefore capable of forming the basis of a thin or minimal version of global justice. But controversy over the kinds of rights that are important, and the ways in which they might best be defended, is very much apparent. The two *Covenants* of 1966, for instance, were strongly implicated in the ideological struggle of the Cold War, with the *Covenant on Civil and Political Rights* largely advancing the liberal capitalist perspective of the West; the *Covenant on Social, Economic and Cultural Rights*, on the other hand, was very much the child of the Soviet Union and to this day has not been accepted by the US (Dower 2003: 61). Even today, Mignolo (2002) observes that human rights are a critical counter in struggles over coloniality, gender and culture. Human rights talk was a defining feature of resistance and liberation movements in 'developing' countries, and many movements for social and economic justice in the global South have turned to the language of rights as an alternative to the managerialist and depoliticised language of 'development' (Cornwall and Nyamu-Musembi 2004). For some, human rights provide a valuable language for calling prominent world powers such as the USA to account (see e.g. Mertus 2003), especially at a time when civil and political rights are under increasing threat in the supposed home of democracy and freedom (Stephens 2004). On the other hand, NGOs from the global South have attempted to use human rights as a tool for the restructuring of the global order (see Van Ness 1999). For others, human rights are a Western imperialist invention, designed to eradicate alternatives to the one true path of liberal capitalism (see Bell *et al.* 2001), whilst for others still, although rights are important, the fact that the discourse of human rights exerts such sway over debates on the parameters of global justice is deeply regrettable (Baker 2002). Suffice to say, then, that rights are contested; behind this contestation, moreover, lie a series of struggles to define the nature of world community and of human identity; in the words of one defence of human rights, they are responsible for the very 'inventing of humanity' (Booth and Dunne 1999). In this section I can only hope to outline some of the most prominent areas of controversy, though I will return to some of these issues at the end of this chapter.

Rights and dualism

It is important to recognise at the outset that the dominant discourse on rights is characterised by a typically liberal dualism between civil/political and socio-economic rights. Furthermore, the very status of socio-economic rights as core elements of human rights or global citizenship is highly contested: within human rights politics, a liberal consensus has ensured that 'socioeconomic rights are rarely given the same status as liberal freedoms associated with civil and political rights' (Evans 2002: 197). Whereas these latter rights are seen as paramount and inviolable, socio-economic rights are usually reduced to the level of 'aspirations', and responsibility for their enforcement is generally placed at the door of 'local' national governments. More pressingly still, the delivery of socio-economic rights has often been made far more difficult by the imposition of policies such as the World Bank's Structural Adjustment Programmes, as a result of which 'the human rights to food, health, education and social assistance are abandoned in favour of privileging global financial and corporate interests' (Evans 2002: 209). The emphasis on the fundamental primacy of civil/political rights – including individual private property rights and the right to trade freely – in practice impels cutbacks on 'unproductive social expenditure', with disproportionate effects on women and children (Pettman 1999: 211).

As with Rawls and Marshall, this division of rights into two (or three) species is deeply unfortunate in many ways, for such a division potentially disguises the socio-economic salience of civil/political rights, at the same time as downplaying the role of political participation in defining or achieving socio-economic provisions. As a response to the pernicious effects of this dualism, the 1993 World Conference on Human Rights in Vienna asserted the interdependence, indivisibility and non-hierarchical nature of all of these rights. This is an important argument for several reasons – foremost among them that civil and political rights have huge economic consequences. As Evans (2002) observes, civil and political rights are often treated as the practical and achievable cousins of socio-economic rights precisely because they are cost-free (cf. Marshall 1950; Rawls 1971). But no rights are cost-free, as Shue (1980) ably shows, since even basic civil and political rights need to be defended by complex systems of crime control, judiciaries and prisons: the free market, as Thatcherism illustrated, requires many policemen. More to the point, even specific conceptions of property rights, though often treated as natural and unexceptionable, in fact require fundamental transformations of social relations in order to take force.[1] Given property regimes do not spring from the earth, but are the product, and the cause, of violent and exclusionary processes. True to form, specific conceptions of (individual, private) property did not arise smoothly within Western countries, but were the product of centuries of coercion and dispossession, and the same is true of many parts of the contemporary world. Liberal property rights are still in the process of being extended, often violently, across dimensions of both space and type, with ever-widening classes of goods, services and other social artefacts coming under their remit. But as Andreasson (2006: 3–4) puts it, 'Taking for granted the value of property rights prevents critical inquiry into their origins and how they are used to extend systems of oppression and exploitation globally.' Although such rights are often presented as harbingers of freedom, a 'historical "accounting" of the means by which propertied classes worldwide have acquired their possessions would become unpleasant indeed for those interested in preserving the status quo of global inequality and the "rights" which impede any radical rectification thereof' (Andreasson 2006: 10).

Although in recent years the language of socio-economic rights has begun to be taken up by institutions such as the World Bank, the lucky few that are defended seem to behave curiously like liberal property rights. A good example of this would be the World Bank's implementation of a water programme in Brazil, Chile, Indonesia, the Philippines and Yemen (and soon to be extended elsewhere) under the title of 'rights-based water sharing'. Though framed in the language of (socio-economic) human rights, this system in fact represents 'no more than a system of tradable permits in water', with such a trading system favouring large commercial users. What is represented as empowerment through human rights in fact amounts to the commodification and privatisation of an asset that was previously owned in common (albeit with unequal access). People 'have now been transformed from "passive beneficiaries" to "rights-holders"', but the effect of this process has been neither egalitarian nor emancipatory in practice (see Cornwall and Nyamu-Musembi 2004: 1427–34); such a transformation may be more widely emblematic of the emergence of the liberal rights-bearing subject.

Rights and responsibilities

As centrist politicians are fond of reminding us, an account of individual rights is dependent in practice on an accompanying set of obligations. It has been widely observed that the biggest obstacle preventing human rights having real critical bite may be the weakness of a corresponding discourse of responsibilities. As Nigel Dower notes, in the *Universal Declaration of Human Rights* 'not much is made of the correlative obligations and who or what institutions are to implement them'. As a result, a key aspiration of radical activists and NGOs has been to supplement this document with a 'Declaration of Human Responsibilities' (Dower 2003: 59) which places at least some of the burden on citizens of richer states. Legally speaking, at present the bulk of responsibilities under human rights law are certainly focused on the states in which human rights violations or 'shortfalls' might take place. Socio-economic rights in particular are usually depicted as standards to be striven towards by the hard work of less developed countries, and do not generate enforceable claims on the resources of more privileged states, even when there are clearly observable flows of money and resources from poorer to richer countries. As in Rawls's account (Rawls 1999b), the 'failures' of poor states are treated as if they were rooted in domestic mismanagement rather than global exploitation. For Evans (2002) this is all too convenient for the liberal consensus, since credit can be claimed for defending socio-economic rights morally, whilst at the same time casting scorn on their applicability, and denying a link between the rights of the world's poor and any putative responsibilities of the world's rich (see also Donnelly 1999: 91).

Despite their apparently universal and decontextualised nature, the logic of human rights therefore remains state-centric in at least two ways. For one thing, whether an action *counts* as a human rights violation often depends on whether it is directly linked to the state apparatus – so that an assault by a fellow citizen is a crime, but an assault by an on-duty policeman is a human rights violation (Donnelly 1999: 86). Secondly, under the UN system most *responsibilities* for upholding rights are directed at 'local' states, rather than some universal or transcendental community, and states owe rights primarily to their 'own' citizens, not to aliens (Donnelly 1999: 85). As a result, universal declarations on rights – given the difficulties poorer countries may face upholding them for a variety of reasons – can serve as a stick with which powerful countries can beat less powerful ones, rather than vice versa. In the contemporary world the very term universal human rights might be a misnomer: instead at present we seem to have a universally imposed system of domestic rights and responsibilities, and one, moreover, which has been applied selectively and hypocritically by major powers. As such, as David Chandler puts it, 'the imperative of action to defend the human rights of cosmopolitan citizens ironically entails a realpolitik which is highly state-centric' (2003: 338).

None of this is to reject the idea of human rights, or to deny the fact that gains have been made even by selectively pressuring weaker states (as well as more powerful ones) to uphold values of democracy and equal treatment. But taken as a whole, it is clear that if human rights are to figure in a genuinely critical vision of global citizenship, this is an inauspicious start. Within international law and the major global institutions the dominant discourse of rights reopens the liberal chasm Marx observed, where a line of indemnity is drawn between the socio-economic rights of the poor, and the civil (and particularly property) rights of the rich. If the global regime of human rights represents an embryonic form of global citizenship, it is citizenship in the most neoliberal form, where property rights reign supreme, and social rights represent little more than exhortations to industrious self-reliance. In this instance any ideal of collective or structural responsibility is largely absent, and instead the presumption of state responsibility serves as an injunction to conform to a neoliberal model of development, or bear the consequences alone. Nevertheless, there is space for the assertion of alternative conceptions of rights and responsibilities, and indeed in the current global order even underscoring a relatively thin set of rights could be transformative, depending on how they are interpreted and at whose door responsibility for upholding those rights is laid. At the end of this chapter I will outline just a few of the current areas of contention over rights, each of which reveals competing attempts to define the terms of global citizenship, or the 'human' in human rights.

2 Civility, radicalism and global democracy: two perspectives on 'global civil society'

If a global regime of citizenship is in the process of emerging, at what sites does the political participation of citizens take place? Where, precisely, is the 'politics' in global citizen politics? For most cosmopolitan theorists, the status of the nation-state as the locus of real power is fast eroding if not altogether terminated, and the real focal points of power in the contemporary world lie with international organisations and powerful economic actors (see e.g. Held 1995). If this is the case, national citizenship can no longer operate as the site of a viable form of democracy or equality, and other possibilities, which are closer to the seats of real power, must be found. One possibility lies with democratic reform of existing institutions such as the UN, taking the form perhaps of a directly globally elected UN parliament (Linklater 2002: 329; see also Young 2000). Such a project is worthwhile, but could be expected to have radical implications only if we assume that bodies such as the UN are crucial sites of transnational power. Far from it, in the current global order multinational corporations and institutions such as the World Bank, International Monetary Fund (IMF) and World Trade Organisation (WTO) appear to many to represent the embodiment of such power. For a growing number of commentators, the democratic participation of citizens is and should therefore be expressed through the intermediaries of international non-governmental organisations (INGOs), which are able to interact with, and hopefully influence, international governmental institutions (IGOs) such as the UN, IMF, WTO or World Bank. In re-linking global power with the concerns of individual citizens across the globe, and injecting an element of accountability and transparency into 'global governance', these INGOs represent the crucial focus of an emerging 'global civil society'. For Linklater (2002: 329) 'attempts by INGOs to build a worldwide public sphere by participating, albeit sporadically, in global events, running parallel to major United Nations conferences such as those held in Beijing and Rio de Janeiro advance the claim that global institutions should comply with principles of democratic legitimacy'. Whereas the suited and limousined executives who attend global summits represent the real princes of global power, the colourful eruptions of popular democratic will that picket them represent their consciences, and sometimes at least succeed in making their voices heard. In this section I will examine two opposed narratives on the role of global civil society, before reaching some tentative conclusions about its potential for substantiating a form of democratic global citizenship.

[*172*]

Global civil society as counterweight to globalisation

only 'global civil society' can be posed as a counterweight to globalisation. (Anheier *et al.* 2001: 17)

the advantage of the language of civil society is precisely its *political* content, its implications for participation and citizenship. It adds to the human rights discourse the notion of individual responsibility for respect of human rights through public action. (Kaldor 1999: 211)

A newly emerging global civil society (hereafter GCS) is usually constituted as a 'third zone', beyond formal politics and the market, or at least a zone where 'civic initiative' mingles with 'market forces' and the power-play of 'state inter-action' (Keane 2001: 35). This GCS forms an essential counterbalance to the exclusionary, inegalitarian and undemocratic nature of global power. Some rather grand claims have been made about the potential of GCS to 'civilise' glob-alisation: that it produces the key to the delivery of human rights, by supplementing that discourse with an effective account of individual responsi-bility (Kaldor 1999), that it supplies an 'answer to war' by defusing conflict between major powers, and that it can provide 'a check both on the power and arbitrariness of the contemporary state and on the power of unbridled capital-ism' (Kaldor 2003: 21). Indeed civil society at the global level is ethically superior to its seedbeds at the national level, for GCS overcomes the exclusion-ary tendencies of Westphalian citizenship (Linklater 1998). Such is the potential legitimising role of GCS within global politics that, for Daniele Archibugi (1998) it is the existence of GCS alone that provides the authority for global institutions to interfere in the domestic affairs of nation-states. Whereas global institutions such as the UN suffer from obvious 'democratic deficits', the democratic ener-gies of GCS can act as a legitimating force for their actions and re-couple economic and military power with the authority of democratic citizenship.

If a global citizenry is emerging, then, GCS represents one of its primary manifestations. Naidoo and Tandon (1999: 6–7) have described it as 'the network of autonomous institutions that rights-bearing and responsibility-laden citizens voluntarily create to address common problems, advance shared interests and promote collective aspirations'. GCS is the place where human rights connect with human responsibilities, as individuals and groups seek to mediate the terms of global integration and interdependence. This much is also averred by many of the component organisations of GCS which explicitly use the language of citizenship to frame their concerns and mode of operation (such as Civicus and the various Citizens' Forums; the organisers of the oppositional World Social Forum have also claimed that it represents a key element of an emerging 'universal planetary citizenry'). There is an odd slippage in the litera-ture, however, on the question of whether global civil society *expresses* the emergence of global citizenship, or in fact *engineers* that emergence. Here prominent accounts of global civil society become somewhat circular, for many defenders of global civil society do see it as playing a role in *creating* global citizens. As Anheier, Glasius and Kaldor (2001: 17) put it, 'global civil society can be seen as an aspiration to reach and include citizens everywhere and to enable them to think and act as global citizens'. This implies a critical (and very liberal) distancing from national traditions and identities: in the new globalised world, Held and McGrew (2002: 107) tell us, 'Each citizen of a state will have to learn to become a "cosmopolitan citizen" as well; that is, a person capable of mediating between national traditions and alternative forms of life'. For Linklater (1998: 181) transnational political communities are necessary to 'promote a transnational citizenry with multiple political allegiances', and not just to give expression to those allegiances. For Keane (2001: 43), even more bluntly, global public spheres 'enable citizens to shake off bad habits of parochialism'.

Although GCS begins to look like a tremendously powerful and progressive force on this dominant narrative, its supporters do feel the need to address three tricky issues. The first is the Western bias of the nascent global civil society. As Gideon Baker (2002: 937) puts it, 'most "global" civil society organisations are actually thoroughly Western ... and the majority of the world's "citizens" are more adequately conceptualised as objects rather than subjects of such organisations'. Even its champions admit that the INGOs that constitute GCS are 'heavily concentrated in north-western Europe' (Anheier *et al.* 2001: 7; see also Linklater 2002: 329). Keane (2001: 24) in fact tells us that there are 'no-go areas for civil society' at the global level, where GCS has barely been able to put down roots at all (and where 'parochialism' presumably still rules). But for supporters of GCS this is generally identified as a *transitional* problem: in time, the organisations and practices of GCS will become more vocal and powerful in the global South, thereby confirming its legitimacy. The second tricky issue concerns what 'counts' as GCS and what does not. Do we include right-wing organisations such as transnational fundamentalist and even terrorist organisations, or organisations that challenge the basic principles of human rights, for instance? Opinion here is divided; some are happy to boldly define GCS as 'a complex multi-organizational field that explicitly excludes reactionary – racist, fascist or fundamentalist – organizations and movements' (Taylor 2004: 4), whereas others are more circumspect. But a commitment to existing ideals of human rights do seem to be hardwired into the definitions of theorists such as Kaldor and Linklater. Finally, just how independent from the powers-that-be does GCS have to be to represent a corrective to their undemocratic tendencies? Should financial organisations, corporations and/or economic lobbying organisations themselves be included in the definition of GCS? Held and McGrew (2002: 70) themselves point to 'a significant privatisation of aspects of global governance [representing] the expanding influence of private interests in the formulation as well as the delivery of global policies'. Some have responded to this fact by defining GCS in such a way that it does not include these private voices, but it is not clear that its independence can be secured by such 'definitional fiat' (Munck 2004). On a related theme, should the INGOs considered to comprise GCS be autonomously organised by citizens, and funded by concerned individuals, or may they be sponsored, organised or even paid for, by states and transnational organisations (as many are) and still preserve their role as the democratic 'policemen' of world politics? For defenders of GCS these are difficult questions, but the claim stands that GCS – however constituted – represents the best hope for reinserting democratic politics into the global order.

Global civil society as disciplinary agent

To increase the efficiency of adjustment and solidify the political foundations of neoliberalism, global regulatory agencies began [in the 1980s] to concern themselves with political and social processes beyond crude impressment, and began to structure their relationship with NGOs and other would-be representatives of global civil society ... 'Global governance' is an attempt to invent a political interlocutor with whom globalizing elites might negotiate sustainable terms for global accumulation. (Drainville 2002: 23)

The second perspective views the narrative above with considerable suspicion, and considers global civil society as principally an agent or conduit of neoliberal governance. Many radical critics will already come to the notion of civil society with a measure of suspicion of course, given that within nation-states it is the 'civil society' of voluntary organisations, corporations, lobbying groups and quasi-state organisations that neoliberalism has turned to in 'rolling back the frontiers' both of the state and of democracy. Thus 'whilst "progressive" forces look to civil society as a site for mounting challenges to globalisation, it is important to remember that a strengthened civil society is itself a goal of neoliberal forces' (Robinson 2003: 169). For Gramscian critics in particular it is no surprise that 'the activities of "global civil society" – meaning the civil society that is seen and heard – are thus neither autonomous from nor particularly challenging to the processes of globalisation' (Robinson 2003: 170).

On the harshest assessment, then, GCS stands 'coopted as the "social" wing of neoliberal global capitalism' (Munck 2004: 20), an agent of inequality rather than equality. But what does this mean in practice? David Chandler (2004: 332–4) considers GCS an exemplar of 'courtier politics', and claims that rather than GCS pressuring institutions such as the UN, the UN has 'been largely responsible for creating a global activist network' around itself. For Andre Drainville the engagement of institutions such as the IMF and World Bank with GCS has been highly instrumental, aimed at gathering legitimacy for neoliberal economic policies, and 'putting in place the social and political infrastructure of a sustainable global order free of irritants and resistance' (Drainville 2004: 136;

see also Thirkell-White 2004 for a careful assessment). Whereas large numbers of INGOs have existed for decades at least, it was only during the 1980s that the IMF and World Bank began to engage with – and even to nurture and bankroll – such 'automous' institutions. On Drainville's (2002) account, this has little to do with any interest in democracy and accountability, but a good deal to do with increased fears about the smooth progress of the global financial system (as a result of anti-IMF riots in the 1980s, the removal of neoliberal leaders in Latin America, and more recently financial crises in Asia and Mexico, for example). The colourful spectacle of GCS is wheeled out every time a major summit is held, but the real function of GCS is to negotiate and then propagate 'back home' a 'reformist' version of neoliberalism which institutions such as the IMF and World Bank believe is in the best interests of global capital anyway. Although Drainville is fiercely, and perhaps immoderately, critical of the crucial potential of GCS, he is not alone in his suspicions here. For Jacqueline Best (2003: 378) we are witnessing the birth of 'a strange new kind of embedded liberalism', which springs from a recognition of the limits of an unstable and unpopular 'disembedded liberalism' for the stability of global accumulation. The freedom given to finance capital in the 1970s and 1980s proved just too risky in practice, as unrestrained speculation triggered a series of economic and political crises. The IMF and World Bank are now instead engaged in seeking a new top-down 'consensus' on financial management which aims to 'reform' these excesses, and although they are securing it by using apparently consensual terms such as 'civility', 'civilising globalisation', and the need for 'good financial citizenship' (Best 2003: 363), the reality is that GCS has been turned to as a legitimating tool for global neoliberalism, 'a means of making the global political economy governable in particular ways' (Amoore and Langley 2004: 90).

Resistance and civility

The second narrative begs the question, and forcefully, of whether GCS as currently conceived is part of the solution, as opposed to part of the project of global neoliberal hegemony. Is global civil society the velvet glove that covers the iron fist of a racist, patriarchal and militaristic capitalism? For Drainville (1998: 37) GCS has functioned as a tool for 'the making of a compliant citizenry', and not as the entry point for real challenges to the global order. The 'new agoras' of the global order attempt to 'make new citizens, unsullied by context, immaculately conceived' (Drainville 2004: 23), whereby the sheer dirtiness, messiness and complexity of individuals' lives and perspectives is erased – and this ambition does seem to resonate with the claims of GCS's champions about its ability to oblige citizens to transcend their particular and parochial obsessions. As a result, global citizenship brings to bear precisely the vision of universal citizenship that Iris Young (1998) earlier criticised for pulling a rug of 'impartiality' over the distasteful facts of oppression and cultural imperialism. If what characterises global citizens is their ability to transcend their parochialism, might this not also undercut the possibility of radical critique and of the solidarity formed by the experience of oppression? These concerns are well taken; nevertheless even the sceptical voices cited above acknowledge that a transnational politics independent of both state and economic institutions is possible. The devil, as ever, is in the detail: most critics of GCS do not recoil so much from the aspiration it expresses, but are, rather, highly sceptical of the dominant narratives of how, and to what extent, it is manifested at present. The elitist and Western bias of GCS is not denied – though it may be downplayed – even by many of its defenders, and there is considerable justification for Munck's (2004: 23, 17) assertion that GCS is 'hegemonized by Western liberal notions of civility and citizenship', so that '"Enlightenment man" is seen as the privileged actor in the GCS play we are asked to support'. The danger of co-option is real, and the independence – and therefore critical import – of much of what goes under the heading of GCS is highly dubious. For Pasha and Blaney (1998: 420), 'a failure to attend to the mutually constitutive relationship of civil society, capitalism, and the liberal state will misguide our assessments of the emancipatory possibilities of associational life'; although a critical global civil society is possible, it does not necessarily exist in the places where supporters of the first narrative have preferred to look (see also Jaggar 2005).

The sheer diversity of the so-called GCS does make blanket condemnations appear misguided, and in the end some of the sternest critics of GCS turn out to favour a somewhat different set of actors to the dominant narrative, but to still hold out the possibility of independent and critical global action. It would of course be far too sweeping to dismiss the movements that have protested at Rio, Seattle, Beijing, Quebec City or Davos as mere elite proxies, and in the final analysis critics of GCS tend to retreat from such a claim. Thus Drainville, one of GCS's harshest judges, does acknowledge that some INGOs have altered the policy of IGOs, and been instrumental in, for instance, increasing levels of development aid, and establishing international covenants on torture (Drainville 2004: 109). And indeed the movements Drainville does champion – (spontaneous movements against sweatshops, for abortion rights, against the trafficking of women, for tougher labour standards) may also fall under the GCS rubric, although they show considerably less 'respect' for dominant norms of civility and cooperation with the vested interests that stand foremost on the global stage. This implies that the problem does not lie with the 'globality' or with the 'societal' elements of GCS, but with the dominant ideas of 'civility' that characterise it, and which serve to narrow the political agenda and exclude many dissonant voices (Pasha and Blaney 1998). A second cause for concern is that, for all that Linklater, Kaldor *et al.* appear to champion democratic involvement in the fight for human rights and global justice, the rights and the principles of justice too often seem to come before the politics. Democratic contestation over the substance of those rights and principles frequently seems to be as distant from the politics of GCS as substantial democratic control over the basic policies, orientations and even existence of institutions such as the IMF, WTO or World Bank. Cosmopolitan law/adjustment comes first, and democratic participation/good governance comes later, but in each case this ordering serves to displace more profound questions over the nature of the contemporary global order. Although a critical counter-hegemonic politics is possible, its existence may be more fleeting and fragile than has been assumed, and dependent on a far broader notion of politics than that held out by mainstream advocates of global civil society.

3   Either/Or? The politics of global citizenship

If a commitment to equal citizenship is to provide a framework for struggles against global inequalities, such a project appears highly precarious. The claim that a meaningful global regime of citizenship is emerging – and that it represents the seedbed for a new global democratic egalitarianism – should be treated with caution, for two reasons. Firstly, to the extent that such a citizenship regime is represented by the discourse of human rights and the vibrancy of so-called global civil society its egalitarian credentials look far from certain, and as a whole the global order exhibits what Santos (1999) calls 'low intensity human rights [plus] low intensity democracy'. In fact, the narratives of human rights and global civil society have often been employed – though never without resistance – as tools in the continuing development of neoliberalism, as well as in the more limited realpolitik of powerful states and economic actors. Secondly, the supposedly 'global' elements of global citizenship turn out on closer inspection to be far less universal and transcendental than is often implied. The imperatives of the current capitalist global order demand not a world in which all is global, but a world in which some things (capital, goods, information, economic elites, human rights) are constituted as 'global', but some things (national borders, the poor, responsibilities for 'development' and human rights) remain resolutely 'local'. The contemporary world is a world of deep chasms between the supposedly global and the resolutely local, and people, democracy and critical possibilities often fall through the cracks.

By the same token, globalisation appears to have transformed the terms of national citizenship, rather than rendering it obsolete as a category of political and economic life. To be sure, the social rights of the welfarist state are becoming more and more conditional and incentivised, and social solidarity is increasingly secured instead by emphasising the common threats posed by insecurity, lawlessness, immigration and the competitive global economy. But the relation between state power and the power of transnational economic forces is complex and variable, and some states – and perhaps most notably the UK –

have been far more 'proactive' in 'meeting the challenges' of globalisation than others. In many Western countries the narrative of globalisation has been deployed as a lever with which to legitimise recent transformations of national citizenship, and even such equality and diversity as the modern state can still muster often serves as a useful tool for the 'rebranding' of its workforce.[2] It may well be that the logic of state sovereignty has been transformed, but proclamations of the death of the state and of nation-state citizenship are premature, and eager acceptance of such ideas may be all too convenient for the political leaders beloved of the rhetoric of global necessity, peddling what Ulrich Beck has called 'the rebirth of Marxism as management ideology' (quoted in Steger 2005: 19). It seems, therefore, that what best characterises the contemporary world is not a move from national to global citizenship as such, but the (often shifting) coexistence between a variety of citizenship forms, which enable mobility and choice for some, but which imply 'stability' and compulsion for others. Aihwa Ong's account of 'flexible citizenship' provides perhaps the most illuminating analysis of these developments. For Ong (1999: 216) what we have witnessed is the emergence of a system of 'graduated sovereignty, whereby citizens in zones that are differently articulated to global production and financial circuits are subjected to different kinds of surveillance and in practice enjoy different sets of civil, political and economic rights'. There are differing degrees of mobility between these citizenship regimes, and such mobility is highly stratified according to class, gender and ethnicity. This sounds like a dystopian version of Held's (1995) world of 'multiple citizenships', but it might be closer to the reality for most of the world's people. At the same time effective power over economic and political life, though clearly open to challenge at various institutional locations, cannot adequately be grasped at any one of them. In effect this 'system of graduated zones [thereby] protects against pockets of political unrest' (Ong 1999: 216).

All of this suggests that recourse to the ideal of equal citizenship will not be a straightforward affair at the global level. But this is not to reject the idea, as some theorists have done. Thus communitarians and liberal nationalists remind us that the nation-state remains a crucial locus of identity, social meaning and to some extent political power. Such theorists object to a regime of global citizenship because of sincere concerns over the dangers of theoretical imperialism: in a diverse and pluralist world, adherence to an abstract cosmopolitan citizenship regime amounts to complicity in the erasure of cultural difference. But the communitarian position is vulnerable to a series of powerful criticisms itself: communitarians offer no adequate response to the genuine power of multinationals and global economic institutions, and defend images of the nation that deny the (new but also very old) fact that the nation-state has never been a simple container for political identity. The assertion of the 'unnaturalness' of global citizenship depends on a naturalisation of national citizenship which does not bear up under historical scrutiny (Behnke 1997). Moreover such theorists inexcusably neglect the strong connections between the citizenship privileges enjoyed in wealthy Western democracies and the place of rich states in a hugely unequal global economic system. To worry about theoretical imperialism without seriously addressing the imperialism of liberal capitalism is odd to say the least, and serves to legitimise the privileges of wealthy states and citizens: to maintain inequality under the guise of 'respect'.[3] In the contemporary world we could say in fact that the distinction between 'internal' and 'external' outsiders described by Isin (2002) and Yeatman (1994) is blurring considerably, so that the ways of life, expectations and privileges of citizens in one country are increasingly dependent on those who live outside the official geographical bounds of a given community, and the privileges of citizenship in the West are therefore intimately bound up in exclusionary processes in the global South. On a mundane level my right to health care as a British citizen is underwritten by the presence of thousands of foreign workers within the NHS. On a more profound level, my 'identity' as a privileged white male citizen has been shaped not in isolation but in relation to a series of encounters with a variety of 'others', and a history of colonialism, racism and economic exploitation on a transnational scale.

Although mainstream discourses of globalisation often obscure, legitimate or even facilitate the brutal realities of global 'interdependence' (and displace more longstanding concerns with capitalism, imperialism and domination), the autarchy supposed by communitarian theorists remains untenable in the current global order. Even if a revolt against global capital appeared on the communitarian horizon, and all the lines of global cultural interpenetration and inter-definition were severed, the trump card of many cosmopolitan theorists – the challenge of ecological degradation – would still demand both global principles of justice and a transformation of 'domestic' citizenship practices. This is not to downplay the importance of 'local' action, but it is to say that the world 'out there' is in practice a world of grand narratives and transformative visions; it just happens that the dominant visions are those of neoliberalism and the new world order (see Tormey 2001). In this context even national borders are global institutions, and require defending by force as well as by moral argument.

In fact, it is likely that global inequalities cannot be adequately tackled at *either* the nation-state *or* the global level, and instead demand action at both levels simultaneously (see Harvey 2000: 50; Sassen 2004). As a result, it may be that the opposition between cosmopolitanism on the one hand and nationalism/communitarianism on the other is deceptive and unhelpful. Rather, the suspicion is that an attack on the inequalities that characterise the global system does not by definition necessitate an attack on 'the nation' in all its forms. It may turn out that, if it is a useful political term at all, cosmopolitanism makes sense not in terms of resistance to nationalism per se, but in terms of resistance to racism, sexism, capitalism, and the reckless transformation of the ecology of the planet we live in.

But as Bhikhu Parekh puts it, this does suggest that even if we reject a system of global citizenship, some form of 'globally-oriented citizenship' is a minimal requirement. One of the arguments of this book has been that equal citizenship is opposed to hierarchy and to oppression, whether of 'internal' or 'external' outsiders. A vivid example of this line of thinking emerged in the aftermath of the terrible Asian tsunami of 26 December 2004. Writing in *El Pais*, Jose Cerda (2005) commiserated with the victims, but berated Western governments for their hypocrisy: specifically, he compared the everyday effects of indebtedness and world poverty to a second tsunami, only an ongoing one, and one to which richer states willingly contribute. But 'As citizens', Cerda asserted, 'we do not want to contribute to this new exploitation of misery.' This declaration could be taken in two senses. The first counterposes citizen to state, for the response of 'ordinary' citizens to the humanitarian disaster was faster and more profound than that of political leaders (and indeed the majority of global aid generally does come from non-state sources). The second (and compatible) reading is that the notion of citizenship is being opposed here to the existence of hierarchy. As citizens of wealthy Western countries we benefit from exploitative economic relations with the global South, and this fact undermines even the egalitarian aspiration of 'our own' citizenship.

As a result, one component in this turn to 'globally-oriented' or 'worldly' citizenship is likely to be a far more substantial account of responsibility than we find in the communitarian literature, and even in much of the dominant cosmopolitan literature. In Chapter 4, I argued for the salience of the concept of 'privileged irresponsibility' found in feminist theory, and applied it to issues of economic justice, care, and ecological justice, and Iris Young has more recently developed an account of 'structural responsibility' which shares many of the same concerns. For Young (2004), individuals who benefit from global inequalities of wealth and power have a responsibility to act in order to combat such exploitative relations, regardless of national boundaries (cf. Pogge 2004). Such responsibilities cannot easily be traced back to individual actions, but derive from the facts of 'interdependence', from privilege and from complicity in oppression. Such an idea could potentially be interpreted much more broadly; certainly parallel arguments are also common in ecological theory, where ideals of (citizenly) 'ecological virtue' have been defended that strongly challenge the consumption and production choices of 'private' individuals (see e.g. Dobson 2003). We could also apply the notion of 'privileged irresponsibility', as Tronto (1993) intimates, to reveal and to frame the struggle against processes of racial and sexual hierarchy at a transnational level.

But I also want to suggest that the egalitarian aspiration expressed in the ideal of citizenship cannot cease at national borders. If, as seems likely, the development of some very thin version of world citizenship continues, then theorists need to critically engage with this development in order to seek out the points of tension, and to make the most of the potential it offers for immanent critique. If not, then an embryonic world citizenship regime will remain dualistic, hierarchical and inegalitarian, and an opportunity for critical intervention(s) will have been lost. At the same time, an egalitarian cosmopolitanism cannot simply be 'deduced' by theoretical reason.[4] It has by now become common to differentiate between cosmopolitanisms 'from above' and 'from below', and recently theorists have suggested the need for 'vernacular', 'dialogical', 'embedded' or 'popular' cosmopolitanisms. One of the points behind such arguments, as I take it, is to resist the abstraction and rationalism of dominant (and pre-eminently liberal) versions of cosmopolitanism, which paradoxically remain exclusionary at the same time as posing themselves as 'universal'. Whereas dominant cosmopolitanisms have deduced universal principles via the dictates of 'abstract' reason, the hope of these alternative positions is that by attending to the diverse and concrete struggles against oppression that characterise the contemporary world, we might be able to 'build', rather than 'discover' a basis for a viable cosmopolitanism, and one that is less hostile to difference.[5] Such a vision has long been more apparent in feminist and anti-racist struggle, perhaps, than in the confines of academic cosmopolitanism.

Contesting citizenships

One of the sites at which contestation over the nature of an embryonic form of global citizenship might take place is that of human rights. For some, the fact that debates over global citizenship and civil society have aggregated around the issue of rights is deeply regrettable in itself (see e.g. Baker 2002). There is much to be said for this view, and it is doubtful that an account of egalitarian citizenship can be built wholly on the back of the language of rights. Nevertheless, it may still be the case that a more radical and democratic contestation of the politics of human rights does provide one avenue for levering open the neoliberal conceptualisation of global citizenship. Struggles over rights also represent struggles to define humanity, the individual and world community, and refusing the language of human rights as inherently Western, imperialist or totalising may represent, for the theorist, an odd kind of complicity in that totalising project. Rather than surrendering 'the universal' or the 'human' to liberalism and neoliberalism, a more critical engagement with the discourse of human rights might open up possibilities to frame resistance to neoliberalism, racism and sexism (see Eisenstein 2004: 36), for instance. Such contestations might represent the very beginning of what Fraser (1989) has called the democratic process of need interpretation, in which the prerequisites of equal citizenship are contested and enacted in an open-ended and democratic process, though we need to be cautious about such claims. But what remains of this section will briefly detail some of the arenas in which the terms of a 'thin' neoliberal regime of global citizenship are being contested.

Property-owning citizens? What is the relationship between humanity and property? A series of hugely significant debates are currently being waged over the subject of property rights, and the struggles here betoken a contestation of the boundaries of public and private, individual and society, and the individual citizen itself. Just a few examples might include debates over intellectual property rights in the genetic codes of varieties of cereal crops that have been grown for generations in Asia; over private ownership of the air, the water, and even extra-terrestrial artefacts; struggles over land ownership and dispossession in Latin America or Southern Africa; and debates about private ownership or copyright of human genetic information which bring to bear significant questions about the very nature and boundaries of personhood. Although some of these debates have been the preserve of activists and transnational social movements, the status and nature of universal property rights have also been considered by prominent cosmopolitan political theorists, including those of a broadly liberal variety. The foremost example here would be Thomas Pogge, who has criticised what he calls the 'international resource and borrowing privileges that allow any person or group exercising effective power in a developing country to sell its resources and to borrow money in its name' (2004: 6). In the prevailing political and economic order, as Pogge observes, Western powers are usually content to trade mineral resources, for instance, with anyone who is prepared and willing to sell them on the global market, even if they are associated with brutality and dispossession within their own states. As a result the development of internationally sanctioned property rights within poor countries is intimately linked to substantial flows of wealth to rich countries, mediated by local elites and multinational corporations, and to exclusion and repression 'back home'. As a bulwark against this Pogge (2002, 2004) recommends what he calls a Global Resources Dividend, which would 'compensate' for the removal of 'common' property by taxing globally traded material resources at 1 per cent, thereby producing an estimated $300 billion per year, enough to bring everyone in the world above the $2 per day level, the World Bank's current benchmark for poverty. The impact of this would be very positive, and yet would not, presumably, 'disturb' the global economic system unduly (Pogge 2002: 92).[6] Nevertheless, Pogge's suggestion is interesting for the issues it opens up: the legitimacy, and effects, of notions of private property which remain uncontroversial much of the time, and the possibility of property regimes other than those imagined within the possessive individualist account of neoliberal theory (see also Andreasson 2006). Struggles over land ownership and intellectual property rights raise many of the same issues.

Social citizens? Are the ingredients of substantial economic change already implied by existing discourses on socio-economic rights? For some activists the answer is yes: one example might be the 'right to development' included in the UN's *Declaration on the Right to Development* of 1986, which aimed to create a 'New International Economic Order' that was fairer to poor countries, implying a substantial readjustment of trade rules. The US has fiercely resisted any 'right to development', focusing instead on states' responsibilities to develop themselves, and their obligation to liberalise markets (Marks 2004), and many other Western countries have viewed this Declaration as an 'invasion into what should be ... the discretionary/voluntary field of development assistance, where spelling out precise obligations is anathema' (Cornwall and Nyamu-Musembi 2004: 1422). It may be that this 'right' is of limited value, but some socio-economic rights are evident even in articles 22 through to 26 of the 1948 Declaration of Human Rights itself. Even implementing the economic rights of this Declaration (including the right to work, to favourable remuneration to preserve human dignity, to unionisation, social protection and so on) would require radical transformations of existing practices and patterns of wealth distribution, and of the economic hierarchies that characterise our world. As David Harvey (2000: 90) puts it, for instance, 'strict enforcement of these rights would entail massive and in some sense revolutionary transformations in the political economy of capitalism'. In particular, Harvey advocates a 'living wage' as a plank of resistance to globalising capitalism (see also Hardt and Negri 2000; Drainville 2004); such a policy has also been a key goal of movements such as the World and European Social Forums. Such a goal may be emblematic of the struggle to close the 'dualism' of global citizenship practices, which proclaim human equality in the face of desperate inequalities and protect the privileges of powerful economic actors over the less powerful.

Healthy citizens?

> AIDS has become the new anti-apartheid movement demanding drugs and health for all. Sick and dying bodies are the signs of our greedy times, when wealthy nations exploit others ... this could be a new democratic beginning of sorts ... a politics which rejects global riches at the expense of people's health and bodies. (Eisenstein 2004: 47)

In many ways rights to health are amongst the least secure of all the rights proclaimed by the UN, and the conventional assertion that it is the responsibility of states to safeguard the health of 'their own' citizens serves to conceal the inegalitarian effects of neoliberalism on global health, and the impact of structural adjustment policies on domestic health-care systems (see e.g. Fort *et al.* 2004). Nevertheless for Evans (2002) the human right to health accepted under international law is potentially a lever for radical change, and particularly for resisting the narrow version of rights inherent in global liberalism. Problems of health are strongly linked to poverty, and given this fact even a basic commitment to the right to health is potentially radical in its implications. The conflict between the rights to health and to private property is powerfully on display in debates over HIV/AIDS, as Zillah Eisenstein suggests. The current US administration, for instance, has tended to adopt a neoconservative strategy on the AIDS epidemic, treating it as an issue of national security and strategic interests rather than 'humanitarian' concern. It has broadly underplayed the human right to health, focusing instead on the rights of African citizens, for example, to expect 'good governance' from their own nation-states (Fidler 2004: 128). And finally, it has also attempted to defend private intellectual property rights in antiretroviral drugs over the socio-economic right to health, in resisting the ability of African countries to produce cheaper versions of drugs patented in the US. Nevertheless, several African states, along with NGOs, have scored some small but significant victories in overturning US policy here; this may be a grudging defeat for a US regime determined to avoid responsibility for health on a global scale (Fidler 2004: 132), or it might represent a crack in the armour of neoliberal citizenship.

Sexed and raced citizens?   Despite erstwhile fears over the dangers of universalism, a belief in the progressive potential of human rights discourse is increasingly evident in some feminist circles. Feminist activists have appealed, for example, to the language of reproductive rights (see e.g. Madden 1999), as well as the human rights of trafficked women in order to advance the struggle against sexism in all its forms. More recently critics have explored the links between sexuality and human rights discourse, in seeking to uncover and challenge the conceptions of the individual and the family present in international jurisprudence. Two currently contentious issues include the legal recognition of transgendered individuals and relationships (Whittle 1999), and the issue of whether oppression on the basis of sexuality provides good grounds for claiming refugee status (Millbank 2004). Generally, progress here has been slow: the European Court of Human Rights, for instance, has until now refused to recognise same-sex partnerships as 'families' within its provisions on 'privacy and family life', and has often refused to rule against discrimination against homosexuals (Wintemute 1995). The same is true of international human rights law more generally, where recent decisions have affirmed the ability of homosexuals to 'avoid' persecution by acting with discretion and propriety (Millbank 2004), thus promoting on a global scale an image of what Smith (1994) has called the 'good homosexual'. Debates on human rights are therefore implicated in competing definitions of sexual propriety, the family, and the (public or private) place of sexuality; nevertheless opposition to more egalitarian conceptions may be shifting, and activists with many states have appealed to human rights law against the intransigence of their own governments. More broadly, for some critics the ingredients of radical resistance to sexism are contained within discourses on human rights. Kate Nash (2002), for instance, has argued that the idea of 'degendering' implicit in the Convention on the Elimination of all forms of Discrimination Against Women (adopted by the UN in 1979) is compatible with a post-structuralist model of gender equality involving 'the continual disruption of gender inequalities without penalty or disadvantage to any person' (though it is worth noting that this is the Convention with the most state 'reservations'). Similar conclusions have been reached on race and culture, with some commentators pointing to the emancipatory potential of the World Conferences Against Racism, heralding perhaps a more 'polyversal humanity' beyond racism (Eisenstein 2004). Such an argument runs close to Paul Gilroy's (2000) argument for a critical cosmopolitan imagination as an essential element in constructing a 'planetary humanism' which will resist racism. Indeed there may be some precursors for this in the transnational anti-apartheid and anti-slavery coalitions (Klotz 2002). Ultimately, this approach implies a version of what I have called a critical group principle of equality, and a widening struggle to disaggregate rewards, privileges and roles from hierarchical constructions of sexual or racial difference (see Chapter 5).

Ecological citizens? Recent years have witnessed increasing interest in the ideal of citizenship on the part of green theorists and activists (see e.g. Dobson 2003), and some theorists have mobilised the idea of 'citizenship of planet Earth' in order to gesture towards a culture of responsibility, personal activism and egal-itarian community (see e.g. Steward 1991). For Falk (1994), the language of world citizenship is an essential tool with which to intervene to 'redesign polit-ical choices', and transform political behaviour, on the basis of an ecological sense of sustainability. The progress of ecological concerns into human rights law has been more difficult, but there are some signs of success (including the incorporation of a right to a safe environment into the African and soon the American Conventions on Human Rights). It has been argued that this right to a safe environment might focus resistance to 'threats to human life and health from technological and industrial processes' (Nickel and Viola 2003: 472), and as such bolster a commitment to equality and democracy; some indeed have seen environmental justice as 'only one aspect of a far wider project that involves social justice, democratization and demilitarization' (Falk 2001: 222). Some of the issues that are currently being debated within this field bring to bear fundamental issues of justice and subjectivity: in terms of justice, currently contentious issues include the boundaries of intellectual property rights; the rights of ecological refugees; the rights of indigenous peoples and land rights; rights to use non-renewable resources or to draw on the earth's finite capacity to absorb pollutants. Each of these potentially challenges the focuses of existing human rights law – which may be one reason why their implementation has been resisted so far – and in each case the arguments of ecologists often dovetail with the claims of radical egalitarians (see e.g. Singer 2002). In terms of subjectivity, struggles over ecological rights signal the contestation of what counts as the 'human' of human rights, as illustrated by debates over intergenerational justice (are the 'humans' in human rights those living now, or prospective humans?) and animal rights (can apes be citizens?), whilst ecological arguments more broadly challenge the ascendancy of the masculine, possessive individualist subject of discourses of human rights. Indeed it may be that ecological arguments present the most wide-ranging challenge, and the site of greatest resistance, to neoliberal visions of global citizenship.

Notes

1 For some commentators, the spread of liberal rights also transforms – or even produces – the individual itself. Yeatman (2000), a supporter of the universal discourse of human rights, celebrates the fact that the global human rights regime can be credited with 'the creation of individuality as such'. Others are less satisfied with the results of this process. Discussing the case of Africa, Tom Young (1995: 531) argues that '"free individuals" and the rest of the liberal agenda do not emerge "naturally", but are the result of political and social processes which are often coercive in nature'. A '"radical disengagement" opens the prospect of "self-remaking"'; as 'such "emancipated" individuals can more easily be welded into collectivities and subjected to various forms of social discipline' (Young 1995: 531). On this view, the only identity protected by the dominant human rights discourse is the identity of the competitive, unique, utility maximiser. If so, as Hopgood (2000: 21) aptly puts it, 'Human rights do not protect identities, they open them up for the process of complete transformation. Acknowledging this fact is vital, at the very least, to creating a space for those critical of liberalism, and those engaged in actual resistance to it, to undermine the natural, truth-like status of human rights claims.'

2 Indeed one of the tools which neoliberal politicians deploy to rise to the challenges of globalisation may even be national identity itself. The project of 'rebranding Britain' is perhaps the foremost example, but such trends are notable elsewhere. Mark Laffey makes this point well in his analysis of debates over national identity in New Zealand, concluding that 'As workforces are internationalised and states seek "high quality" and "hybridised" subjects as assets in pursuit of global competitiveness, so narratives of place and belonging, of self and other, become a potential object of state strategy, to be reworked or not, according to circumstance and need' (Laffey 1999: 257).

3 Thus Walzer (1996) is certainly right, for instance, that a global welfare system would ride rough-shod over the norms and traditions of diverse communities, but then so does the global economic system on a daily basis, especially when 'the cultural particularities of other countries are viewed as xenophobic barriers to the expansion of capital' (Gill 1995: 410). The work of communitarians and liberal nationalists is unfortunately characterised by a spirited condemnation of the abstract universalism of cosmopolitan theory, and timid condemnations of global capitalism that imply we could best 'domesticate' it by refraining from just some of the most visible forms of exploitation. 'Resolving' things in this way allows global capitalism to have its cake and eat it, and misses, on my analysis, an opportunity to turn the immanent value of the ideal of equal citizenship to radical effect.

4 On a related theme, Kate Nash has lamented the fact that within the literature on cosmopolitanism, the dominant approach is predominantly 'rationalist': little is said about the significance of 'emotional' attachments to other humans, as opposed to the power of universalising 'reason'. In particular Nash shows how 'Identification with a national community is typically associated with "hot" emotions, and opposed to "cool" cosmopolitanism as an ideal' (Nash 2003: 506). This is clearly observable in the liberal cosmopolitan literature, where 'The emotional "coolness" of neo-Kantian cosmopolitanism is related to its basis in liberal-democratic human rights rather than in political community' (Nash 2002: 508). This idea needs to be resisted, though, as 'the dichotomy makes it difficult to see how "warm" cosmopolitanism is actually developing in political communities organized by western national states'. In developing the grounds for an ethic of global responsibility and transnational solidarities, we may need to look closer at what Lamont and Aksartova (2002) call 'ordinary cosmopolitanisms'.

5 On this point, Craig Calhoun is right to observe that 'the political theory of cosmopolitanism is shaped by liberalism's poorly drawn fight with communitarianism and thus left lacking a strong account of solidarity' (Calhoun 2003: 88); it is unfortunate that within the 'liberal-communitarian debate' ideas of community, solidarity and identity have been monopolised by communitarian (or nationalist) positions, at the same time as they have been deleted altogether from liberal positions. If a viable cosmopolitanism is to develop, as Calhoun argues, we will need precisely an account of how social solidarities might emerge in order to provide the basis for a less exclusionary form of citizenship (Calhoun 2003: 96). What such a project seems to require is an account of solidarity in the face of diversity, and Young's notion of 'differentiated solidarity' may provide the beginnings of such an account. For Young, whilst solidarity can arise on the basis of common problems and common social institutions (in the sense of a common, though complex, basic structure of capitalism, sexism, racism and so on), such a solidarity can only be built, and not assumed, given the diversity and hybridity of contemporary allegiances and identities (2000: 221–5).

6 Pogge also supports the idea of a Tobin Tax – a half per cent levy on international currency trading. Such an idea has been approved by the Canadian Parliament as a result of campaigns by NGOs, but clearly depends on multilateral support to gain force. The Tax was the original rallying-point for the transnational movement ATTAC (Association for the Taxation of financial Transactions for the Aid of Citizens), which has now gone on to campaign for more radical political and economic change.

Conclusion

THIS BOOK has covered a good deal of ground, and so in the Conclusion I will briefly summarise the major arguments that have been defended, and indicate some future challenges for the approach I have taken to egalitarian theory. Carol Bacchi (1999) has argued that any policy-related discourse (and the egalitarian literature meets that definition, at least most of the time) depends upon a particular framing of the social or political 'problem' it tries to solve. Though the terms of this framing are often implicit, we can learn a lot by bringing to the surface the precise ways in which the relevant problem is understood. Some framings may in the end turn out to be unhelpful or obfuscatory, whereas framing a political problem in a novel way can open up new horizons of inquiry and may make different political remedies look more attractive. Seen in this light, we could say that the task this book set itself has been to contribute towards a reframing, or reorientation of the political theory of equality. It began by drawing a distinction between two such framings: the approach which is prevalent in the 'equality of what?' literature, and an alternative approach that is made possible by conceiving equality and inequality in relation to the ideal of equal citizenship. Broadly speaking, the arguments of Part I of the book sought to criticise – and ultimately reject – the ways in which inequality (and therefore equality) have been framed within the liberal egalitarian literature, whereas Part II sought to interrogate how equality and inequality might be conceived in more productive ways.

Although Part I saw a number of diverse criticisms levelled at the theories of Rawls, Dworkin and the luck egalitarians, these chapters had three broad goals. The first set of concerns were more theoretical, insofar as I sought to question whether the theoretical arsenal of modern liberal egalitarianism is really up to the task of theorising (and hence responding to) the complex inequalities that characterise contemporary societies. Amongst other things, in the first three chapters I examined the inadequate response to structural inequalities presented by Rawls, Dworkin and the luck egalitarians. To be sure, this problem manifests itself in different ways: in Rawls, for example, it is apparent in the failure to take group-based inequalities as well as global injustices seriously as elements of the basic structure of contemporary society. In the work of Dworkin and the luck egalitarians, the problem is reflected in the difficulty of subsuming a variety of inequalities under one potentially misleading choice/chance distinction. Although the liberal debate on egalitarian justice has been lively and prolific, if we understand equality as involving (at least in part) the struggle against racism, sexism, and the neoliberal transformation of society, for instance, then these theories have made far less impressive contributions.

The second set of concerns were more 'political' in the conventional sense, insofar as they addressed, amongst other things, the way in which liberal (and especially luck) egalitarians have positioned themselves in relation to their ideological opponents. Following the halcyon days of social welfarism, a New Right (or more broadly, neoliberal) onslaught has succeeded to a large extent in redefining the terms of citizenship and the appropriate role of the state. Universal social provisions have been lambasted for generating the moral hazard of dependency and for robbing the industrious to pay for the feckless; in the face of such a critique, equality begins to look like the 'endangered species' (Dworkin 2000: 1) of the ideological arena. This critique has not passed liberal egalitarians by. Rather, by their own admission it has provided an impetus for the development of a 'new' egalitarianism which would avoid the mistakes of the 'old' variety (see e.g. Dworkin 2000).

My analysis of this 'new' egalitarianism has been broadly critical: whilst political gains are supposedly made by incorporating the values of choice and responsibility from New Right or neoliberal rhetoric, the protagonists in the luck egalitarian debate have not properly interrogated the ways in which these ideas are deployed within neoliberal discourse, and the problems of the neoliberal account have not, therefore, been adequately resisted. Chapter 2 argued that Dworkin's theory incorporates a neoliberal sensibility, defending a mixture of private and public provision on the basis of individuals' variable ability to manage risk prudently, rather than on the values of community and solidarity that underpinned the social state (and Rawls's theory) in the era of social citizenship. It was not my contention that Dworkin's account equates to, or has no major differences with, neoliberal discourse. But it has been argued that Dworkin's account shares an 'elective affinity' with certain neoliberal ideas that means his theory possesses very few resources with which to challenge its ideological ascendancy. Chapter 3 took these arguments a little further by drawing a comparison between luck equality and another noteworthy attempt to head off the New Right critique by co-opting some of its core elements: namely, the New Labour vision of social inclusion. Coding equality as inclusion, and inequality as exclusion, New Labour has developed a set of policies which define inequality primarily in terms of the inability or unwillingness to participate in the formal economy. As such equality becomes a 'gatekeeping' concept, whereby individuals are exhorted to make prudent choices under conditions of (some) equality of opportunity, but as a result of which radical critique of social or economic institutions takes a back seat. The task of this chapter was not to argue for any simple equivalence between the two discourses, though their fascination with the interlinked concepts of opportunity, responsibility and choice is remarkably similar. But the point was to say that if New Labour has ultimately accommodated itself to neoliberalism, as Hall (2003) has argued, then liberal egalitarians also threaten to make such an accommodation.

Given this book's preoccupation with the theme of citizenship, my third concern was to analyse the ways in which liberal approaches to equality intersect with existing practices or discourses of citizenship. Rawls of course was explicit about the regulatory role the ideal of equal citizenship plays in his theory, but told us very little about how that ideal resembled or diverged from either pre-existing theories or real-world practices of citizenship, and by and large the critical literature has followed his lead. I tried to remedy this disjuncture in Chapter 1 by analysing Rawls's theory alongside the discourse of social citizenship. The overarching goal of Rawls's project appears to be that of closing the (political/economic) dualism of liberal citizenship. It is highly questionable whether this goal is achieved, though, since (like Marshall) Rawls remained ambiguous on the precise economic implications of his theory. Furthermore, the account is hampered by its inadequate theorisation of the many forms of inequality that afflict present-day societies. We could say that although Rawls tried earnestly to tackle the political/economic dualism that Marx diagnosed, he failed to acknowledge, and therefore was unable to respond to, the other major dualisms that have inflected Western citizenship practices (between men/women, black/white, gay/straight, insider/outsider and so on). As a result Rawls (again, like Marshall) failed to recognise just how transformative a project a genuinely equal citizenship would be.

One of the key arguments of Part I was that the development of post-Rawlsian liberal egalitarian theory, on the other hand, clearly parallels the transition from social citizenship to the neoliberal vision of active citizenship. Recent decades have witnessed a neoliberal onslaught on the social state, entailing a hollowing-out of social rights and provisions, a move to two-tierist, public/private provision, an exhortation on citizens to behave prudently and to take an entrepreneurial approach to the risks we all face. All of these trends come to the fore, in various ways, in Dworkin's much more theoretical writings, and have their parallels in the liberal luck egalitarian literature he has inspired. The neoliberal vision of active citizenship places huge emphasis on the importance of individual choice but, like the luck egalitarian account, understands this to mean choice within the market and not within meaningful democratic institutions, for instance. This vision of active citizenship has not gone unchallenged, however, and feminists, disabled activists and other radical egalitarians have instead suggested an opposing conception of active citizenship that focuses on the importance of political participation, democratic self-determination and the drive to further embed the 'democratic revolution' described by Mouffe (1993). Whilst the discourses of social citizenship and of active citizenship are to be found wanting, both may offer resources for theorists and activists seeking to entrench and deepen the commitment to equality and to democracy.

Whereas the arguments of Part I were mainly critical, the chapters that make up Part II sought to commence a reframing of the problem of inequality which would highlight the interconnections between equality, inequality and the modern ideal of citizenship. Though these chapters dealt with a range of issues, the guiding thread of the argument has been that transformative approaches to citizenship provide powerful resources for framing a more satisfactory variety of egalitarian politics. Chapters 4 and 5 examined two of the characteristic preoccupations of much contemporary egalitarian argument: opportunity and responsibility. Chapter 4 set out to delineate at least the beginnings of a more critical egalitarian approach to the issue of responsibility. The goal was to generate an account of responsibility that might be mobilised against, rather than with, neoliberalism, by opening out that concept and interpreting it in more politically challenging ways. Whereas luck egalitarians have assumed that a relatively narrow conception of responsibility can provide the basis for egalitarian theory, in this chapter I employed the notion of privileged irresponsibility in order to assess how egalitarians could integrate a concern for responsibilities to care, and for ecological, corporate and global responsibilities. Chapter 5, by contrast, examined the role that the ideal of opportunity should play in a satisfactory egalitarian theory. It was argued here that equality of opportunity is not capable of fully fleshing out the ambitions of egalitarians, and that as a regulatory ideal it encounters serious problems. A concern for equal citizenship will grant that opportunities are important, but insist that they are not all that matters. Drawing on the work of Young and Phillips, I argued instead for a critical group-oriented principle of equality, which indicates that a critical egalitarian politics should seek to end substantial equalities in incomes *and* social roles such as caring aggregating around hierarchical constructions of race or ethnicity, or binary constructions of sex and sexuality, for instance. In addition a critical egalitarian defence of citizenship suggests a continual scrutiny of established hierarchies of respect and reward within the major institutions of society.

In Chapter 6, I examined Fraser's account of participatory parity, which asserts the moral equality of all members of a democratic community, and sets about the task of interpreting the prerequisites for that common status to become meaningful. In response to the pervasive dualisms and hierarchies of citizenship practices, the ideal of equal citizenship offers a location where diverse claims for equality can be played out and negotiated. This is also an open-ended ideal: although parity of participation or equal citizenship will continually function as the reference point of political struggle, it is an ideal that is flexible and open-ended, not one that points towards a predetermined destination. Although the claims for justice of cultural, ethnic or sexual minorities, for example, may appear to be self-serving, each potentially pushes us in the direction of a more equal citizenship for all, by challenging the way in which equality (and citizenship) is presently defined in such a manner as to serve the interests of dominant groups. As Smith (1998: 135) has put it, citizenship serves as an 'articulating principle' through which our diverse commitments and radical impulses are mediated, the 'nodal point' for a critical politics which aims to deliver on the promise of equality for all.

Chapter 6 also cast doubt on Fraser's recognition/redistribution framework, however, and argued instead for the centrality of hierarchy and oppression as the key targets of egalitarian politics. Whilst the idea of resistance to oppression is familiar enough to those acquainted with the work of Young (1990), for example, the argument that equal citizenship is opposed to hierarchy may be less familiar. My claim here is not that we should aim to obliterate all forms of hierarchy, because after all some hierarchies are useful and necessary. Rather, my argument is that egalitarianism involves a continual suspicion of institutional hierarchies, and a commitment to mitigating their inegalitarian effects. There are many ways in which this idea might be applied. One concerns the hierarchies of economic life which were discussed in Chapter 5. Another case is that of 'identity': although such an argument is missing from liberal theory, I would argue that egalitarian politics implies the goal of mitigating the impact that the hierarchical construction of difference has on the lives of individuals, and even targeting those symbolic hierarchies themselves. Finally, and at the broadest level, the resistance to hierarchy involves a struggle against the way in which membership or citizenship is based around the exclusion or marginalisation of others, whose energies are required to sustain the way of life of citizens but who are excluded from the possibility of becoming full citizens themselves. In the context of citizenship the opposition to hierarchy implies a commitment to resisting the dependence of one person's full membership on someone else's exclusion or 'otherness', and the continual interrogation of the ways in which citizenship practices depend on unequal relations with 'internal' and 'external' others.

Whilst the citizenship-oriented approach allows us to avoid some of the problems of the 'equality of what' debate, it clearly brings to bear its own problems and challenges, and Chapter 7 addressed one of the most significant of these challenges. Specifically, this final chapter examined the potential of global citizenship to act as a vehicle for egalitarian concerns. Here, it became clear that the project of employing the ideal of equal citizenship as a vehicle for egalitarian aspirations is not going to be a straightforward affair at the global level.

Indeed, many recent proclamations about the emergence of a meaningful form of global citizenship politics need to be treated with considerable caution. Rather, a thin conception of global citizenship – comprising a liberal interpretation of human rights focused on capitalist economic rights, allied with a thin notion of both human responsibilities and of common political action – has proven a useful resource for defending and entrenching the growing inequalities that disfigure the global scene. Nevertheless, even this thin discourse of citizenship does provide some critical resources, and in this final chapter I gestured towards some of the ways in which the notion of privileged irresponsibility, as well as the discourse of human rights, might be enlisted in the ongoing struggle against neoliberalism, racism, sexism and the other forms of structural injustice that characterise the contemporary world.

All of the above suggests two things. The first is that it is worthwhile, and indeed necessary, for theorists to try to think further beyond the narrow confines of the 'equality of what' debate, and to continue to question the philosophical and political assumptions that are often taken for granted there. Given the current preoccupations of that literature, this will involve continuing reflection on the usefulness or otherwise of the various components that make up much contemporary egalitarian discourse – among them the concepts of opportunity, choice and responsibility. Given their pre-eminence in some of the dominant political discourses of our times, such concepts cannot simply be ignored, and it is to the credit of egalitarian theory over the last quarter of a century that such concepts have been grappled with at all. But in much of the preceding argument I have tried to open out these concepts, to refuse to take them at face value, and to ask to what other purposes, beyond the obsessions of neoliberals, they might be put. At the same time, though, I have argued that these concepts cannot flesh out an adequate egalitarian account, and that in sketching the contours of a more satisfactory approach we will need to look elsewhere too: and specifically towards a vision of a genuinely inclusive, egalitarian and democratic form of citizenship.

Theorising equality in relation to citizenship is not, as I observed in the Introduction to this book, entirely new. In that sense it might be appropriate to describe this project as one of retrieval, or of recovering a link which has been partially lost within the liberal egalitarian debate of recent years (see also Levine 1998; Anderson 1999a; Scheffler 2003). But such an exercise cannot only be one of recovery, for it is the contemporary revival in critical work on citizenship, perhaps, which presents the greatest resources – and challenges – to contemporary egalitarian theory. This book has tried in its own way to stage a kind of encounter between the contemporary literatures on equality and on citizenship, but has only begun such a project. My second suggestion, then, is that egalitarians can continue to draw inspiration from critical work on citizenship: from feminist efforts to 'rechart the terrain of citizenship' (Jaggar 2005: 4), from disabled activists' critiques of the exclusion of disabled people from full citizenship (Oliver 1990), from analyses and reformulations of citizenship practices as they relate to sexuality (Monro and Warren 2004), to ethnicity or race (see e.g. Werbner 1999), and from critiques of the emptiness of political citizenship in the face of widening economic inequalities (see e.g. Phillips 1999; Pateman 2005). And in line with the arguments of the final chapter, egalitarian theorists need to pay close attention to the challenges and possibilities that are held out by contemporary transformations of citizenship practices, and by the dismantling of the package of nation-state, identity, community and power that has underpinned equality politics in recent decades. Whilst an emphasis on citizenship may provide shape and force to egalitarian commitments, egalitarians may themselves play a useful role in imagining citizenship practices that are less marked by exclusion, oppression and hierarchy.

References

Ackerman, Bruce (1980) *Social Justice in a Liberal State*, New Haven: Yale University Press.

Alejandro, Roberto (1996) 'What Is Political About Rawls's Political Liberalism?', *Journal of Politics* 58(1): 1–24.

_____ (1998) *The Limits of Rawlsian Justice*, Baltimore: Johns Hopkins University Press.

Alund, Aleksandra (1999) 'Feminism, Multiculturalism, Essentialism', in Nira Yuval-Davis and Pnina Werbner (eds) *Women, Citizenship and Difference*, London: Zed Books, pp. 147–61.

Amoore, Louise and Paul Langley (2004) 'Ambiguities of Global Civil Society', *Review of International Studies* 30(1): 89–110.

Anderson, Elizabeth (1999a) 'What Is the Point of Equality?', *Ethics* 109: 287–337.

_____ (1999b) *Reply to Arneson*, online paper on Brown University Department of Philosophy's BEARS website. Can be found at: www.brown.edu/Departments/Philosophy/bears/9912ande.html.

Andreasson, Stefan (2006 forthcoming) 'Stand and Deliver: Private Property and the Politics of Global Dispossession', *Political Studies*.

Anheier, Helmut, Marlies Glasius and Mary Kaldor (2001) 'Introducing Global Civil Society', in Anheier, Glasius and Kaldor (eds) *Global Civil Society 2001*, Oxford: Oxford University Press, pp. 3–22.

Archibugi, Daniele (1998) 'Principles of Cosmopolitan Democracy', in Daniele Archibugi, David Held and Martin Kohler (eds) *Reimagining Political Community*, Cambridge: Polity, pp. 198–228.

Arestis, Philip and Malcolm Sawyer (2005) 'Neoliberalism and the Third Way', in Alfredo Saad-Filho and Deborah Johnston (eds) *Neoliberalism: A Critical Reader*, London: Pluto, pp. 177–83.

Armstrong, Chris (2002) 'Complex Equality: Beyond Equality and Difference', *Feminist Theory* 3(1), 67–82.

_____ (2003a) 'Opportunity, Responsibility and the Market: Interrogating

References

Liberal Equality', *Economy and Society* 32(3): 410–27.

_____ (2003b) 'Some Reflections on Equality of Power', *Imprints* 7(1): 44–53.

_____ (2003c) 'Equality, Recognition and the Distributive Paradigm', *Critical Review of International Social and Political Philosophy* 6(3): 154–64.

Arneson, Richard (1989) 'Equality and Equality of Opportunity for Welfare', *Philosophical Studies* 56: 77–93.

_____ (1997a) 'Egalitarianism and the Undeserving Poor', *Journal of Political Philosophy* 5(4): 327–50.

_____ (1997b) 'Postscript – 1995', in Louis Pojman and Robert Westmoreland (eds) *Equality: Selected Readings*, Oxford: Oxford University Press, pp. 238–41.

_____ (1999) 'Equality of Opportunity for Welfare Defended and Recanted', *Journal of Political Philosophy* 7: 488–97.

_____ (2000a) 'Egalitarian Justice versus the Right to Privacy', *Social Philosophy and Policy* 17(2): 91–119.

_____ (2000b) 'Luck Egalitarianism and Prioritarianism', *Ethics* 110: 339–49.

_____ (2001) 'Luck and Equality', *Proceedings of the Aristotelian Society Supplement*, pp. 73–90.

Bacchi, Carol Lee (1996) *The Politics of Affirmative Action: 'Women', Equality and Category Politics*, London: Sage.

_____ (1999) *Women, Policy and Politics: The Construction of Policy and Politics*, London: Sage.

Bader, Veit (1995) 'Citizenship and Exclusion: Radical Democracy, Community and Justice', *Political Theory* 23(2): 211–46.

Baker, Gideon (2002) 'Problems in the Theorisation of Global Civil Society', *Political Studies* 50(5): 928–43.

Baker, John (1987) *Arguing for Equality*, London: Verso.

_____ (1990) 'What Equality Is Not'. Online paper, can be found on the Equality Exchange website: http://aran.univ-pau.fr/ee/page3.html.

_____ (1997) 'Studying Equality', *Imprints* 2(1): 57–71.

Baker, John, Kathleen Lynch, Sara Cantillon and Judy Walsh (2004) *Equality: From Theory to Practice*, London: Palgrave Macmillan.

Baker, Tom and Jonathan Simon (2002) 'Embracing Risk', in Baker and Simon (eds) *Embracing Risk: The Changing Culture of Insurance and Responsibility*, Chicago: Chicago University Press, pp. 1–25.

Balibar, Etienne (2002) *Politics and the Other Scene*, London: Verso.

Barbalet, J.M. (1994) 'Citizenship, Class Inequality and Resentment', in Bryan Turner (ed.) *Citizenship and Social Theory*, London: Sage, pp. 36–56.

Barber, Benjamin (1989) 'Justifying Justice: Problems of Psychology, Politics and Measurement in Rawls', in Norman Daniels (ed.) *Reading Rawls*, Oxford: Blackwell, pp. 292–318.

Barry, Brian (1973) 'John Rawls and the Priority of Liberty', *Philosophy and Public Affairs* 2: 274–90.

References

_____ (1989) *Theories of Justice*, London: Harvester Wheatsheaf.

_____ (1991) 'Chance, Choice and Justice', in *Liberty and Justice: Essays in Political Theory 2*, Oxford: Clarendon Press, pp. 142–58.

_____ (2001) *Culture and Equality. An Egalitarian Critique of Multiculturalism*, Cambridge: Polity Press.

_____ (2005) *Why Social Justice Matters*, Cambridge: Polity Press.

De Beauvoir, Simone (1997) *The Second Sex*, London: Virago.

Bebchuk, Lucian, Jesse Fried and David Walker (2002) 'Managerial Power and Rent Extraction in the Design of Executive Compensation', *University of Chicago Law Review* 69: 751–846.

Behnke, Andreas (1997) 'Citizenship, Nationhood and the Production of Political Space', *Citizenship Studies* 1(2): 243–66.

Beitz, Charles (1979) *Political Theory and International Relations*, Princeton: Princeton University Press.

_____ (2000) 'Rawls's Law of Peoples', *Ethics* 110(4): 669–96.

Bell, Lynda, Andrew Nathan and Ilan Peleg (eds) (2001) *Negotiating Culture and Human Rights*, New York: Columbia University Press.

Beneria, Lourdes (1979) 'Reproduction, Production and the Sexual Division of Labor', *Cambridge Journal of Economics* 3: 203–25

Benhabib, Seyla (2001) 'Transformations of Citizenship: The Case of Contemporary Europe', *Government and Opposition* 37(4): 439–65.

_____ (2002) *The Claims of Culture: Equality and Diversity in the Global Era*, Princeton: Princeton University Press.

Benn, S.I. and R.S. Peters (1959) *Social Principles and the Democratic State*, London: Allen & Unwin.

Best, Jacqueline (2003) 'From the Top Down: The New Financial Architecture and the Re-embedding of Global Finance', *New Political Economy* 8(3): 363–84.

Bhatt, Chetan (1994) 'New Foundations: Contingency, Indeterminacy and Black Translocality', in Jeffrey Weeks (ed.) *The Lesser Evil and the Greater Good*, London: Rivers Oram Press, pp. 138–64.

Blair, Tony (1992) Interview in *The Guardian Newspaper*, 30 June.

_____ (2002) Speech in Hackney, 18 September.

_____ (2004) Labour Annual Conference speech, 28 September.

Blair, Tony and Gerhard Schroeder (1999) *Europe: The Third Way/Die Neue Mitte*, joint policy paper launched on 8 June.

Blake, Michael and Mathias Risse (2004) 'Two Models of Equality and Responsibility'. Paper presented at Harvard University conference on The Theory and Practice of Equality, April.

Booth, Ken and Tim Dunne (1999) 'Learning Beyond Frontiers', in Tim Dunne and Nicholas Wheeler (eds) *Human Rights in Global Politics*, Cambridge: Cambridge University Press, pp. 303–28.

References

Brighouse, Harry and Erik Olin Wright (2002) 'On Alex Callinicos's Equality', *Historical Materialism* 10(1): 193–222.

Brown, Chris (2001) 'Cosmopolitanism, World Citizenship and Civil Society', in Simon Caney and Peter Jones (eds) *Human Rights and Global Diversity*, London: Frank Cass, pp. 7–26.

Brubaker, Rogers (ed.) (1989) *Immigration and the Politics of Citizenship in Europe and North America*, Lanham: University Press of America.

Bryson, Valerie (2004) 'Marxism and Feminism: can the "Unhappy Marriage" Be Saved?', *Journal of Political Ideologies* 9(1): 13–30.

Burchell, David (1995) 'The Attributes of Citizens: Virtues, Manners and the Activity of Citizenship', *Economy and Society* 24(4): 540–68.

Butler, Judith (1995) 'For a Careful Reading', in Linda Nicholson (ed.) *Feminist Contentions: A Philosophical Exchange*, London: Routledge, pp. 127–43.

_____ (1998) 'Merely Cultural', *New Left Review* 227: 33–44.

Butler, Judith, Ernesto Laclau and Slavoj Žižek (2000) *Contingency, Hegemony, Universality*, London: Verso.

Calhoun, Craig (2003) 'The Class Consciousness of Frequent Travellers: Towards a Critique of Actually Existing Cosmopolitanism', in Daniele Archibugi (ed.) *Debating Cosmopolitics*, London: Verso, pp. 86–116.

Callinicos, Alex (2000) *Equality*, Cambridge: Polity Press.

_____ (2001a) *Against the Third Way*, Cambridge: Polity Press.

_____ (2001b) 'Review Essay on Cohen, Dworkin and Roemer', *Historical Materialism* 9: 169–95.

Casal, Paula and Andrew Williams (2004) 'Equality of Resources and Procreative Justice', in Justine Burley (ed.) *Dworkin and His Critics*, Oxford: Blackwell, pp. 150–69.

Cerda, Jose Ortega (2005) 'It Is also a European Tragedy', in *The Guardian* Newspaper, 5 January (reprinted from an article originally published in *El Pais*, Madrid).

Cerny, Philip (1995) 'Globalization and the Changing Logic of Collective Action', *International Organisation* 49(4): 595–625.

Chandler, David (2003) 'New Rights for Old? Cosmopolitan Citizenship and the Critique of State Sovereignty', *Political Studies* 51(2): 332–49.

_____ (2004) 'Building Global Civil Society "From Below"', *Millennium: Journal of International Studies* 33(2): 313–40.

Chunn, Dorothy and Shelley Gavigan (2004) 'Welfare Law, Welfare Fraud, and the Moral Regulation of the "Never Deserving" Poor', *Social and Legal Studies* 13(2): 219–43.

Cohen, G. A. (1989) 'On the Currency of Egalitarian Justice', *Ethics* 99: 906–44.

_____ (1992) 'Incentives, Inequality and Community', in G. Peterson (ed.) *The Tanner Lectures on Human Values* 13, Salt Lake City: University of Utah Press, pp. 261–329.

References

_____ (2000) *If You're an Egalitarian, How Come You're So Rich?*, Cambridge, Massachusetts: Harvard University Press.

_____ (2004) 'Expensive Taste Rides Again', in Justine Burley (ed.) *Dworkin and His Critics*, Oxford: Blackwell, pp. 3–29.

Collins, Patricia Hill (1999) 'Producing the Mothers of the Nation: Race, Class and Contemporary US Population Policies', in Nira Yuval-Davis and Pnina Werbner (eds) *Women, Citizenship and Difference*, London: Zed Books, pp. 118–29.

Connell, R.W. (2002) *Gender*, Cambridge: Polity.

Connolly, William (1991) *Identity/Difference*, Ithaca: Cornell University Press.

_____ (1999) *Why I Am Not a Secularist*, Minneapolis: University of Minnesota Press.

Conover, Pamela, Donald Searing and Ivor Crewe (2004) 'The Elusive Ideal of Equal Citizenship: Political Theory and Political Pschology in the United States and Great Britain', *Journal of Politics* 66(4): 1036–68.

Cook, Robin (2003) 'France Need Not Fear Schoolgirls in Headscarves: Britain's Multicultural Approach Enriches Our Lives and Gives Us a Competitive Advantage in the Global Economy', *The Independent Newspaper*, 19 December.

Cooper, Davina (2000) '"And You Can't Find Me Nowhere": Relocating Identity and Structure Within Equality Jurisprudence', *Journal of Law and Society* 27(2): 249–72.

_____ (2004) *Challenging Diversity: Rethinking Equality and the Value of Difference*, Cambridge: Cambridge University Press.

Cornwall, Andrea and Celestine Nyamu-Musembi (2004) 'Putting the "Rights-Based Approach" to Development into Perspective', *Third World Quarterly* 25(8): 1415–38.

Corrigan, Philip and Derek Sayer (1985) *The Great Arch: English State Formation as Cultural Revolution*, London: Basil Blackwell.

Danermark, Berth and Lotta Gellerstedt (2004) 'Social Justice: Redistribution and Recognition: a Non-reductionist Perspective on Disability', *Disability & Society* 19(4): 339–53.

Daniels, Norman (1989) 'Equal Liberty and Unequal Worth of Liberty', in Daniels (ed.) *Reading Rawls*, Oxford: Blackwell, pp. 253–81.

_____ (2003) 'Democratic Equality: Rawls's Complex Egalitarianism', in Samuel Freeman (ed.) *The Cambridge Companion to Rawls*, Cambridge: Cambridge University Press, pp. 241–76.

Dean, Hartley (2003) 'The Third Way and Social Welfare: The Myth of Post-emotionalism', *Social Policy and Administration* 37(7): 695–708.

Desai, Meghnad and Yahia Said (2001) 'The New Anti-capitalist Movement: Money and Global Civil Society', in Anheier, Glasius and Kaldor (eds) *Global Civil Society 2001*, Oxford: Oxford University Press, pp. 51–78.

References

Dietz, Mary (1987) 'Context Is All: Feminism and Theories of Citizenship', *Daedalus* 116(4): 1–24.

Dobson, Andrew (2003) *Citizenship and the Environment*, Oxford: Oxford University Press.

Donnelly, Jack (1999) 'The Social Construction of International Human Rights', in Tim Dunne and Nicholas Wheeler (eds) *Human Rights in Global Politics*, Cambridge: Cambridge University Press, pp. 71–102.

Doppelt, Gerrard (1981) 'Rawls's System of Justice: A Critique from the Left, *Nous* 15: 259–307.

Dower, Nigel (2003) *An Introduction to Global Citizenship*, Edinburgh: Edinburgh University Press.

Drainville, Andre (1995) 'Of Social Spaces, Citizenship, and the Nature of Power in the World Economy', *Alternatives* 20(1): 51–79.

_____ (1998) 'The Fetishism of Global Civil Society: Global Governance, Transnational Urbanism and Sustainable Capitalism in the World Economy', in Michael Smith and Luis Guarnizo (eds) *Transnationalism From Below*, London: Transaction Publishers, pp. 35–63.

_____ (2002) 'Quebec City and the Making of Transnational Subjects', *The Socialist Register*, 15–43.

_____ (2004) *Contesting Globalization: Space and Place in the World Economy*, London: Routledge.

Duggan, Lisa (2003) *The Twilight of Equality: Neoliberalism, Cultural Politics and the Attack on Democracy*, Boston: Beacon Press.

Duxbury, Neil (1999) *Random Justice: On Lotteries and Legal Decision-Making*, Oxford: Oxford University Press.

Dworkin, Ronald (1985) *A Matter of Principle*, Cambridge, Massachusetts: Harvard University Press.

_____ (1989) 'The Original Position', in Norman Daniels (ed.) *Reading Rawls*, Stanford, California: Stanford University Press, pp. 16–52.

_____ (2000) *Sovereign Virtue: The Theory and Practice of Equality*, Cambridge, Massachusetts: Harvard University Press.

_____ (2002) 'Sovereign Virtue Revisited', *Ethics* 113: 106–43.

_____ (2003a) 'Equality, Luck and Hierarchy', *Philosophy and Public Affairs* 31(2): 190–8.

_____ (2003b) 'Law, Morality and Equality [interview]', in Herlinde Pauer-Studer (ed.) *Constructions of Practical Reason: Interviews on Moral and Political Philosophy*, Stanford: Stanford University Press, pp. 128–47.

Eisenstein, Zillah (2004) *Against Empire: Feminisms, Racism and the West*, London: Zed Books.

Ericson, Richard, Dean Barry and Aaron Doyle (2000) 'The Moral Hazards of Neoliberalism: Lessons from the Private Insurance Industry', *Economy and Society* 29(4): 532–58.

Eriksen, Erik and Jarle Weigard (2000) 'The End of Citizenship? New Roles Challenging the Political Order', in Catriona McKinnon and Iain Hampsher-Monk (eds) *The Demands of Citizenship*, London: Continuum, pp. 13–34.

Estlund, David (1998) 'Liberalism, Equality and Fraternity in Cohen's Critique of Rawls', *Journal of Political Philosophy* 6: 99–112.

Evans, David (1993) *Sexual Citizenship: The Material Construction of Sexualities*, London: Routledge.

Evans, Tom (2002) 'A Human Right to Health?', *Third World Quarterly* 23(2): 197–215.

Falk, Richard (1994) 'The Making of Global Citizenship', in Bart van Steenbergen (ed.) *The Condition of Citizenship*, London: Sage, pp. 127–40.

_____ (2001) 'Humane Governance and the Environment: Overcoming Neoliberalism', in Brendan Gleeson and Nicholas Low (eds) *Governing for the Environment*, Basingstoke: Palgrave, pp. 221–36.

Faulks, Keith (1998) *Citizenship in Modern Britain*, Edinburgh: Edinburgh University Press.

Feldman, Leonard (2002) 'Recognition, Redistribution and the State: The Irreducibly Political Dimension of Justice', *Political Theory* 30(3): 410–40.

Fidler, David (2004) 'Fighting the Axis of Illness: HIV/AIDS, Human Rights, and US Foreign Policy', *Harvard Human Rights Journal* 17(1): 99–136.

Finlayson, Alan (2003) *Making Sense of New Labour*, London: Lawrence and Wishart.

Fisher, Bernice and Joan Tronto (1990) 'Toward a Feminist Theory of Caring', in Emily Abel and Margaret Nelson (eds) *Circles of Care: Work and Identity in Women's Lives*, New York: State University of New York Press, pp. 35–62.

Flax, Jane (1992) 'Beyond Equality: Gender, Justice and Difference', in Gisela Bock and Susan James (eds) *Beyond Equality and Difference: Feminist Politics and Female Subjectivity*, London: Routledge, pp. 193–210.

Fletcher, Don (1998) 'Iris Marion Young: The Politics of Justice, Difference and Democracy' in April Carter and Geoffrey Stokes (eds) *Liberal Democracy and Its Critics*, Cambridge: Polity, pp. 196–215.

Fleurbaey, Marc (2002) 'Equality of Resources Revisited', *Ethics* 113: 82–105.

Fort, Meredith, Mary Mercer and Oscar Gish (eds) (2004) *Sickness and Wealth: The Corporate Assault on Global Health*, South End: South End Press.

Foucault, Michel (1994) *Ethics: The Essential Works, Volume 1* (edited by Paul Rabinow), London: Penguin.

Fraser, Nancy (1989) *Unruly Practices: Power, Discourse and Gender in Contemporary Social Theory*, Minneapolis: Minnesota University Press.

_____ (1995) 'Recognition or Redistribution? A Critical Reading of Iris Young's "Justice and the Politics of Difference"', *Journal of Political Philosophy* 3(2): 166–80.

_____ (1996) 'Gender Equity and the Welfare State: A Postindustrial Thought

Experiment', in Seyla Benhabib (ed.) *Democracy and Difference: Contesting the Boundaries of the Political*, Princeton: Princeton University Press, pp. 218–41.

_____ (1997a) *Justice Interruptus: Critical Reflections on the 'Postsocialist' Condition*, London: Routledge.

_____ (1997b) 'A Rejoinder to Iris Young', *New Left Review* 223: 126–9.

_____ (1998) 'From Redistribution to Recognition? Dilemmas of Justice in a "Post-Socialist" Age', in Anne Phillips (ed.) *Feminism & Politics*, Oxford: Oxford University Press, pp. 430–60.

_____ (2000) 'Rethinking Recognition', *New Left Review* 3(May/June): 107–20.

_____ (2001) 'Recognition Without Ethics?', *Theory, Culture and Society* 18(2–3): 21–42.

_____ (2003a) 'Social Justice in the Age of Identity Politics: Recognition, Redistribution and Participation' in Nancy Fraser and Axel Honneth, *Redistribution or Recognition? A Political-philosophical Debate*, London: Verso, pp. 7–109.

_____ (2003b) 'Social Justice in Globalisation', *Eurozine* online magazine. Can be found at: www.eurozine.com/article/2003–01–24–fraser-en.html.

_____ (2003c) 'Distorted Beyond All Recognition', in Nancy Fraser and Axel Honneth, *Redistribution or Recognition? A Political-philosophical Exchange*, London: Verso, pp. 198–236.

_____ (2004) 'Institutionalizing Democratic Justice: Redistribution, Recognition and Participation', in Seyla Benhabib and Nancy Fraser (eds) *Pragmatism, Critique, Judgement: Essays for Richard J. Bernstein*, London: MIT Press, pp. 125–47.

_____ (2005) 'Transnationalizing the Public Sphere', in Max Pensky (ed.) *Globalizing Critical Theory*, London: Rowman and Littlefield, pp. 37–47.

Fraser, Nancy and Linda Gordon (1992) 'Contract-versus-Charity: Why is there No Social Citizenship in the United States?' *Socialist Review* 22: (3): 45–68.

_____ (1994) 'A Genealogy of "Dependency": Tracing a Keyword of the US Welfare State', *Signs* 19(2): 309–36.

Frazer, Elizabeth and Nicola Lacey (1993) *The Politics of Community: A Feminist Critique of the Liberal-communitarian Debate*, Toronto: University of Toronto Press.

Freeman, Samuel (1998) 'Response to John Kekes'. Online paper on Brown University Department of Philosophy's BEARS website. Can be found at: www.brown.edu/Departments/Philosophy/bears/9802free.html.

Giddens, Anthony (1998) *The Third Way*, Cambridge: Polity Press.

_____ (1999) 'Risk and Responsibility', *Modern Law Review* 62: 1–10.

Gill, Stephen (1995) 'Globalisation, Market Civilisation, and Disciplinary Neoliberalism', *Millennium: Journal of International Studies* 24(3): 399–423.

References

Gilroy, Paul (2000) *Against Race: Imagining Political Culture beyond the Color Line*, Cambridge Massachusetts: Belknap Press.

Gordon, Paul (1989) *Citizenship for Some? Race and Government Policy 1979–1989*, London: Runnymede Trust.

Gorz, Andre (1999) *Reclaiming Work: Beyond the Wage-Based Society*, Cambridge: Polity Press.

Gowan, Peter (2003) 'The New Liberal Cosmopolitanism', in Daniele Archibugi (ed.) *Debating Cosmopolitics*, London: Verso, pp. 51–66.

Green, Philip (1998) *Equality and Democracy*, New York: New Press.

Gutmann, Amy (1980) *Liberal Equality*, Cambridge: Cambridge University Press.

Habermas, Jürgen (1987) *The Theory of Communicative Action, Vol. 2 Lifeworld and System*, Boston: Beacon Press.

_____ (1995) 'Reconciliation through the Public Use of Reason: Remarks on John Rawls's Political Liberalism', *Journal of Philosophy* 92: 109–31.

Hall, Stuart (1983) 'The Great Moving Right Show', in Stuart Hall and Martin Jacques (eds) *The Politics of Thatcherism*, London: Lawrence and Wishart, pp. 19–39.

_____ (2003) 'New Labour Has Picked Up Where Thatcherism Left Off', *The Guardian Newspaper* 6 August.

Hardt, Michael and Antonio Negri (2000) *Empire*, Harvard: Harvard University Press.

Harsanyi, John (1975) 'Can the Maximin Principle Serve as a Basis for Morality?', *American Political Science Review* 69: 594–606.

Hart, H.L.A. (1989) 'Rawls on Liberty and Its Priority', in Norman Daniels (ed.) *Reading Rawls*, Stanford: Stanford University Press, pp. 230–52.

Harvey, David (2000) *Spaces of Hope*, Edinburgh: Edinburgh University Press.

Hay, Colin (2004) 'The Normalizing Role of Rationalist Assumptions in the Institutional Embedding of Neoliberalism', *Economy and Society* 33(4): 500–27.

Hayek, Friedrich (1976) *Law, Legislation and Liberty, Vol. 2*, London: Routledge.

Heimer, Carol (2002) 'Insuring More, Ensuring Less: The Costs and Benefits of Private Regulation through Insurance', in Tom Baker and Jonathan Simon (eds) *Embracing Risk*, Chicago: Chicago University Press, pp. 116–45.

Held, David (1995) *Democracy and the Global Order: From the Modern State to Cosmopolitan Governance*, Cambridge: Polity.

Held, David and Anthony McGrew (2002) *Globalization/Antiglobalization*, Cambridge: Polity.

Henderson, Jeanette and Liz Forbrat (2002) 'Relationship-based Social Policy: Personal and Policy Constructions of "Care"', *Critical Social Policy* 22(4): 669–87.

Hindess, Barry (1994) 'Citizenship in the Modern West', in Bryan Turner (ed.)

Citizenship and Social Theory, London: Sage, pp. 19–35.

Hobson, Barbara (2003) 'Introduction', in Hobson (ed.) *Recognition Struggles and Social Movements*, Cambridge: Cambridge University Press, pp. 1–17.

Hobson, Barbara (ed.) (2003) *Recognition Struggles and Social Movements*, Cambridge: Cambridge University Press.

Hoffman, John (2004) *Citizenship Beyond the State*, London: Sage.

Honderich, Ted (1999) 'Yes, Tony's Talking that Equality Talk', *The Guardian Newspaper*, 1 October.

Honig, Bonnie (1993) *Political Theory and the Displacement of Politics*, Ithaca, New York: Cornell University Press.

Honneth, Axel (1992) 'Integrity and Disrespect: Principles of a Conception of Morality Based on the Theory of Recognition', *Political Theory* 20(2): 187–201.

_____ (2001) 'Recognition or Redistribution? Changing Perspectives on the Moral Order of Society', *Theory, Culture and Society* 18(2–3): 43–55.

_____ (2003) 'Redistribution as Recognition: A Response to Nancy Fraser' in Nancy Fraser and Axel Honneth, *Redistribution or Recognition? A Political-Philosophical Exchange*, London: Verso, pp. 110–97.

Hopgood, Stephen (2000) 'Reading the Small Print in Global Civil Society: The Inexorable Hegemony of the Liberal Self', *Millennium: Journal of International Studies* 29(1): 1–25.

Hugemark, Agneta and Christine Roman (2002) *Disability, Gender and Social Justice*. Working Paper Series 2001/2, Uppsala University Department of Sociology.

Hughes, Bill, Linda McKie, Debra Hopkins and Nick Watson (2005) 'Love's Labour Lost? Feminism, the Disabled People's Movement and an Ethic of Care', *Sociology* 39(2): 259–75.

Hurley, Susan (2001) 'Luck and Equality', in *Proceedings of the Aristotelian Society Supplement*, pp. 51–72.

_____ (2003) *Justice, Luck and Knowledge*, Cambridge, Massachusetts: Harvard University Press.

_____ (2006 forthcoming) 'Choice and Incentive Inequality', in Christine Sypnowich (ed.) *The Egalitarian Conscience: Essays in Honour of G.A. Cohen*, Oxford: Oxford University Press.

Iorns, Catherine (1993) 'A Feminist Looks at Ronald Dworkin's Theory of Equality', *Murdoch University Electronic Journal of Law* 1(1). Can be found at: www.murdoch.edu.au/elaw/issues/v1n1/iorns113.html.

Isin, Engin (2002) *Becoming Political: Genealogies of Citizenship*, London: University of Minnesota Press.

Isin, Engin and Patricia Wood (1999) *Citizenship and Identity*. London: Sage.

Jaggar, Alison (2005) 'Arenas of Citizenship: Civil Society, State and the Global Order', *International Feminist Journal of Politics* 7(1): 3–25.

References

Jessop, Bob (2004) 'Critical Semiotic Analysis and Cultural Political Economy'. Online paper, can be found at: www.comp.lancs/sociology/rjessop.html.

Jewson, Nick and David Mason (1986) 'The Theory and Practices of Equal Opportunities Policies: Liberal and Radical Approaches', *Sociological Review* 34(2): 307–33.

Jordan, Bill (1996) *A Theory of Poverty and Social Exclusion*, Cambridge: Polity.

Kaldor, Mary (1999) 'Transnational Civil Society', in Tim Dunne and Nicholas Wheeler (eds) *Human Rights in Global Politics*, Cambridge: Cambridge University Press, pp. 195–213.

_____ (2003) *Global Civil Society: an Answer to War*, Cambridge: Polity.

Kantola, Ann (2003) 'Loyalties in Flux: The Changing Politics of Citizenship', *European Journal of Cultural Studies* 6(2): 203–17.

Kaufman, Alexander (2004) 'Choice, Responsibility and Equality', *Political Studies* 52(4): 819–36.

Keane, John (2001) 'Global Civil Society?' in Anheier, Glasius and Kaldor (eds) *Global Civil Society 2001*, Oxford: Oxford University Press, pp. 23–47.

Kelly, Paul (2002) 'Defending Some Dodos: Equality and/or Liberty?', in Paul Kelly (ed.) *Multiculturalism Reconsidered*, Cambridge: Polity Press, pp. 62–80.

Kim, Hee-Hang (2001) 'Women, Equality and Fortune: A Feminist Critique of Ronald Dworkin's Theory of Equality', paper presented at the American Political Science Association, Boston, August.

Klotz, Audie (2002) 'Transnational Activism and Global Transformations: the Anti-Apartheid and Abolitionist Experiences', *European Journal of International Relations* 8(1): 49–76.

Kutz, Christopher (2003) 'Groups, Equality and the Promise of Democratic Politics', *Issues in Legal Scholarship*, Article 13. Can be found at: www.bepress.com/ils/iss2/art13/.

Kymlicka, Will (1998) 'Introduction: an Emerging Consensus?', *Ethical Theory and Moral Practice* 1: 143–57.

_____ (2001) 'Review of Ronald Dworkin: Sovereign Virtue', *Canadian Journal of Policy Research* 2(1). Can be found at: www.isuma.net/v02n01/kymlicka/kymlicka_e.shtml.

_____ (2002) *Contemporary Political Philosophy*, second edition, Oxford: Oxford University Press.

Kymlicka, Will and Wayne Norman (1994) 'Return of the Citizen: A Survey of Recent Work on Citizenship Theory', *Ethics* 104(2): 352–81.

Lacey, Nicola (1998) *Unspeakable Subjects: Feminist Essays in Legal and Social Theory*, Oxford: Hart Publishing.

Laden, Anthony Simon (2003) 'The House that Jack Built: Thirty Years of Reading Rawls', *Ethics* 113: 367–90.

Laffey, Mark (1999) 'Adding an Asian Strand: Neoliberalism and the Politics of Culture in New Zealand, 1984–97', in Jutta Weldes, Mark Laffey, Hugh

Gusterson and Raymond Duvall (eds) *Cultures of Insecurity*, London: University of Minnesota Press, pp. 233–60.

Lake, Christopher (2001) *Equality and Responsibility*, Oxford: Oxford University Press.

Lamont, Julian (1997) 'Incentive Income, Deserved Income and Economic Rents', *Journal of Political Philosophy* 5(1): 26–46.

Lamont, Michele and Sadsa Aksartova (2002) 'Ordinary Cosmopolitanisms: Strategies for Bridging Racial Boundaries among Working-class Men', *Theory, Culture and Society* 19(4): 1–25.

Lessnoff, Michael (1999) *Political Philosophers of the Twentieth Century*, Oxford: Blackwell.

Levine, Andrew (1998) *Rethinking Liberal Equality: From a 'Utopian' Point of View*, Ithaca, New York: Cornell University Press.

_____ (1999) 'Rewarding Effort', *Journal of Political Philosophy* 7(4): 404–18.

Levitas, Ruth (1998) *The Inclusive Society? Social Exclusion and New Labour*, Basingstoke: Palgrave.

_____ (2001) 'Against Work: A Utopian Incursion into Social Policy', *Critical Social Policy* 21(4): 449–65.

_____ (2004) *Shuffling Back to Equality*, Compass Online. Can be found at: www.compassonline.org.uk/documents/05s25levitas.pdf.

Linklater, Andrew (1998) *The Transformation of Political Community*, Cambridge: Polity.

_____ (2002) 'Cosmopolitan Citizenship', in Bryan Turner and Engin Isin (eds) *Citizenship Studies: A Handbook*, London: Sage, pp. 317–22.

Lister, Ruth (2001) 'Towards a Citizens' Welfare State: the 3 + 2 "R"s of Welfare Reform', *Theory, Culture and Society* 18(2–3): 91–111.

_____ (2002) 'The Dilemmas of Pendulum Politics: Balancing Paid Work, Care and Citizenship', *Economy and Society* 31(4): 520–32.

_____ (2003) *Citizenship: Feminist Perspectives*, second edition, London: Palgrave Macmillan.

Longo, Patrizia (2001) 'Revisiting the Equality/Difference Debate: Redefining Citizenship for the New Millennium', *Citizenship Studies* 5(3): 269–84.

Love, Nancy (2003) 'Rawlsian Harmonies: Overlapping Consensus Symphony Orchestra', *Theory, Culture and Society* 20(6): 121–40.

MacLeod, Colin (1998) *Liberalism, Justice and Markets: A Critique of Liberal Equality*, Oxford: Oxford University Press.

_____ (2003) 'Agency, Goodness and Endorsement: Why We Can't Be Forced to Flourish', *Imprints* 7(2): 131–59.

MacPherson, C.B. (1973) *Democratic Theory: Essays in Retrieval*, Oxford: Oxford University Press.

Madden, Deirdre (1999) 'Reproductive Rights and Assisted Conception', in Angela Hegarty and Siobhan Leonard (eds) *Human Rights: an Agenda for the*

References

21st Century, London: Cavendish, pp. 217–29.

Mann, Michael (1987) 'Ruling Class Strategies and Citizenship', *Sociology* 21: 339–54.

Markell, Patchen (2000) 'The Recognition of Politics: A Comment on Emcke and Tully', *Constellations* 7(4): 496–506.

Marks, Stephen (2004) 'The Human Right to Development: Between Rhetoric and Reality', *Harvard Human Rights Journal* 17(1): 137–68.

Marshall, Gordon, Adam Swift and Stephen Roberts (1997) *Against the Odds? Social Class and Social Justice in Industrial Societies*, Oxford: Clarendon Press.

Marshall, T.H. (1950) *Citizenship and Social Class*, Cambridge: Cambridge University Press.

_____ (1964) *Class, Citizenship and Social Development*, New York: Doubleday.

Marx, Karl (1994) 'On the Jewish Question', in Joseph O'Malley (ed.) *Marx: Early Political Writings*, Cambridge: Cambridge University Press, pp. 28–56.

Mason, Andrew (2000) 'Equality, Personal Responsibility, and Gender Socialisation', *Proceedings of the Aristotelian Society* 100(1): 227–46.

_____ (2006) *Equal Opportunity for All: On Levelling the Playing Field*, Oxford: Oxford University Press.

Matravers, Matt (2002) 'Luck, Responsibility and "the Jumble of Lotteries that Constitutes Human Life"', *Imprints* 6(1): 28–43.

McKay, Ailsa (2001) 'Rethinking Work and Income Maintenance Policy: Promoting Gender Equality Through a Citizen's Basic Income', *Feminist Economics* 7(1): 97–118.

Meckled-Garcia, Saladin (2002) 'Why Work Harder? Equality, Social Duty and the Market', *Political Studies* 50(4): 779–93.

Mendus, Susan (2000) *Feminism and Emotion: Readings in Moral and Political Philosophy*, London: Macmillan.

_____ (2002) 'Chance, Choice and Multiculturalism', in Paul Kelly (ed.) *Multiculturalism Reconsidered*, Cambridge: Polity, pp. 31–44.

Mertus, Julie (2003) 'The New U.S. Human Rights Policy: A Radical Departure', *International Studies Perspectives* 4(4): 371–84.

Mignolo, Walter (2002) 'The Many Faces of Cosmo-polis: Border Thinking and Critical Cosmopolitanism', in Pollock *et al.* (eds) *Cosmopolitanism*, London: Duke University Press, pp. 157–88.

Mill, John Stuart (1991) 'On Liberty', in John Gray (ed.) *On Liberty and Other Essays*, Oxford: Oxford University Press, pp. 1–128.

Millbank, Jenni (2004) 'The Project of Rights in Asylum Claims Based on Sexual Orientation', *Human Rights Law Review* 4(2): 193–228.

Miller, David (1997) 'What Kind of Equality Should the Left Pursue?', in Jane Franklin (ed.) *Equality*, London: IPPR Publishing, pp. 83–99.

_____ (1999a) *Principles of Social Justice*, Cambridge, Massachusetts: Harvard

University Press.

_____ (1999b) 'Bounded Citizenship', in Kimberley Hutchings and Roland Dannreuther (eds) *Cosmopolitan Citizenship*, Basingstoke: Macmillan, pp. 61–80.

_____ (2000) *Citizenship and National Identity*, Cambridge: Polity.

Minogue, Kenneth (1990) 'Equality: A Response', in G.K. Hunt, (ed.) *Philosophy and Politics* (Royal Institute of Philosophy Supplement 2: 6), pp. 99–108.

Monro, Surya and Lorna Warren (2004) 'Transgendering Citizenship', *Sexualities* 7(3): 345–62.

Moss, Jeremy and Catriona McKinnon (eds) (2004) 'Philosophical Justifications of Workfare', special issue of *Journal of Applied Philosophy* 21(3).

Mouffe, Chantal (1993) *The Return of the Political*, London: Verso.

_____ (1996) 'On the Itineraries of Democracy: An Interview with Chantal Mouffe', *Studies in Political Economy* 49: 131–48.

Munck, Ronaldo (2004) 'Global Civil Society: Myths and Prospects', in Rupert Taylor (ed.) *Creating a Better World: Interpreting Global Civil Society*, Bloomfield: Kumarian Press, pp. 13–26.

Nagel, Thomas (1989) 'Rawls on Justice', in Norman Daniels (ed.) *Reading Rawls*, Oxford: Blackwell, pp. 1–17.

Naidoo, Kumi and Rajesh Tandon (1999) 'The Promise of Civil Society', in Naidoo (ed.) *Civil Society at the Millennium*, Bloomfield: Kumaman Press, pp. 1–16.

Narayan, Uma (1997) 'Towards a Feminist Vision of Citizenship', in Mary Lyndon Shanley and Uma Narayan (eds) *Reconstructing Political Theory: Feminist Perspectives*, Cambridge: Polity, pp. 48–67.

Nash, Kate (2002) 'Human Rights for Women: An Argument for "Deconstructive Equality"', *Economy and Society* 31(3): 414–33.

_____ (2003) 'Cosmopolitan Political Community: Why Does It Feel So Right?' *Constellations* 10(4): 506–18.

Nickel, James and Eduardo Viola (2003) 'Integrating Environmentalism and Human Rights', in Andrew Light and Holmes Rolston (eds) *Environmental Ethics*, Oxford: Blackwell, pp. 472–6.

Norman, Richard (1987) *Free and Equal*, Oxford: Oxford University Press.

Nozick, Robert (1974) *Anarchy, State and Utopia*, Oxford: Blackwell.

Nussbaum, Martha (1992) 'Human Functioning and Social Justice: In Defense of Aristotelian Essentialism', *Political Theory* 20: 202–46.

_____ (2000) *Women and Human Development: The Capabilities Approach*, Cambridge: Cambridge University Press.

_____ (2001) 'Adaptive Preferences and Women's Options', *Economics and Philosophy* 17: 67–88.

_____ (2002) 'Women and the Law of Peoples', *Politics, Philosophy and*

Economics 1(3): 283–306.

O'Brien, Mary (1981) *The Politics of Reproduction*, London: Routledge.

O'Brien, Ruth (2005) 'Other Voices at the Workplace: Gender, Disability and an Alternative Ethic of Care', *Signs* 30(2): 1529–56.

Okin, Susan Moller (1989) *Justice, Gender and the Family*, New York: Basic Books.

⸻ (1994) 'Political Liberalism, Justice and Gender', *Ethics* 105: 23–43.

Oliver, Michael (1990) *The Politics of Disablement*, London: Macmillan.

Olson, Kevin (2001) 'Distributive Justice and the Politics of Difference', *Critical Horizons* 2(1): 5–32.

O'Malley, Pat (1996) 'Risk and Responsibility', in Andrew Barry, Thomas Osborne and Nikolas Rose (eds) *Foucault and Political Reason*, London: UCL Press, pp. 189–208.

O'Neill, John (2000) 'Review of Colin MacLeod: Liberalism, Justice and Markets', *Journal of Applied Philosophy* 17(3): 303–7.

O'Neill, Shane (1997) *Impartiality in Context: Grounding Justice in a Pluralist World*, New York: State University of New York Press.

⸻ (2004) 'The Equalization of Effective Communicative Freedom: Democratic Justice in the Constitutional State and Beyond', *Canadian Journal of Law and Jurisprudence* 27(1): 83–99.

Ong, Aihwa (1999) *Flexible Citizenship: the Cultural Logic of Transnationality*, Durham: Duke University Press.

Paden, Roger (1998) 'Democracy and Distribution', *Social Theory and Practice* 24(3): 419–47.

Parekh, Bhikhu (2003) 'Cosmopolitanism and Global Citizenship', *Review of International Studies* 29(1): 3–27.

Pasha, Mustapha Kamal and David Blaney (1998) 'Elusive Paradise: The Promise and Peril of Global Civil Society', *Alternatives* 23(3): 417–50.

Pateman, Carole (1988) *The Sexual Contract*, Stanford: Stanford University Press.

⸻ (1989) *The Disorder of Women*, Cambridge: Polity.

⸻ (1992) 'Equality, Difference, Subordination: The Politics of Motherhood and Women's Citizenship', in Gisela Bock and Susan James (eds) *Beyond Equality and Difference*, New York: Routledge, pp. 17–31.

⸻ (2005) 'Democratizing Citizenship: Some Advantages of a Basic Income', *Politics & Society* 32(1): 89–105.

Peter, Fabienne (2001) 'Health, Equity and Social Justice', *Applied Philosophy* 18(2): 159–70.

Petersen, Alan, Ian Barns, Janice Dudley and Patricia Harris (1999) *Poststructuralism, Citizenship and Social Policy*, London: Routledge.

Pettman, Jan Jindy (1999) 'Globalisation and the Gendered Politics of Citizenship', in Nira Yuval-Davis and Pnina Werbner (eds) *Women,*

Citizenship and Difference, London: Zed Books, pp. 207–220.

Phillips, Anne (1992) 'Feminism, Equality and Difference,' in Linda McDowell and Rosemary Pringle (eds) *Defining Women: Social Institutions and Gender Divisions*, Cambridge: Polity Press, pp. 205–22.

_____ (1997) 'What Has Socialism to Do With Sexual Equality?', in Jane Franklin (ed.) *Equality*, London: Institute for Public Policy Research, pp. 101–22.

_____ (1999) *Which Equalities Matter?* Cambridge: Polity Press.

_____ (2000) 'Equality, Pluralism, Universality: Current Concerns in Normative Theory', *British Journal of Politics and International Relations* 2(2): 237–55.

_____ (2001a) 'Not as Individuals but in Pairs', *Theory, Culture and Society* 18(4): 123–7.

_____ (2001b) 'Feminism and Liberalism Revisited: Has Martha Nussbaum Got It Right?', *Constellations* 8(2): 249–66.

_____ (2003) 'Recognition and the Struggle for Political Voice', in Barbara Hobson (ed.) *Recognition Struggles and Social Movements: Contested Identities*, Cambridge: Cambridge University Press, pp. 263–73.

_____ (2004) 'Defending Equality of Outcome', *Journal of Political Philosophy* 12(1): 1–19.

Pieterse, Jan Nederveen (2002) 'Global Inequality: Bringing Politics Back In', *Third World Quarterly* 23(6): 1023–46.

Player, Stewart and Allyson Pollock (2001) 'Long-term Care: from Public Responsibility to Private Good', *Critical Social Policy* 21(2): 231–55.

Pogge, Thomas (1989) *Realizing Rawls*, New York: Cornell University Press.

_____ (2000) 'On the Site of Distributive Justice: Reflections on Cohen and Murphy', *Philosophy and Public Affairs* 29: 137–69.

_____ (2002) *World Poverty and Human Rights*, Cambridge: Polity Press.

_____ (2004) 'What Is Transnational Citizenship?', paper presented at Campbell Public Affairs Institute, Syracuse, 30 April.

Purcell, Mark (2003) 'Citizenship and the Right to the Global City: Reimagining the Capitalist World Order', *International Journal of Urban and Regional Research* 27(3): 564–90.

Rakowski, Eric (1991) *Equal Justice*, Oxford: Clarendon Press.

_____ (2002) 'Who Should Pay for Bad Genes?', *California Law Review* 90: 1345–1414.

Ramsay, Maureen (2004) 'Equality and Responsibility', *Imprints* 7(3): 269–96.

Rawls, John (1971) *A Theory of Justice*, Oxford: Oxford University Press.

_____ (1980) 'Kantian Constructivism in Moral Theory', *Journal of Philosophy* 77: 515–72.

_____ (1982) 'Social Unity and Primary Goods', in Amartya Sen and Bernard Williams (eds.) *Utilitarianism and Beyond*, Cambridge: Cambridge University

References

Press, pp. 159–85.

_____ (1987) 'The Idea of an Overlapping Consensus', *Oxford Journal of Legal Studies* 7: 1–25.

_____ (1993) *Political Liberalism*, New York: Columbia University Press.

_____ (1999a) *Collected Papers*, Cambridge, Massachusetts: Harvard University Press.

_____ (1999b) *The Law of Peoples with the Idea of Public Reason Revisited*, Cambridge, Massachusetts: Harvard University Press.

_____ (2001) *Justice as Fairness: A Restatement*, Cambridge, Massachusetts: Harvard University Press.

Reus-Smith, Christian (2001) 'Human Rights and the Social Construction of Sovereignty', *Review of International Studies* 27: 519–38.

Richardson, Diane (2000) 'Claiming Citizenship? Sexuality, Citizenship and Lesbian/Feminist Theory', *Sexualities* 3(2): 255–72.

Robeyns, Ingrid (2003) 'Is Nancy Fraser's Critique of Theories of Distributive Justice Justified?', *Constellations* 10(4): 538–53.

Robinson, Fiona (2003) 'Human Rights and the Global Politics of Resistance: Feminist Perspectives', *Review of International Studies* 29: 161–80.

Roemer, John (1994) *Egalitarian Perspectives: Essays in Philosophical Economics*, Cambridge: Cambridge University Press.

_____ (1996) *Theories of Distributive Justice*, Cambridge, Massachusetts: Harvard University Press.

_____ (1998) *Equality of Opportunity*, Cambridge: Cambridge University Press.

Rosanvallon, Pierre (2000) *The New Social Question: Rethinking the Welfare State*, Princeton: Princeton University Press.

Rose, Nikolas (1996) 'Governing "Advanced" Liberal Democracies', in Andrew Barry, Thomas Osborne and Nikolas Rose (eds) *Foucault and Political Reason*, London: UCL Press, pp. 37–65.

_____ (1999) *Powers of Freedom: Reframing Political Thought*, Cambridge: Cambridge University Press.

_____ (2000) 'Community, Citizenship and the Third Way', *American Behavioral Scientist* 43(9): 1395–411.

Roseneil, Sasha (ed.) (2004) 'Beyond the Conventional Family: Care, Community and Intimacy in the 21st Century', special edition of *Current Sociology*.

Rousseau, Jean-Jacques (1978) *On the Social Contract*, trans J.R. Masters, New York: St Martin's Press.

Rubenstein, Kim and Daniel Adler (2000) 'International Citizenship: The Future of Nationality in a Globalized World', *Indiana Journal of Global Legal Studies* 7(2): 519–48.

Santos, Boaventura De Sousa (1999) 'A Multicultural Conception of Human

Rights', in Mark Featherstone and Scott Lash (eds) *Spaces of Culture*, London: Sage, pp. 214–29.

Sargent, Lydia (ed.) (1981) *Women and Revolution: The Unhappy Marriage of Marxism and Feminism*, London: Pluto Press.

Sassen, Saskia (2003) 'The State and Globalization', *Interventions* 5(2): 241–8.

_____ (2004) 'The Repositioning of Citizenship: Toward New Types of Subjects and Spaces for Politics', paper presented at Campbell Public Affairs Institute, Syracuse, 30 April.

Scheffler, Samuel (2003) 'What Is Egalitarianism?', *Philosophy and Public Affairs* 31(1): 5–39.

_____ (2005) 'Choice, Circumstance and the Value of Equality', *Politics, Philosophy and Economics* 4(1): 5–28.

Schmid, Gunther (1984) 'The Political Economy of Labour Market Discrimination', in G. Schmid and R. Weitzel (eds) *Sex Discrimination and Equal Opportunity*, Aldershot: Gower, pp. 44–67.

Schwartzmann, Lisa (2000) 'Liberal Abstraction and Social Inequality: A Critique of Dworkin', in Cheryl Hughes and Yeager Hudson (eds) *Social Philosophy Today* 22(15): 229–43.

Sen, Amartya (1992) *Inequality Re-examined*, Oxford: Clarendon Press.

_____ (1993) 'Capability and Well-being', in Amartya Sen and Martha Nussbaum (eds) *The Quality of Life*, Oxford: Oxford University Press, pp. 30–53.

_____ (2000) 'Equality of What?', in David Johnston (ed.) *Equality*, Indianapolis: Hackett, pp. 160–77.

_____ (2004) 'Why We Should Preserve the Spotted Owl', *London Review of Books* 26(3), 5 February.

Sevenhuijsen, Selma (1998) *Citizenship and the Ethics of Care*, London: Routledge.

_____ (2000) 'Caring in the Third Way: The Relation Between Obligation, Responsibility and Care in Third Way Discourse', *Critical Social Policy* 20(1): 5–38.

Shafir, Gershon and Yoav Peled (1998) 'Citizenship and Stratification in an Ethnic Democracy', *Ethnic and Racial Studies* 21(3): 408–27.

Shapiro, Ian (1999) *Democratic Justice*, New Haven: Yale University Press.

Short, Clare (2003) 'Interview with Andrew Grice', *The Independent* newspaper, London, 28 July: 1.

Shue, Henry (1980) *Basic Rights: Subsistence, Affluence and US Foreign Policy*, New York: Basic Books.

Siim, Birte (2000) *Gender and Citizenship: Power and Agency in France, Britain and Denmark*, Cambridge: Cambridge University Press.

Simhony, Avital and David Weinstein (eds) (2001) *The New Liberalism: Reconciling Liberty and Community*, Cambridge: Cambridge University Press.

Simpson, Evan (1980) 'The Subject of Justice', *Ethics* 90: 490–501.

Singer, Peter (2002) *One World: The Ethics of Globalization*, Yale: Yale University Press.

Smilansky, Saul (2001) 'Egalitarianism, Free Will and Ultimate Injustice', unpublished paper. Can be found at The Equality Exchange, http://aran .univ-pau.fr/ee/page3.html.

Smith, Anna Marie (1994) *New Right Discourse on Race and Sexuality*, Cambridge: Cambridge University Press.

_____ (1998) *Laclau and Mouffe: The Radical Democratic Imaginary*, London: Routledge.

Smith, Steven and Mike O'Neill (1997) '"Equality" of What and the Disability Rights Movement', *Imprints* 2(2): 123–44.

Smith, Susan (1989) *The Politics of 'Race' and Residence: Citizenship, Segregation and White Supremacy in Britain*, Cambridge: Polity.

Soysal, Yasemin (2001) *The Limits of Citizenship: Migrants and Postnational Membership in Europe*, Chicago: University of Chicago Press.

Squires, Judith (1994) 'Ordering the City: Public Spaces and Political Participation', in Jeffrey Weeks (ed.) *The Lesser Evil and the Greater Good*, London: Rivers Oram Press, pp. 79–99.

_____ (1999) *Gender in Political Theory*, Cambridge: Polity Press.

_____ (2006 forthcoming) 'Equality and Difference', in John Dryzek, Bonnie Honig and Anne Phillips (eds) *The Oxford Handbook of Political Theory*.

Steger, Manfred (2005) 'Ideologies of Globalization', *Journal of Political Ideologies* 10(1): 11–30.

Stephens, Beth (2004) 'Upsetting Checks and Balances: The Bush Administration's Efforts to Limit Human Rights Litigation', *Harvard Human Rights Journal* 17(1): 169–205.

Stevens, Jacob (2001) 'G.A. Cohen's Revolution in Morals', *New Left Review* 7 (Jan./Feb.), pp. 145–50.

Stevens, Jacqueline (1999) *Reproducing the State*, Princeton: Princeton University Press.

Steward, Fred (1991) 'Citizens of Planet Earth', in Geoff Andrews (ed.) *Citizenship*, London: Lawrence and Wishart, pp. 65–75.

Swift, Adam (2001) *Political Philosophy*, Cambridge: Polity.

Talisse, Robert (2001) *On Rawls*, Belmont, California: Wadsworth.

Tawney, R.H. (1921) *The Acquisitive Society*, London: Bell.

_____ (2000) 'Equality in Historical Perspective', in David Johnston (ed.) *Equality*, Indianapolis: Hackett Publishing, pp. 90–106.

Taylor, Charles (1989) *Sources of the Self: The Making of Modern Identity*, Cambridge Massachusetts: Harvard University Press.

Taylor, Robert S. (2003) 'Rawls's Defense of the Priority of Liberty: A Kantian Reconstruction', *Philosophy and Public Affairs* 31(3): 246–71.

Taylor, Rupert (2004) 'Interpreting Global Civil Society', in Rupert Taylor (ed.)

Creating a Better World: Interpreting Global Civil Society, Bloomfield: Kumarian Press, pp. 1–12.

Thirkell-White, Ben (2004) 'The International Monetary Fund and Civil Society', *New Political Economy* 9(4): 251–70.

Thompson, Simon (2006) *The Political Theory of Recognition*, Cambridge: Polity Press.

Tormey, Simon (2001) 'Do We Need "Identity Politics?"? Postmarxism and the Critique of "Pure Particularism"', paper presented at the European Consortium for Political Research, Grenoble, April.

Tremain, Shelley (1996) 'Dworkin on Disablement and Resources', *Canadian Journal of Law and Jurisprudence* 9(2): 343–59.

Tronto, Joan (1993) *Moral Boundaries: A Political Argument for an Ethic of Care*, London: Routledge.

Turner, Bryan (1986) *Equality*, London: Tavistock Publications Limited.

_____ (1994) 'Contemporary Problems in the Theory of Citizenship', in Bryan Turner (ed.) *Citizenship and Social Theory*, London: Sage, pp. 1–18.

_____ (2001) 'The Erosion of Citizenship', *British Journal of Sociology* 52(2): 189–209.

Van Der Veen, Robert (1999) 'The Adjudicating Citizen: On Equal Membership in Walzer's Theory of Justice', *British Journal of Political Science* 29: 225–58.

_____ (2002) 'Equality of Talent: Procedures or Outcomes?', *Ethics* 113: 55–81.

Van Ness, Peter (ed.) (1999) *Debating Human Rights: Critical Essays from the United States and Asia*, London: Routledge.

Van Parijs, Philippe (1990) 'Equal Endowments as Undominated Diversity', *Recherches Economiques de Louvain* 56: 327–356.

_____ (1993) 'Rawlsians, Christians and Patriots: Maximin Justice and Individual Ethics', *European Journal of Philosophy* 1(3): 309–42.

_____ (1995) *Real Freedom for All: What (If Anything) Can Justify Capitalism?* Oxford: Clarendon Press.

Van Parijs, Philippe (ed.) (1992) *Arguing for Basic Income: Ethical Foundations for a Radical Reform*, London: Verso.

Voet, Rian (1998) *Feminism and Citizenship*, London: Sage.

Vogel, Ursula (1991) 'Is Citizenship Gendered?', in Ursula Vogel and Michael Moran (eds) *The Frontiers of Citizenship*, London: Macmillan, pp. 58–85.

Waites, Matthew (1996) 'Lesbian and Gay Theory, Sexuality and Citizenship', *Contemporary Politics* 2(3): 139–49.

Walzer, Michael (1983) *Spheres of Justice: A Defense of Pluralism and Equality*, New York: Basic Books.

_____ (1996) 'Spheres of Affection', in Joshua Cohen (ed.) *For Love of Country: Debating the Limits of Patriotism*, Boston: Beacon Press, pp. 125–7.

References

Warren, Paul (1997) 'Should Marxists Be Liberal Egalitarians?', *Journal of Political Philosophy* 5(1): 47–68.

Werbner, Pnina (1999) 'Political Motherhood and the Feminisation of Citizenship: Women's Activism and the Transformation of the Public Sphere', in Pnina Werbner and Nira Yuval-Davis (eds) *Women, Citizenship and Difference*, London: Zed Books, pp. 221–45.

Werbner, Pnina and Nira Yuval-Davis (1999) 'Introduction', in Pnina Werbner and Nira Yuval-Davis (eds) *Women, Citizenship and Difference*, London: Zed Books, pp. 1–38.

White, Stuart (2001) 'Liberal Equality, Exploitation, and the Case for an Unconditional Basic Income', *Political Studies* 45(4): 312–26.

Whittle, Stephen (1999) 'Transgender Rights', in Angela Hegarty and Siobhan Leonard (eds) *Human Rights: An Agenda for the 21st Century*, London: Cavendish, pp. 201–16.

Williams, Fiona (1999) 'Good-enough Principles for Welfare', *Journal of Social Policy* 28(4): 667–87.

_____ (2001) 'In and Beyond New Labour: Towards a New Political Ethics of Care', *Critical Social Policy* 21(4): 467–93.

Wintemute, Robert (1995) *Sexual Orientation and Human Rights*, Oxford: Clarendon.

Wintour, Patrick and Michael White (2005) 'Citizens' Pension Plan to Lift Nearly Million out of Poverty', *The Guardian Newspaper*, 29 January.

Wolff, Jonathan (1998) 'Fairness, Respect and the Egalitarian Ethos', *Philosophy & Public Affairs* 27(2): 97–122.

Wolff, Robert Paul (1977) *Understanding Rawls*, Princeton: Princeton University Press.

Yar, Majid (2001) 'Beyond Nancy Fraser's "Perspectival Dualism"', *Economy and Society* 30(3): 288–303.

Yeatman, Anna (1994) *Postmodern Revisionings of the Political*, London: Routledge.

_____ (2000) 'Who Is the Subject of Human Rights?', *American Behavioral Scientist* 43(9): 1498–513.

Young, Iris (1981a) 'Toward a Critical Theory of Justice', *Social Theory and Practice* 7: 172–82.

_____ (1981b) 'Beyond the Unhappy Marriage: A Critique of the Dual Systems Theory', in Sargent, Lydia (ed.) *Women and Revolution: The Unhappy Marriage of Marxism and Feminism*, London: Pluto Press, pp. 43–69.

_____ (1990) *Justice and the Politics of Difference*, Princeton: Princeton University Press.

_____ (1995) 'Survey Article: Rawls's Political Liberalism', *Journal of Political Philosophy* 3(2): 181–90.

_____ (1997a) 'Unruly Categories: A Critique of Nancy Fraser's Dual Systems

References

Theory', *New Left Review* 222: 147–60.

_____ (1997b) *Intersecting Voices: Dilemmas of Gender, Political Philosophy, and Policy*, Princeton: Princeton University Press.

_____ (1998) 'Polity and Group Difference: A Critique of the Ideal of Universal Citizenship', in Anne Phillips (ed.) *Feminism and Politics*, Oxford: Oxford University Press, pp. 401–29.

_____ (2000) *Inclusion and Democracy*, Oxford: Oxford University Press.

_____ (2001) 'Equality of Whom? Social Groups and Judgments of Injustice', *Journal of Political Philosophy* 9(1): 1–18.

_____ (2002a) 'Status Inequality and Social Groups', *Issues in Legal Scholarship*, article 9. Can be found at: www.bepress.com/ils/iss2/art9/.

_____ (2002b) 'Reply to Tebble', *Political Theory* 30(2): 282–8.

_____ (2004) 'Responsibility and Global Labour Justice', *Journal of Political Philosophy* 12(4): 365–88.

Young, Michael (1961) *The Rise of the Meritocracy, 1870–2033*, London: Harmondsworth.

Young, Tom (1995) '"A Project to be Realized": Global Realism and Contemporary Africa', *Millennium: Journal of International Studies* 24(3): 527–46.

Yuval-Davis, Nira (1999) 'The "Multi-Layered Citizen"', *International Feminist Journal of Politics* 1(1): 119–36.

Žižek, Slavoj (1997) 'Multiculturalism, or, the Cultural Logic of Multinational Capitalism', *New Left Review* 225: 28–51.

Zurn, Christopher (2003a) 'Identity or Status? Struggles over "Recognition" in Fraser, Honneth, and Taylor', *Constellations* 10(4): 519–37.

_____ (2003b) 'Arguing over Participatory Parity', paper presented at SPEP conference, Boston, 6 November. Can be found at: www.uky.edu /~cfzurn/CZonNFJustice.pdf.

Index

Index